Cinema, Suffering and Psychoanalysis

Cinema, Suffering and Psychoanalysis

The Mechanism of Self

Laura Stephenson

BLOOMSBURY ACADEMIC
NEW YORK • LONDON • OXFORD • NEW DELHI • SYDNEY

BLOOMSBURY ACADEMIC
Bloomsbury Publishing Inc
1385 Broadway, New York, NY 10018, USA
50 Bedford Square, London, WC1B 3DP, UK
29 Earlsfort Terrace, Dublin 2, Ireland

BLOOMSBURY, BLOOMSBURY ACADEMIC and the Diana logo
are trademarks of Bloomsbury Publishing Plc

First published in the United States of America 2024
Paperback edition published 2025

Copyright © Laura Stephenson, 2024

Cover design: Eleanor Rose
Cover images © Getty Images

All rights reserved. No part of this publication may be reproduced or transmitted in any form or by any means, electronic or mechanical, including photocopying, recording, or any information storage or retrieval system, without prior permission in writing from the publishers.

Bloomsbury Publishing Inc does not have any control over, or responsibility for, any third-party websites referred to or in this book. All internet addresses given in this book were correct at the time of going to press. The author and publisher regret any inconvenience caused if addresses have changed or sites have ceased to exist, but can accept no responsibility for any such changes.

A catalog record for this book is available from the Library of Congress.

Library of Congress Cataloging-in-Publication Data

Names: Stephenson, Laura (Lecturer in film and media), author.
Title: Cinema, suffering and psychoanalysis : the mechanism of self / Laura Stephenson.
Description: New York : Bloomsbury Academic, 2024. | Includes bibliographical references and index.
Identifiers: LCCN 2023025699 (print) | LCCN 2023025700 (ebook) | ISBN 9798765105665 (hardback) | ISBN 9798765105672 (paperback) | ISBN 9798765105634 (epub) | ISBN 9798765105641 (pdf) | ISBN 9798765105658 (ebook other)
Subjects: LCSH: Mental illness in motion pictures. | Motion pictures--21st century--History. | Psychoanalysis and motion pictures.
Classification: LCC PN1995.9.M463 S74 2024 (print) | LCC PN1995.9.M463 (ebook) | DDC 791.43/653–dc23/eng/20230801
LC record available at https://lccn.loc.gov/2023025699
LC ebook record available at https://lccn.loc.gov/2023025700

ISBN: HB: 979-8-7651-0566-5
PB: 979-8-7651-0567-2
ePDF: 979-8-7651-0564-1
eBook: 979-8-7651-0563-4

Typeset by Integra Software Services Pvt. Ltd.

To find out more about our authors and books visit www.bloomsbury.com and sign up for our newsletters.

For my mum and my dad.
For Nina, Reznik, Lisbeth, Michael, Helen and Quoyle – I see you.
I am also seen by you.

Contents

Introduction	1
1 *Black Swan* (2010)	25
Introduction to psychosis and *Black Swan*	25
The early years and the mirror stage	27
Mother/child libidinal relationship and the Oedipus complex	31
Foreclosure, the Name-of-the-Father and psychosis	34
The conscious unconscious and the breaking of boundaries	38
Agony and ecstasy: Jouissance	44
Conclusion: The agency of the reflection	46
2 *The Machinist* (2004)	49
Introduction to insomnia and *The Machinist*	49
Reznik's memory: The unknown known	51
Insomnia as a psychological and social issue	53
Sleep and the (living) death of insomnia	56
Emaciation: Reznik's body as canvas	58
Dual meanings: Repetition and obsession	60
Dual meanings: Written language	61
Paranoia and persecution	62
Hallucinations: Marie, the superego and the 'dream'	65
Hallucinations: Ivan, the superego and the doppelgänger	67
Conclusion: Destructive guilt and the stepping stone symptoms	73
3 *The Girl with the Dragon Tattoo* (2009)	75
Introduction to PTSD and *The Girl with the Dragon Tattoo*	75
The mental impact of trauma: Repetition	78
The mental impact of trauma: Belatedness and latency	81
The mental impact of trauma: Complex PTSD	84
The mental impact of trauma: Memory and the honorary silence	87
The mental impact of trauma: Identification and unexpected agency	89

	The physical effect of trauma: The raped body, abjection and temporality	92
	The physical effect of trauma: Boundaries and behaviours	96
	The physical effect of trauma: The second skin and tattooing	98
	Conclusion: The changed subject – trauma and survival	101
4	*Brødre* (2004)	103
	Introduction to adjustment disorder, emotional detachment and *Brødre*	103
	The post-9/11 subgenre and West/Other dichotomy	107
	Jouissance and the pleasurable pain of transgression	111
	The event and the act	113
	Silence and witnessing	116
	Guilt: Origin	119
	Guilt: Mechanism	121
	Guilt: Displacement and projection	123
	Survival anger and the link with jouissance	125
	The time travelling captive and traumatized speech	127
	Suicide as the only successful act	130
	Conclusion: Return of the repressed, return of the connection and reparation	131
5	*Copycat* (1995)	133
	Introduction to agoraphobia and *Copycat*	133
	The mirror stage reversed	137
	Anxiety speaks through bodily symptoms	141
	The agoraphobic paradox and zones	145
	Fear as the 'felt reality' of future threat	149
	The phobia conduit: Linking fear, anxiety and threat	152
	The third mirror stage	154
	Suddenly, successfully beyond the boundary	156
	Conclusion: The *Copycat* method in returning to the symbolic	158
6	*The Shipping News* (2001)	161
	Introduction to melancholia, depression and *The Shipping News*	161

Symptoms and affect of melancholia: Suffering, sadness, self-hate and speech	164
Symptoms and affect of melancholia: An alternative temporal reality	166
Cause of melancholia	168
Mechanism of asymbolia	171
The melancholic 'in love' but suicidal	173
The female narcissist: Petal	175
Love and loss: Wavey	177
The void, the thing and the lack	180
Writing, the move away from asymbolia and melancholia	181
Death and surprising survival	184
Conclusion: The struggle with sadness and subtle shift	187
Conclusion	189
Works cited	200
Index	215

Introduction

Psychological suffering as human experience

This book acknowledges psychological disorder as part of human subjectivity; as belonging to the normative spectrum of our lived experience. My work does not seek to categorize people, nor pathologize or define them. Rather, it acknowledges significant moments of human experience through an exploration of psychological suffering.

The Mechanism of Self is an exploration of the mind, as narrativized through film. Recognizing film as a socially situated medium, this book investigates some of the more common psychological disorders in the contemporary era. Six films heralding from the United States, Denmark and Sweden are investigated, each with a central character suffering from psychological distress. Modern, clinical psychology is first used to identify the disordered psychology the character is experiencing, and psychoanalysis then provides the methodology for an in-depth exploration of the disorder's cause/s (origin), evolution (mechanism) and symptoms (affect). Together, the three strands of clinical psychology, psychoanalysis and cinema acknowledge that psychological disorder and suffering is a prominent element of the contemporary human lived experience; psychoanalysis recognizes the inherent suffering encountered by each subject due to developmental phases; psychology applies specific categorization to how this suffering manifests; cinema depicts that suffering through a combination of visual and aural elements.

My work is motivated in part by the recognition that suffering, as a pan-human condition, is, paradoxically, both an isolating and unifying experience. The individual who experiences psychological disorder is frequently enveloped by the sense they go through this 'abnormality' alone. Indeed, part of the suffering connected with psychological disorder is the misconception that the suffering subject is isolated, detached and even ostracized from everyone else. Yet, the medical literature indicates that, for many people of varied ages, ethnicities, cultures, genders, sexualities, education and income levels, psychological disorder is a part of their lives, whether temporarily or chronically (World Health Organization [WHO] 2020).

The painful experience of psychological disorder as unique and isolating is perpetuated by the notion that psychological disorder and psychological health constitute a deviant versus normative dichotomy. Contrary to many clinical approaches (Capps and Ochs 23; Cooper x; Frances 98; Kinghorn 48–51; Paris vi; Sadler 21) this book refutes the notion that psychological disorder and psychological health exist in a binary. Instead, it posits that psychological status is a spectrum, with multiple variations dependent on the individual, and thereby acknowledges psychological disorder as a cultural diagnostic, rather than an anomaly. Key literature by Sigmund Freud and Jacques Lacan suggests that psychoanalysis is open to an exploration of psychological suffering beyond the confines of diagnosis and treatment. Indeed, Lacan, Julia Kristeva and Slavoj Žižek – the latter two themselves heavily influenced by Lacan – argue that the lived experience intrinsically involves suffering because of the subject's self-alienation; it recognizes that psychological suffering is not extraneous to the normal lived experience, but inherent to it.

Two strands: Clinical psychology and psychoanalysis

Modern clinical psychology, such as cognitive behavioural therapy [CBT], dialectical behavioural therapy [DBT] and mindfulness-based cognitive therapy [MBCT], works in collaboration with a literary diagnostic tool primarily designed for use by practitioners and physicians. In the vast majority of countries this tool is either the Diagnostic and Statistical Manual [DSM], which is published by the American Psychiatric Association, or the International Statistical Classification of Diseases and Health Related Problems [ICD], which is supported by the World Health Organization [WHO]. While the ICD is sanctioned for use in any country belonging to the United Nations, the DSM is often favoured or used in conjunction (Cooper x–xi), because the ICD covers all human health problems (including all physical problems, population health and group health), and therefore does not specialize in psychological disorder to the extent that the DSM does. Additionally, the most recent version of the DSM (the DSM-V-TR) was published in 2022, with updates almost every decade,[1] while the latest ICD (the ICD-11) was made available in 2019, more than a quarter of a century since the last formal development between 1992 and 1994.

While clinical psychology lays emphasis on the processes of diagnosis and treatment (hence the categorization of psychological disorder using the DSM-V), psychoanalysis is more engaged with subjectivity and the overall process of human development (Brazil 300–9). Driven by the guidelines of a diagnostic tool, clinical psychology often engages on a broad, social level (Lerner, Fisher and Weinberg 11–20), compared to psychoanalysis, which is predominantly focused on the individual (Weiss 106). It is important to reinforce that my work is not an attempt to trace mass movements in psychological health, but is an analysis of various individual psychological states. For this reason, I have chosen psychoanalysis as the primary analytical framework, while clinical psychology provides a template from which to recognize, diagnose and organize the central characters within these films.

Psychoanalysis is fitting for this book because of its emphasis on the psychical processes of the individual (what I frequently refer to as the 'mechanism') and because mental illness is experienced as separating the individual from the group by isolating the individual in their experience of suffering. Moreover, some difficult life experiences generate psychological disorder, while others don't. Psychoanalysis provides an explanation for why the long-term process of disorder occurs, and also why such a process can lead to fundamental changes in the subject. Most importantly this work acknowledges psychological disorder and suffering as part of human subjectivity, rather than extraneous to it.

Many authors believe there is little connection between psychoanalysis and clinical psychology (Chiesa 99; De Vos 354–72; Friman, Allen, Kerin and Larzalere 658–64; Ouweneel 1; Shepherdson xvi), citing fundamental differences between the two schools of thought. However, while I acknowledge these differences I also refute the idea that they can't be used in conjunction; Why shouldn't a combination of scientific inquiry and philosophy be used together? Indeed, an approach which uses both of these elements seems much better equipped to investigate the variation within humanity and the lived experience than an approach which uses only one or the other. A theoretical framework, which combines classification and diagnosis with psychical mechanism and

---

[1] The DSM is now in its fifth iteration [DSM-V], having been revised almost once each decade since the publication of the DSM-I in 1952. The DSM-II was published in 1968, the DSM-III in 1980, and the DSM-IV in 1994 (Shorter 6–8, 15).

subjectivity, employs the 'best of both worlds' for an intricate understanding of psychological disorder and suffering.

There are other benefits to employing a combination of clinical psychology and psychoanalysis (Midgley 225). For example, modern psychology lends a categorizing feature (articulated by the DSM) to the discussion that psychoanalysis lacks. In turn, psychoanalysis enhances clinical psychology by looking at something other than fixed categories. Fixed categories, when anchored by symptomatology are ineffective at exploring details of the subject's total experience with the disorder, such as cause and development. Where clinical psychology emphasizes the goal of recovering and returning to a state of 'mental health' (Miller *Suffering Psychology* 39–69), psychoanalysis eschews normalizing the patient or returning them to a 'better' state of well-being (Capps and Ochs 19). In psychoanalysis the primary goal is an improved self-knowledge (Szabados 691–707) ('*wo es war, soll ich werden*', as Freud says of the relation between the id and the ego), and therefore the reparative effects of reflexivity are a measure of the success of the treatment.

The major limitation of modern psychology's categorizing feature is that it has a normalizing function, which helps to perpetuate the deviant versus normative dichotomy previously mentioned, while psychoanalysis goes in the other direction and argues that everyone is abnormal to some extent. For example, psychoanalysis, which queries where suffering stems from (Why is it there? When did it start? What initiated it? How did it evolve?), inherently unpacks the experiences of the subject's life cycle, including stages such as the pre-Oedipal dyad, the Mirror Stage, separation from the mother and entrance into the Symbolic, and the internalization of the Name-of-the-Father paternal metaphor as superego. As each person is liable to encounter suffering at any of these life stages, or *because* of these life stages, psychoanalysis suggests that simply to live is to encounter a struggle with psychological suffering and that everyone is therefore 'abnormal' in going through this. Clinical psychology's DSM-V, which instead queries how that suffering manifests (What behaviours have changed? What new or different thought processes are occurring? How is daily functioning impacted?), inherently erects a divide between the subject's experience before and after the onset of symptoms. This reinforces the notion of a binary of healthy and unhealthy psychological states, as opposed to recognition that psychological changes are intrinsically a part of the individual's subjectivity, rather than extraneous to it.

A framework which combines cause and development *with* symptomatology and diagnosis employs the strengths of two schools of thought for the most rounded comprehension of the suffering subject. This philosophy, which argues that origin, development, manifestation and classification are best acknowledged as an interconnected group, also reveals that the lived experience consists of a multitude of psychological states (as opposed to a binary between 'mentally ill' and 'mentally healthy'), and these states may lie dormant, manifest or resolve themselves at any point in the life cycle. Accordingly, for this book I have specifically chosen three psychoanalytic theorists – Jacques Lacan, Julia Kristeva and Slavoj Žižek – whose scholarly work is based on the understanding that the lived experience involves suffering because of the subject's self-alienation. In addition to acknowledging the strength of combining two schools of thought, this book also employs film as part of the methodological framework, functioning as a culturally reflexive medium through which the two philosophies (modern psychology and psychoanalysis) can be applied.

The films analysed here reflect a sensitivity to the nature of psychological disorder, as opposed to recovery, whilst also maintaining a focus on the central character (and their suffering), rather than a narrative which is dominated by the drama between characters. The psychoanalysis of these film characters does not attempt to define recovery or even suggest a point at which this might occur. Instead, this work is interested in understanding the internal mechanisms and external conditions which induce psychological disturbance. Acknowledging these characters' psychological disorder as an existential process, as opposed to problems to be fixed by the medical profession, helps to solidify psychological disorder as part of the human condition.

These films also consider *how* psychological disturbance is experienced by the individual character through a variety of filmic techniques; as an audio-visual medium, film is able to narrativize these experiences through a combination of cinematographic, mise-en-scène, edit, sound, score and dialogue choices – elements specific to filmmaking which are useful in contributing to the accurate depiction of various psychological disorders. These elements of filmmaking can work separately or in combination to convey states of psychological distress such as confusion, fear, rage, sadness or despondency.

The third strand: Film as analysand of contemporary context

Psychological disorder can be studied from the perspective of clinical case studies, but I have chosen to use film as a mediating element because philosophical issues can be uniquely engaged with through filmic analysis; the film medium is a particularly powerful vehicle for representing an issue regarding the human condition, given (a) the intensity of the viewing experience and (b) the popularity of film consumption in contemporary society. Additionally, clinical case studies are limited by the professional discourse between patient and analyst and rest heavily on the analyst's ability to observe, record and write effectively and accurately; using 'character' as a pedagogical tool avoids such clinical restrictions and permits the viewer considerably more access to the lived experience than through case-notes alone. Close textual analysis of cinema provides insight into the experience of psychological disorders that may not be revealed through clinically based research because it is a medium which appeals to both aural and visual senses *and* an awareness of temporality (through imagery, sound and editing) (Simpson, Utterson and Shepherdson 1–22). Therefore, it is especially adept at portraying complicated internal states including psychological disorder and suffering.

While the medium of film provides aural and visual representations of the experience of psychological disorder, admittedly these representations are placed within an intensive, limited-length framework (none of the films analysed in this book are over 3 hours). Even a more extended screen representation (such as a lengthy television series covering 60–70 hours) fails to truly encapsulate the lived reality of psychological disorder; the diegesis of the text may span five decades, but as long as the viewer consumes it within the space of several hours, the representation of psychological suffering fails to be temporally accurate. And yet, because of film's combining of aural elements and moving visual elements, it's the closest option we have to 'the real thing'.

It is also important to acknowledge that films are influenced by the socio-cultural context of their production and serve as vehicles for cultural reflexivity. Therefore, a selection of recent films reflects the prevalence of psychological disorder and suffering in contemporary society (which is why only films from the most recent 25-year period have been used in this book). Furthermore, film can be viewed as both an art form and a cultural phenomenon, providing a strong sociological basis on which individual characters function as representations of the lived experience with/of particular psychological disorders. For example, Hansen (59–77), Hill (xiii–xv), Kolker (9) and Turner (193–9) each suggest that all artistic works, including film, are situated within the broader context of history. Lackey (271–3), Mercer (17–20) and Miller (*Introduction* 3–4) acknowledge that film specifically reveals information about the cultural climate at the time of production, and as a reflection of contemporary culture, it has the ability to represent human experience. Various scholars cite the merits of film as an educational tool due to its cultural reflexivity and widespread accessibility, which, according to Chow (167–73), makes almost everyone literate in its visual language. However, what I am particularly interested in is how film functions as a medium of fantasy which stages the lived experience and provides a space for the representation of psychological disorder specifically. Pearson (70), Hickam and Meixner (40–6) for instance, claim that film can illuminate unique ideas in a way that theoretical literature does not – through a combination of acoustic and optical content which transcends the written word, and represents desire on a stage otherwise only accessible via the unconscious in dreams.

The subject of psychological disorder appears to have significant appeal for filmgoers because many modern films which meet this criterion (including *Rain Man* [1988], *What's Eating Gilbert Grape* [1993], *Nell* [1994] and *Shine* [1996]) have been commercially successful (Smith Jr 41). Smith Jr claims that, while madness has been explored in cinema since the era of early silent cinema, films which look specifically at mental illness, learning difficulties or asylums are a relatively recent trend (42–5), and have usually been restricted to the 'serious drama' genre (Noll Zimmerman 43). Yet, as previously stated, many of these 'serious dramas' actually focus on the negative repercussions (the interpersonal fall-out) of an individual's disorder, rather than the internal mechanism of it, thereby lifting the focus off character and onto conflict. Film texts which 'stay with' the trajectory and experience of the individual provide a more nuanced, personal representation of their particular (human) condition, rather than a commentary on the (surrounding) social impact of the disorder. The increase in cinematic texts which explore psychological disorder reveals that modern culture increasingly positions film as an analysand and acknowledges psychological disorder as an aspect of the human condition. Indeed, Masuda and Latzman (435–8) suggest that lingering negative stigmas surrounding mental illness can be combated through a multidimensional approach which includes the accurate representation of psychological disorder in screen media.

Psychoanalysis and screen theory

McGowan (ix) ventures that contemporary film theory suffers from over-contextualization of the subject matter and argues that it is time for film theory to re-embrace textual analysis. Similarly, I have chosen to use textual analysis because I perceive that the inclusion of production and reception details would detract from, rather than add to, a psychoanalytic interpretation by clouding the analysis with information regarding celebrity casting, marketing strategies and promotional budgets, audience reception and box office ratings – elements which contribute nothing to an analysis of, for example, one character's experience of the pre-Oedipal dyad or another character's relationship with guilt and memory loss. Analysis of the context surrounding the films would be superfluous because this book is specifically and deliberately employing film *characters* as representations of the human experience of psychological disorder and suffering. Indeed, of all art forms, film arguably lends itself to a psychoanalytic dissection better than others; Fritz and Poe cite the predominant visual imagery and warping of time and space through editing as key elements which allow 'the motion picture … direct access to the unconscious' (208). The Surrealist theorists of the 1920/1930s were influenced by Freud's theories of the unconscious mind and likened editing techniques, such as slow motion and dissolves, to dreaming (Creed 75–8). Likewise, Allen (125–42) and Baudry (39–47) endorse Jean Goudal's early observations about film as the conscious representative of a dream, believing the combination of location (a dark room), visual imagery and editing transitions make film-going very similar to the experience of dreaming.

Christian Metz and Barbara Creed believe that watching a film allows the spectator to escape the constant sense of lack that an individual feels in real life – because they are there watching the text (with the omnipotent, arguably patriarchal 'gaze' [Mulvey 14–30]), while they themselves are not being watched (Creed 79–88; McGowan 2–3; Metz 42–52). Some psychoanalytic theorists link the editing cut with a symbolic castration, as the cut is a break in the spectator's omnipotent scrutiny of the screen (Allen 140). These theorists, among others, argue that classic Hollywood continuity editing makes transitions as unnoticeable as possible (by cutting on action), thereby hiding the symbolic castration of the cut. However, while the viewer can suspend their disbelief in the representation of reality on screen, they also have an understanding that this particular reality doesn't exist (Metz 42–52). According to Metz, the cinematic image is based on a signifier that represents something which is absent (Easthope *Classic Film* 49–51). In other words, while the cinema appears to present reality to the viewer, it can only ever *re*-present reality because the referent of the screen image is always lacking. Because the film signifies something which isn't there (something that *was*), any relationship between the viewer and the on-screen subject matter is an illusion.

Another mode of psychoanalytic film theory pertains to 'the analogy between the spectator-screen situation and the child-mirror situation' (Kaplan 13). This approach suggests that the cinema screen is equivalent to the mirror in Lacan's mirror-phase theory, where the subject attains self-identification upon first looking into a mirror and seeing their own reflection. Louis Althusser calls this process the 'ideological interpellation of the subject' (cited in McGowan 2), where an individual mis-recognizes themselves in a 'socially given' identity (ibid). In the cinematic equivalent, the spectator, looking at a screen rather than a mirror, develops an affinity with an on-screen character, gaining a sense of self-identification through this image located outside of themselves. I acknowledge that all media analysis is influenced, to an extent, by individualistic factors such as life experience, personality, cultural surroundings and social climate. In other words, no analysis can be purely objective, but operates through the interpretation of the analyst. Therefore, while I don't use spectatorship theory in this book, I recognize that my reading of these films, and the characters within them, comes from my position not only as an academic but also as a spectator. This unavoidable proclivity is another reason not to include contextual details of the films' production and reception within the analysis; the approach already uses three strands (psychoanalysis, psychology and film) in its methodological framework, (a framework which is somewhat further shaped by the analyst – myself); it does not need a fifth element muddying the analytical waters further.

Rather than employing spectatorship theory this book applies a psychoanalytic reading to the film as a text. This reading uses a triple theoretical approach by Jacques Lacan, Julia Kristeva and Slavoj Žižek, who each subscribe to a variation of psychoanalytic philosophy based on Sigmund Freud's theory of the dualistic conscious and unconscious. Using Lacan, Žižek and Kristeva encompasses both earlier and more modern psychoanalytic literature and allows for the employment of psychoanalytic philosophies which have been developed by several people over a period of time. Additionally, using all three philosophers (Lacan, Žižek and Kristeva) enables adequate coverage of a broad and varied analytical terrain; Lacan, for instance, writes predominantly about psychosis, anxiety and the Mirror Stage, but barely mentions melancholia, whereas Kristeva has published prolifically on melancholia, and foregrounded the academic rhetoric regarding abjection. Similarly, Žižek's work pulls on Lacan but develops specific 'Žižekian' ideas about the big Other and the Event – both useful concepts for an analysis of several of the films in this book. This approach not only enables a discussion beyond the symptomatology of modern psychology to consider cause, mechanism and affect, but also elicits findings which take into account the complexities of different life stages (infant, adolescent and adult), genders (male and female), and behaviours (six varied disorders). Resultantly, the theoretical scope of this book, while grounded in psychoanalytic theory and narrowed by the DSM classification, is still significantly wide.

From Freud to Lacan: Psychoanalytic roots

Freud first encountered hysteria in Charcot's clinic and he theorized that such irrational behaviour was generated by an unconscious mental state (Allen 124). Freud believed these 'disturbed' states are a result of psychological repression, and irrational behaviour is the manifestation of deep desire and/or trauma which has broken through the preconscious divide and, in hysteria, is expressed through bodily symptoms. If these desires and/or traumas don't break through the preconscious divide, they may instead appear in dreams – a night stage on which fantasies can play out, unable to do so in the conscious mind.

There are three different uses for classic Freudian psychoanalysis: as a science, as a medical practice (the talking cure) and as a tool for analysing texts. However, it was Lacan's psychoanalytic work rather than Freud's which influenced the early film psychoanalysts such as Metz in the 1970s. Kaplan (2–5) states that, too often, film theorists have conflated Freudian and Lacanian psychoanalysis into one model, despite their having distinct differences. For example, Freudian analysis, based as it is in clinical studies, eventually moves back from the 'text' of the psyche to the self-authored life (making it a biographical analysis at the roots), whereas Lacan's analytic focus, heavily influenced by continental philosophy, remains with the text (it is purely symbolic). It is for this reason that I have chosen to use Lacan rather than Freud as my grounding psychoanalytic philosopher.

According to Lacanian theory there are three registers of human subjectivity: the Imaginary[2] (the world which the individual ego perceives and 'a chaotic field of early sensory experience' [Reineke 18]), the Symbolic (the organization of signifiers which makes this perception possible) and the Real (the domain of trauma which is unrepresentable by language). Creed (76–7) states that the Imaginary and the Symbolic are particularly highly used aspects of Lacanian theory for post-1970s film analysis, although this book will address all three, due to the inclusion of Žižek's work with the Real.

---

[2] It should be noted that Lacan's use of the term 'Imaginary' has a dual meaning. It refers to something which is both visual and illusory.

As previously stated, Lacan claims identification occurs when an individual first sees either a mirror image of themselves (which occurs at 6–18 months [Lechte 158]) or in some circumstances a similar-looking person. In this moment, the child sees (the image of) itself as more whole and more perfect than the reality actually is, which is where Lacan links with Freud's theories of narcissism. However, because this identification takes place in the Imaginary register, the individual's identity is based on an external image that does not in fact match one's own body. In other words the mirror phase marks the point at which the subject, in the process of ego constitution, mistakes the image for the thing itself (Reineke 18–20). While the child embraces its own completeness in that moment, it is actually a misrecognition (because it's an image, a reflection) and the psyche becomes split. The truth of the subject (as incomplete and split) emerges through motifs such as mirrored images because this is where the difference between the self and the other is revealed. While the ego is bound to the Imaginary, through mis-identification with the image in front of them, the subject is eventually pulled into the 'constraints of the social order' through the subject's use of language (McGowan 2). This shift into the Symbolic occurs with the resolution of the Oedipal complex, whereby the child represses sexual desire for the parent of (usually) the opposite sex, internalizes morality and (eventually) develops a superego.

While the Imaginary (order) is what the individual sees, the Symbolic (order) is a structure which 'supports and regulates the visible world' (McGowan 3). The Symbolic exists in the realm of language, which means that the individual is unable to speak about it objectively and that it is always already present, making it inescapable. While language organizes the world, it is also a symbolic network which an individual is born into, and is unable to escape because of its role as the underlying network for social identity and interaction. As the child enters the Symbolic they acquire language and must obey the laws of society (Creed 76-7). Therefore, entry into the Symbolic signifies the gaining of subjectivity but the loss of freedom (upon entering into law) from a culturally mediated meta-structure (language).

Žižek to Kristeva: Building on Lacan

Žižek acknowledges that confronting the constructed nature of the Symbolic order is psychologically difficult because the Symbolic is fundamental in facilitating subjectivity. Such confrontation can pull at the strings of Lacan's

Borromean knot, untangling the subject to such an extent they unravel the constructed nature of their own subjectivity, coming face-to-face with a universe in which they do not exist.

Much of Žižek's psychoanalytic work revolves around the Real, which is integral to his philosophizing in general (Kay 3). Although Žižek's musings on the Real move along a different trajectory to Lacan's, he attempts to reactivate Lacanian psychoanalysis with both political and philosophical motivation. The Real exists as something which is unrepresentable in the Symbolic. The Real can be viewed as the 'lack' in language or as a realm which resists language. Grant defines the real as 'the traumatic thing which resists symbolization' (145); similarly, Žižek (*Enjoy Your Symptom* 31–6) suggests the Real interrupts the calm closure of the Symbolic order. Kay describes Žižek's real as 'elusive' (4) but also acknowledges that it is constant and all encompassing, neither temporally restricted nor representable. She goes on to label it 'the disgusting, hidden underside of reality'.

Žižek claims the subject is engaged in a constant battle between running from the Real and simultaneously moving towards it in order to be free of its ever-present threat. For example, when the subject feels guilty, that guilt is actually adopted in order to disguise the trauma underneath – the Real (Žižek *Enjoy Your Symptom* 36–8). The key to the traumatic nature of trauma is how inconceivable the event is during the event. Consequently, the mind is unable to process the event into memory, and hence it returns in the form of flashbacks, intrusive thoughts, hallucinations and nightmares. These symptoms are traumatic in themselves, suggesting that the term 'trauma' should be used in reference to events (not an event) which cover several temporalities. Similarly, Žižek concurs with Lacan's analysis that trauma can repeat itself through a seemingly insignificant event in daily life, something as small as a passing comment by a stranger or a particular noise (ibid 9–30). Psychoanalysis (when used as a therapeutic technique) is meant to pull trauma, as unreconstructed memory, out from repression. However, the process of recollection is less about revealing the truth of a historical event than about creating change in the individual's current state, for as Žižek says, 'after accomplishing it [recollection], I am not the same subject as before' (ibid 37).

Like Žižek, Kristeva's psychoanalytic work is heavily influenced by Lacan and she concurs that subjectivity 'is fundamentally enacted by way of language' (Reineke 19). Kristeva suggests that between Lacan's Imaginary and Symbolic orders is the realm of the abject, what Lechte (158) defines as 'the psychoanalytical elaboration of universal horror'. There are two possible responses to an encounter with the abject (Reineke 91): implosive violence (a largely internal process) and explosive violence (ibid). When the subject encounters the abject and responds with explosive violence, involuntary bodily movements of expulsion occur, which are 'ways of protecting the self from contamination and threat' (Kristeva, cited in Pheasant-Kelly *Institutions, Identity* 213). Kristeva says that neither the implosive nor explosive reaction belongs solely to one gender, but she notes in *Powers of Horror* (1982) that subjects who engage in implosive violence are often women, while subjects engaging in explosive violence are often men. Kristeva's discussion of abjection in relation to cinema is usually linked with the horror genre, where blood, gore and bodily malfunction are a staple of the territory (Pheasant-Kelly *Institutions, Identity* 212–13). Despite the classical link between abjection and visceral aesthetics, Pheasant-Kelly argues that abjection has a wide theoretical realm which can also include trans-physical reactions like hysteria and psychotic states (ibid 213).

Kristeva claims the infant experiences ambiguity in the Imaginary phase when it desires to both stay with and separate from the maternal body (ibid 216). Thus, in contrast to traditional psychoanalysis, which favours the paternal function and the phallus as master signifier, Kristeva believes the subject begins the process of individuation through interaction with the pre-Oedipal maternal function prior to the mirror phase or transition into the Symbolic order (Oliver 3). Kristeva thereby articulates the importance of the maternal body in human subjectivity and reasserts the significance of human experience prior to the introduction of language. She also clarifies that the feminine and the maternal are different, that the maternal is neither feminine nor masculine and that, theoretically, the maternal function could be performed by either a man or woman (though in the vast majority of cases it is a woman who provides start-of-life nurturance). For a child to enter into the Symbolic it must separate from the mother and lose her in order to achieve individualization as ego. A descent into melancholia signifies an unsuccessful separation from the mother between the Imaginary and Symbolic stages and a constant mourning for the maternal (Reineke 92). Melancholia represents a withdrawal from life where the melancholic attaches themselves to only one object – sadness, or in Kristeva's terms 'a black sun' (Lechte 185). Resultantly the melancholic doesn't search for meaning, living only with pain, sorrow and despair, and embracing melancholia, a 'living death' (ibid).

Much of Kristeva's *Black Sun* looks at the melancholic subject who struggles with the transition between Imaginary and Symbolic orders, collapsing under the weight of an existence steeped in abjection. Furthermore, the resources in the Symbolic order (language) do not assist the suffering subject (Beardsworth 96). With no linguistic resources at their disposal, sufferers of melancholia encounter an empty sense of 'meaninglessness and nothingness' (ibid 97). When a melancholic becomes predominantly despairing, language retreats (mutism is a symptom of severe depression). This linguistic scarcity includes gaps in speech, silent periods and incomplete phrasing (ibid).

Six films, six characters, six disorders

While this book attempts to recognize socio-cultural trends in mental illness, it also acknowledges there is no definitive categorization of the most common psychological disorders (either globally or in a specifically Western context). However, there have been large studies which look at the prevalence of particular mental illnesses across different cultural environments. One example of such a meta study is WHO's international survey[3] (Demyttenaere et al. 2581–90), which sought to catalogue the prevalence, severity and treatment of psychological disorders using the DSM-IV as the classification guide.

According to WHO's international survey, people living in the Americas (Colombia, Mexico and the United States) suffer more strongly from anxiety-related psychological disorders[4] than Europeans or people living in Africa or the Middle East. Similarly, people living in the Americas also have a higher prevalence of mood disorder,[5] impulse-control disorder[6] and substance disorder[7] than Europeans, Asians, Africans or people living in the Middle East. Ormel and colleagues (1741–8) reinforce some of the findings from the WHO study in their

---

[3] The 2001–3 survey covered fourteen different countries from the Americas, Europe, the Middle East, Africa and Asia.
[4] Anxiety disorders include agoraphobia, generalized anxiety disorder, obsessive compulsive disorder, panic disorder, post-traumatic stress disorder, social phobia and other specific phobias.
[5] Mood disorders include bipolar I and bipolar II, dysthymia and major depressive disorder.
[6] Impulse control disorders include intermittent explosive disorder, attention-deficit hyperactivity disorder, conduct disorder and oppositional-defiant disorder.
[7] Substance disorders include abuse or dependence on alcohol or drug substances.

claim that disability[8] is the highest amongst sufferers of major depression, panic disorder, generalized anxiety and neurasthenia. The findings of the WHO study reveal the most prominent and the most affecting mental illnesses in the modern Western hemisphere, which informs the selection of particular cinematic texts in this book.

The results of the WHO study and Whitaker's (3–11) research reveal that generally psychological disorder is more prevalent in North America than in the other countries surveyed, providing a rationale for the inclusion of film texts from this part of the world. The Hollywood films *Copycat* (1995) (which depicts the anxiety disorder agoraphobia) and *The Shipping News* (2001) (which depicts the mood disorder depression) were appropriate choices given both anxiety and mood disorders are more commonly experienced by Americans than any other people. Additionally, as anxiety disorders and major depression are also found to be more disabling than most other psychological disorders, it was appropriate to include them as representations of how deeply a sufferer can be impacted, thereby contributing to a broader understanding of psychological suffering as part of the lived experience.

Both *Black Swan* (2010) and *The Machinist* (2004) are Hollywood films as well. Although their respective depictions of acute psychotic disorder and insomnia do not fall within the DSM-V classification of anxiety or mood disorders, both central characters within the films (Nina and Reznik) exhibit symptoms and behaviours motivated by strong anxiety (including paranoia, delusions and hallucinations) and changes to mood (Reznik's depressed mood and Nina's increased emotional fragility), meaning that all four Hollywood films reflect some of the most prominent psychological issues to affect Americans in the contemporary era. These films all fit within the broader genre of drama, although *Copycat* may also be considered a thriller, *The Machinist* a psychological thriller, and *Black Swan* a psycho-drama or psychological thriller. Their placement within these genres suggests they fit within the 'serious drama' category previously specified as typical of films about mental illness. That being said, all four films have been included in this book because they are dominated

---

[8] Disability is defined by Ormel and colleagues as 'a restriction or lack of capacity to perform activities as expected in well-defined social roles' (1743). These activities include employment or job searching, volunteer work, housekeeping, study or other daily activities such as exercise, personal hygiene habits and hobbies.

not by inter-character drama, but by the central character's relationship with their own psychological state.

The prevalence of mental illness in Scandinavian countries is lower than in North America. However, closer scrutiny of various results (Singh; Vilhelmsson; The Nordic Council) reveals a paradox whereby, despite high living standards and long life expectancy, Scandinavian populations (Sweden, Denmark and Norway) suffer from disproportionately high levels of depression and anxiety. These statistics provide motivation for the inclusion of Scandinavian films in this study. The prominence of depression in these Scandinavian countries is such that it has been culturally channelled into the creation of a new, dark cinematic genre – Nordic noir. *The Girl with the Dragon Tattoo* (2009) (made in Sweden) and *Brødre* (2004) (made in Denmark) are the two Scandinavian texts chosen in response to these findings.

Given that trauma informs a great deal of Kristeva and Žižek's psychoanalytic philosophy, it was important to include at least one film where the central character's psychological suffering and disorder emerged in response to a specific traumatic episode. Although both *The Machinist* and *Copycat* are films in which the central characters develop a psychological disorder in reaction to a specific event, those disorders (insomnia and agoraphobia, respectively) do not always develop in response to a traumatic incident, sometimes emerging as prodromal[9] or co-morbid[10] disorders and without a clear genesis. Resultantly, I chose *The Girl with the Dragon Tattoo* for analysis, since the central character Lisbeth suffers from post-traumatic stress disorder (PTSD), which, as the name suggests, emerges after a specific event. Kristeva's theories on abjection are heavily employed in the psychoanalytic interpretation of Lisbeth's PTSD.

Brødre is also a text in which the central character suffers in response to a specific incident; Michael develops adjustment disorder with emotional detachment. As the name suggests, adjustment disorder occurs in response to an individual's failure to adjust following a major life change – in Michael's case his traumatic experience as a military officer in Afghanistan. Žižek's

---

[9] Prodromal psychological disorders emerge prior to the onset of another psychological disorder. For example, insomnia often precedes an episode of major depression.
[10] 'Co-morbid' refers to the presence of more than one illness simultaneously present in one person. For example, agoraphobia sometimes presents co-morbidly with obsessive compulsive disorder [OCD].

theories on 'the Act' and the traumatic 'Event' inform a large proportion of the psychoanalytic interpretation of Michael's adjustment disorder. Additionally, *Brødre* was selected for analysis on the basis of its international context as a post-9/11 war film. Numerous American films have depicted the post-9/11 war in Iraq and Afghanistan, with many of them conveying the negative impact that combat has on soldiers' mental health. I wanted to acknowledge this body of films as a particular cinematic trend (which thereby reflects the sociopolitical climate of the contemporary era), but wished to avoid the stereotypical trope of the returned American soldier with PTSD. Therefore, the inclusion of *Brødre* succeeds in recognizing (a) the emergence of a new cinematic sub-genre in the last twenty-five-year period, the post-9/11 war film; (b) that war and combat are aspects of the lived experience which have significant impact on the subject's psychological state; (c) that soldiers suffer from psychological disorders other than PTSD; and (d) that soldiers other than those serving in the American military are effected by time served in war zones.

Following the critical and commercial success of the original Scandinavian productions, both *Dragon Tattoo* and *Brødre* spawned Hollywood remakes, *The Girl with the Dragon Tattoo* (2011, Fincher) and *Brothers* (2009, Sheridan). As previously mentioned, I deliberately included Scandinavian texts in this book to reflect the disproportionately high level of psychological suffering present in modern Scandinavian societies; for this reason the original Danish *Brødre* and Swedish *Dragon Tattoo* were logical choices. However, more specifically I chose to include *Brødre* rather than *Brothers* because the Danish version avoided the cluster of Hollywood films depicting American soldiers with PTSD as an archetypal characterization of the genre; *Brødre* works hard to avoid falling back onto this stereotypical characterization and generalization of the post-combat military man. My reasoning behind choosing the Swedish *Dragon Tattoo* was that Lisbeth's portrayal in the Hollywood remake is notably more gendered and more glamorous than in the original. In the original version her ostracism from society adds to her identity and her suffering, whereas the Hollywood remake seems more interested in coding her 'Otherness' as cool and edgy, making her characterization a commercial tool, rather than an accurate representation of someone living with PTSD.

Films which include psychological disorder as a key element have historically proven to be excellent vehicles for the recognition of an actor's talent, beginning with Joanne Woodward's Academy Award for Best Actress in *The Three Faces* of Eve (1957, Johnson),[11] but such films don't always represent the symptoms of mental illness accurately, foregoing the truth in favour of an intriguing character and a spectacular performance, even when such a depiction contributes to the negative stigma surrounding mental illness. The six films analysed here provide accurate representations of symptomatology: Nina's acute psychotic episode in *Black Swan* is marked by paranoia, delusions and hallucinations; Reznik's insomnia in *The Machinist* conveys a chronic lack of sleep that impacts his cognitive and physical functioning; Lisbeth's PTSD in *Dragon Tattoo* includes all three major symptom groups – re-experiencing, hyper-vigilance and avoidance behaviours; Michael's adjustment disorder in *Brødre* conveys the classic sign of emotional detachment and disproportionate behavioural responses; Helen's agoraphobic symptoms in *Copycat* are very clear depictions of avoidance behaviour and panic attack; Quoyle's depression in *The Shipping News* includes the key symptoms of clinical depression including lack of pleasure, physical and cognitive lethargy, feelings of worthlessness, and thoughts of death.

More broadly speaking what appeals particularly about all six selected films is the way in which they do not attempt to solve, treat or heal the character. While the diagnosis and treatment mode of clinical psychology (formalized through the DSM) suggests that mental health equates to the end of psychological suffering (Bray and Gunnell 333–7), these films are content to portray psychological suffering without a 'return' to mental health or to happiness. Instead they acknowledge that sometimes there is no 'resolution' which restores happiness, and that in some cases the subject learns to live *with* suffering or to negotiate its presence when it arises episodically in their lives. Additionally, the chosen films focus on the trajectory and psychological experience of the central character (rather than the conflict between characters) as they narrativize a change (even when very subtle) between different stages of the disorder.

To cover a sample of the broad spectrum of psychological disorder, each film (and therefore each central character analysed) is selected to represent a different set of symptoms and a different diagnosis. Each of these disorders is recognized by the DSM-V and is attached to a specific set of symptoms, which

---

[11] Woodward portrayed a woman with dissociative identity disorder, formally known as split personality disorder. Sally Field won a Best Lead Actress Primetime Emmy for portraying the same condition in *Sybil* (1976, Petrie); 1988's *Rain Man* (Levinson) won Dustin Hoffman a Best Actor Academy Award for his portrayal of autism; Leonardo DiCaprio was nominated for a Best Supporting Actor Academy Award for his depiction of mental impairment in *What's Eating Gilbert Grape* (1993, Hallstrom); and *Girl Interrupted* (1999, Mangold) won Angelina Jolie the Academy Award for Best Supporting Actress for her portrayal of a sociopath.

the central character in the film meets. Aligning with each DSM-V condition is the psychoanalytic discussion of the disorder, which includes origin, mechanism and affect. The selection of analysed films is taken from North America and Scandinavia in the last twenty-year period (1995–2015) in order to reflect some of the more prevalent psychological disorders from the Western hemisphere during this time frame, including psychosis, sleep disorders, trauma-related disorders, anxiety disorders and mood disorders. I have included an equal combination of male and female characters, who, as a group, reflect that psychological disorder and suffering affects both genders, even while acknowledging that sometimes gender roles or expectations exacerbate the suffering. In addition to meeting the aforementioned basic criteria, the six films favour stories which convey a change in the central character, although the change is not necessarily positive or indicative of 'recovery'.

Chapter 1 is an analysis of *Black Swan* (2010), in which the central character Nina starts off as a successful prima ballerina in New York City. Plagued by the pressures of a career in an image-focused industry, Nina develops brief psychotic disorder (one of the strands of psychosis), which according to Phelan and colleagues (188) ostracizes sufferers from society more than any other mental illness. Nina's increasingly powerful psychological disorder renders her incapable of distinguishing reality from fantasy, which impacts severely on her ability to function personally and professionally. *Black Swan* includes heavy use of props with reflective surfaces (namely mirrors due to its setting in a dance studio), which enables an exploration of the Lacanian mirror phase, where the individual gains a sense of their own identity through self-misrecognition with an external image. Nina's psyche is split by her desire to be perfect (represented by the White Swan as imago) and the emergence of her fractured, incomplete identity (represented by the Black Swan). Nina's psychosis is triggered by the acute stress of striving fruitlessly for perfection while attempting to repress the knowledge of her true subjectivity, predominantly conveyed through her challenging relationship with her own corporeal reality – a relationship which only matures at the very end of the film and the moment of her death.

Chapter 2 examines *The Machinist* (2004), selected for analysis in part because it features a character whose psychological turmoil, like Nina's in *Black Swan*, is visually projected onto an equally disturbed body, further cementing the notion that psychological disorder and suffering are commonly experienced as a challenging relationship with one's own physicality. At first Trevor Reznik's life seems ordinary – he works as a machine operator in a large factory, lives alone in a non-descript apartment and has a casual romantic relationship with a woman. But Reznik's insomnia has been plaguing him for a year and, along with his chronic sleeplessness, he also loses weight. *The Machinist* reveals Reznik as a psychologically and physically suffering subject, someone whose internal disarray is echoed by an increasingly disordered physicality. Reznik's physical state is so altered by his insomnia that he moves through the diegesis of the film with a spectral-like quality, released of the usual temporal restrictions of time and space. Eventually *The Machinist* reveals that rather than Reznik being the victim of a sinister external force, he is actually guilty of a crime, and his destruction (beginning with insomnia) comes from within, not without. Given that Reznik's crime crosses both legal and moral boundaries, this experience serves as an example of an encounter with the Žižekian Real, the horrific underbelly of reality. This text conveys how an encounter with the Real can generate psychological disorder, and how unresolved guilt, after causing the death of another person, has the power to disturb the subject's psyche, body and innate sense of temporality.

Another character who aesthetically and physically manifests psychological disorder is the lead character in *The Girl with the Dragon Tattoo* (*Män Som Hatar Kvinnor*) (2009). *Dragon Tattoo* was chosen in part because it met with an unusual degree of commercial success for a foreign language film, spurring a Hollywood remake, two sequels and a sizeable cult following for the central character Lisbeth Salander. Following several traumatic life experiences, Lisbeth suffers from PTSD. Some of these experiences occur *before* the diegetic narrative begins, while others occur *during* the narrative, thereby making Lisbeth a subject who is changed by psychological disorder before the start of the film, and changed further by it part of the way through. In both cases, *Dragon Tattoo* firmly establishes that trauma profoundly changes the subject by fundamentally altering identity – a change which is visually manifested on and through Lisbeth's physicality. The work of trauma theorist Cathy Caruth is used here to explain how Lisbeth constantly re-encounters her trauma through a series of 're-experiencing symptoms', such as flashbacks and nightmares, which ultimately make Lisbeth's trauma ongoing and inescapable, affirming PTSD's ability to transcend temporal boundaries in its haunting of the subject. This chapter then uses Kristevan theory to analyse how, following trauma, Lisbeth attempts to expel the abject she encountered by outwardly expressing it through an aggressive and confrontational physical aesthetic, solidifying her relationship with her trauma by embodying it – a post-traumatic response to surviving an event which almost killed her.

In the last decade there has been an influx of post-9/11 war films, all dominated by male military characters who, after returning home from service in the Middle East, are afflicted by psychological distress (Dixon 1–28; Markert 209–310; Sanchez-Escalonilla 10–20; Westwell 84). For Chapter 4, I have therefore included the 2004 film *Brødre* [*Brothers*][12] about a Danish veteran experiencing adjustment disorder after returning from service in Afghanistan. Michael begins the film as a high-functioning military leader and family man. However, the unusual circumstances of Michael's time in Afghanistan make his eventual return to Denmark, and to domestic life, difficult to adjust to. Although Michael is able to return to Denmark, the tactics he used to survive his captivity in Afghanistan have negative repercussions on his sense of temporal presence, and he is frequently emotionally pulled back into the time and location of his trauma. The primary symptom of Michael's adjustment disorder is emotional detachment, which sees him emotionally disconnected from his family. This symptom is visually depicted through his unusually rigid physicality and stoic manner, the corporeal manifestation of his psychological disorder. Yet Michael's psychological disorder is not facilitated by trauma in the same sense as Lisbeth's. Rather, his emotional and mental disturbance occurs because, while committing an abhorrent act of violence, he instead encounters freedom and subsequent pleasure – an example of Lacan's notion of jouissance, where the obscene boundary between pain and pleasure is transgressed. A Žižekian analysis argues therefore that the 'real Real' of Michael's time in Afghanistan is not the trauma of brutality, but the joy to be found in transgressing the superego for a few moments of guilt-free violence, in which he narrowly avoids his own death by killing another.

Similar to the high-functioning and professionally successful Michael, Chapter 5 looks at Dr Helen Hudson in *Copycat* (1995). Prior to a violent assault, Helen's work as a forensic psychologist sees her interacting with large numbers

---

[12] A note on the Scandinavian film titles: *The Girl with the Dragon Tattoo* is the English title for this Swedish film, although the Swedish title – *Män Som Hatar Kvinnor* – is not a direct translation (meaning instead, 'Men Who Hate Women'). In this case I have chosen to stay with the English title, as *The Girl with the Dragon Tattoo* refers to the central character under discussion and corresponds with the English title of the book by Stieg Larrson. However, the Danish film *Brødre*, I refer to as *Brødre* (rather than the English translation *Brothers*). This is because, although there is a direct English translation for this title, the 2009 Hollywood remake of the original Danish film also goes by the title *Brothers*. To avoid confusion, within this research I maintain use of the original Danish title.

of people, travelling to different locations and excelling in her field. An attempt on her life by a serial killer at the start of the narrative results in her becoming severely agoraphobic, a particularly difficult disorder for Helen because of its austere and restrictive nature. The attempt on Helen's life at the start of the film, and her continued fear of death, manifests through a number of bodily panic symptoms including hyperventilation, vertigo and extraneous limb movement, as well as avoidance behaviours (namely she never leaves her apartment). Helen's daily functioning is compromised from the outset of her illness (near the start of the film) and her trajectory in *Copycat* therefore involves movement away from dysfunctional behaviour, as opposed to descent into it, as with *Black Swan* and *Brødre*. Lacanian philosophy applied to *Copycat* focuses on the mirror stage and the possibility of the fully functioning adult subject regressing to an earlier developmental phase following trauma, with Helen's agoraphobic safe-zone (her apartment) functioning as a pre-Oedipal space. Therefore, in addition to Helen's encounter with death, and experiencing of symptoms through the body, *Copycat* is also a film which suggests the subject suffering from psychological disorder has an altered relationship with temporality. *Copycat* is included partly because it reinforces that high-functioning individuals can regress to prior stages of psychological development; secondly, because it also suggests that seminal moments in the development of subjectivity can be re-encountered (e.g. Helen has not one but three mirror phases); and thirdly, because anxiety disorders (of which agoraphobia is one variety) are amongst the most prominent mental illnesses in the West and feature a particularly high rate of disability.

As previously discussed mood disorders are highly prevalent in the West (Demyttenaere et al. 2584) with more than 300 million people suffering depression globally (WHO 2018). It is therefore appropriate to include, in the final analysis chapter, *The Shipping News* (2001), featuring a central character (Quoyle) with the most common mood disorder, major depression. The viewer is introduced to Quoyle in an already-depressed state and he appears to move through most of the film in a similar psychological state. Having suffered chronically from low-mood and a constant sense of despair, this final analytical chapter uses Kristeva's theories about melancholia to discuss Quoyle's psychological disorder, including the way in which melancholics embrace a 'living death', physically embodied through lethargy and listlessness and temporally experienced through the sense that life has already passed. Kristeva posits that a subject's melancholia stems from an unsuccessful separation from the mother, upon moving between Lacan's Imaginary and Symbolic stages as an infant. Refusing to accept language as a substitute for the lack (of the mother), Quoyle enters into a life characterized by mourning for the lost object, a life intimately connected to death – the death of the connection with the m(other), the death-drive (which desires a return to the pre-animate, pre-Symbolic state), the death of his lover Petal, and recurrent thoughts of his own suicide. The internal change that Quoyle goes through during this film is arguably the most understated of all the characters in this book. Yet *The Shipping News* suggests, through the realization that the suffering of self-alienation can be alleviated through a command of language, that Quoyle has a changed outlook, built on subtle self-actualization.

Each of these chapters begins with a DSM-V classification and then moves into a psychoanalytic philosophical approach to explore the existential condition. The third strand added to this combination is the use of film (as opposed to clinical case studies) to narrativize the experience of psychological disorder and suffering. Textual analysis of cinema enables unique insight into the experience of psychological disorder and suffering through a combination of visual and aural elements. This ability to convey complex internal states, as well as film's culturally reflexive quality, makes cinema a strong basis for the study of psychological suffering as a human experience. Because the selected films represent some of the more common psychological disorders in the contemporary era, this analysis of them, individually and as a group, will reveal commonalities in cause, mechanism, manifestation and affect, whilst also eliciting insight about how psychological disorder and suffering are intricately connected with the subject's physicality, sense of temporality and relationship with death.

1

Black Swan (2010)

Introduction to psychosis and *Black Swan*

Jacques Lacan provided a solid basis for the discussion of psychosis and highlighted its central importance within psychoanalysis, as opposed to being a sidekick of the more commonly discussed neurosis. Prior to the rise of either psychoanalysis or modern psychology in the nineteenth century, intellectual consideration of psychosis was significantly overshadowed by the generic term 'madness', which saw many people who were exhibiting signs of paranoia (one of the symptoms of psychosis) institutionalized (Lacan *The Psychosis* 4). Even Sigmund Freud's examination of psychosis in the early twentieth century was lacking in depth and can be boiled down to the repression of a homosexual relationship with the father (Grigg *Mechanism of Psychosis* 51).

This investigation of *Black Swan* (Aronofsky 2010) identifies why the phenomenon of psychosis generally induces the experience of suffering and has a significantly adverse impact on the psychological well-being of the individual who experiences it. Taking a psychoanalytic approach to a psychotic film character will reveal the mechanisms behind psychosis and the resultant psychological suffering the character endures. It will also consider how the subject's relationship with reality is disrupted and will confront what is exposed when the fabric of that reality is pulled apart. Additionally, this analysis reveals that psychoanalysis and clinical psychology have similar definitions of psychosis symptoms – both recognizing that psychotics experience an impaired connection with reality through delusions, hallucinations and paranoia (American Psychiatric Association [APA]).

The use of a film character who has almost constant interaction with mirrored surfaces articulates the relationship between image and psychosis, and formally recognizes the destructive power of the image. Such power is multiplied for people who have lifestyles which focus on the visual and the beautiful. Examples of these lifestyles include people with careers in dancing, modelling, gymnastics and acting – people who spend significant time in front of mirrors or have their image recorded, to later be played back to a large audience. I refer to these careers as the 'aesthetic professions'. In these professions there is emphasis on the aesthetic perfection of the performance. There is also pressure to sustain that perfection beyond the stage or frame into other aspects of their lives. This additional stress seems particularly harmful to women in these professions, who suffer from an increased perceived obligation to *be* the image rather than just perform it. This is problematic as it enfolds identity back into image. *Black Swan* is the filmic depiction of the internal unravelling of a woman under the extreme pressure of a career in an aesthetic profession, where the grace, beauty and perfection of the ballet cannot be left on the stage but must be embodied by the ballerina at all times.

Directed by Darren Aronofsky and starring Natalie Portman, *Black Swan* is the story of professional ballerina Nina Sayers, working for the New York City Ballet and desperately trying to achieve prima ballerina status before she retires. She lives with her mother, Erica (Barbara Hershey), also a retired ballerina whose career was cut short by her pregnancy with Nina. Resultantly Erica lives vicariously through Nina, creating additional pressure for Nina to endure. Both their lives are utterly consumed by dance (Sexeny 53). The company's premier production for the year is Swan Lake, which requires a particularly versatile ballerina to perform two roles as Odette, the gentle and beautiful White Swan, and Odile, the dangerous, deceptive Black Swan. While Nina's technical ability and genteel nature make her an ideal White Swan dancer, she has to fight extremely hard to convince the company choreographer that she is capable of also playing the dangerous and seductive Black Swan. Combined with an overbearing mother, diminished self-esteem and physically gruelling training (Tyrer 133), Nina enters a downwards spiral of overwhelming anxiety. Though she does get the role, there is the additional challenge of keeping it and performing it to a nearly impossible standard. This situation results in Nina experiencing a 'brief psychotic disorder', characterized by an episode where she experiences the delusions, hallucinations and paranoia typical of a person who has an impaired connection with reality (APA).[1]

---

[1] In the DSM-V, brief psychotic disorder comes under the category of 'Schizophrenia Spectrum and Other Psychotic Disorders'. Brief psychotic disorder can be diagnosed if there are: (1) delusions, hallucinations, disorganized speech and/or grossly disorganized behaviour; (2) symptoms which last more than one day but less than one month, and the individual returns to a pre-morbid level of functioning afterwards; (3) no evidence of the disturbance being caused by other medical conditions or substances (APA). Nina meets all three of these criteria in *Black Swan*.

The early years and the mirror stage

Lacan's recognition of the centrality of psychosis stems from its particularly deep psychic roots in the early stages of the human life cycle (Grigg *Mechanism of Psychosis* 50). Lacan uses the terms 'repression', 'foreclosure' and 'disavowel' (ibid 48) to discuss the main defence mechanisms of psychological pathology.[2] Each of these pathologies has a differing underlying structure and different mechanism (ibid). Therefore, even if symptoms of, for example, psychosis (which operates through foreclosure) haven't manifested yet, the subject's psyche has some differences to that of a subject who is yet to manifest symptoms of neurosis. And yet, according to Lacan, 'the great secret of psychoanalysis is that there is no psychogenesis' (Lacan *The Psychoses* 7). Because there is no definitive inception ('no genesis'), psychosis is triggered by a response to particular circumstances. In fact, the psychological in general is the subject's response to the surrounding environment, and this much is evident in *Black Swan* when Nina's psychosis materializes as a result of the extraordinary (and unprecedented) pressure she is under personally and professionally.

Lacan suggests that every human goes through a universal development phase between six and eighteen months of age called the mirror stage. This period is articulated by the moment that the infant subject first recognizes itself in a reflection. Specifically, Lacan talks about the infant looking into a mirror, although realistically the subject could enter this phase upon seeing their reflection in any reflective surface. *Black Swan* doesn't depict Nina's first interaction with a reflective surface, but based on her profession the viewer understands that she has, over many years, spent several hours each day in front of a reflective surface, and hence to some extent is constantly re-performing the mirror stage. Lacan acknowledges that humans are born with no mastery of their own body or understanding of their body as a separate entity to their mother's body. They thus spend the months prior to the mirror stage in a state where no sense of unified self has yet developed. Upon seeing a mirror image of themselves (and understanding that the surface is reflective), the subject identifies with that coherent image – providing a sense of mastery of their physical state that had been previously absent. By first identifying with a reflection, the subject forms an identity based on an image. In other words, the innate understanding

---

[2] Lacan's terms are based on Freud's original terms which are *verdrangung* (displacement), *verwerfung* (rejection) and *verleugnung* (denial).

of 'the self' is founded not on 'the self' but on the image of the self, and this is problematic because it suggests that the internalization of an external image and the resultant development of human selfhood merely disguises the pre-mirror phase non-unified subject (Grosz 40).

During the mirror phase, infants are fascinated and entertained by their reflections. Through a series of gestures and movements the child understands the relationship between their own bodily movements and their precise reflections in the virtual world of the mirror. Lacan refers to this moment of interplay between child and image as a 'startling spectacle' causing a 'flutter of jubilant activity' (Lacan *Ecrits* 94–5). What interests me is the way in which this spectacle and activity can be sustained beyond infantile years if the subject engages in an aesthetic profession which puts increased pressure on the understanding of the self through imagery. I use the Lacanian mirror phase to argue that a professional ballerina's ego is actually rooted in her ability to perform herself as bodily image, which means that the mirrors in the dance studio are not only reflections of her athletic skill but also visual depictions of 'her' as an identity based overwhelmingly on an aesthetic. Similarly to the anorexic who looks in the mirror and sees only faults, Nina's hyper-critical gaze is utilized to edit the image of her body into a series of performative flaws which can be supposedly fixed through repetition of the movement – similarly to the toddler who gestures and re-gestures in order to gain understanding of the reflective surface. Such moments are common in *Black Swan* as the film covers multiple technique classes, individual practice sessions, auditions and rehearsals. In these scenes Nina is frequently told to stop her sequence of movement, to start over and to do it better the next time. Sometimes this instruction comes from her trainer or choreographer, and sometimes it is self-administered.

Although the mirror phase is a critical part of early human development, it continues to be negotiated as the infant grows into a child and eventually an adult (ibid 78). While the adult subject has a more complex sense of self than that of the infant who enters the mirror stage, adults continue to look at their reflections from time to time for some confirmation of their ideal ego. If the adult subject constantly refers to the reflection (as is the case with those in the aesthetic professions), the image goes from being a mere confirmation of the ideal ego into the basis of the ego itself. The image gains power by in-forming identity rather than sustaining it (Grosz 40). In other words, a professional dancer such as Nina in *Black Swan* hasn't formed a sense of self which has dependable stability should all reflective surfaces be removed from her life. Nina's reliance on the mirror image disempowers her and this is partially responsible for her inability to function as an adult, the first signal of the relationship between the subject's corporeal reality and psychological state. This interaction with the Lacanian Imaginary register, along with her very stressful life circumstances, helps to trigger the onset of her psychosis. As Lacan insists, however, the Imaginary is only one of three interrelated registers, with the two other registers of human subjectivity, the Symbolic and the Real, also having a role to play in the development and manifestation of psychosis.

The Imaginary both lies beyond tangible reality and is visual, so when the infant subject assumes an image-based sense of ego identity, it is locating its identity in the Imaginary realm. Lacan theorizes that the developmental stage beyond the mirror phase is entry into the second register – the Symbolic. The Symbolic, in contrast to the Imaginary, is the realm of language. As a result, the entry into the Symbolic stage occurs with the individual's use of the pronoun 'I' in reference to the self. Therefore, assuming identity through an image is only the first step in claiming ownership of the self as an individual who is separate from others (and in particular the mother).

The Real is an in-between space that is usually inaccessible to the subject and manifests only as trauma. The understanding that the subject has no self (because the understanding of the self is based on a 'misrecognized' external image) is so unsettling for the ego which has formed out of this misrecognized image that this knowledge exists in the domain of the Real and only emerges at times of massive psychological stress. Such is the case in *Black Swan* where the self as 'fragmented' (Lacan *Ecrits* 78) and incomplete is revealed during acutely stressful moments when Nina's reality is interrupted by the emergence of the Real during a series of hallucinations. This is represented onscreen by horrific bodily malfunctions (Laine *Bodies in Pain* 127–31) which involve the penetration and replacement of her own body parts with that of a Black Swan, another sign that the subject's psychological state is intricately linked with their corporeal reality.

Almost every scene in *Black Swan* features a mirror as part of the set. Mirrors appear not only in the dance studio, of course, but in bathroom settings, changing rooms, restaurants and offices. Because of this Nina is constantly surrounded by her own reflection – the place where her misrecognized ego abides. However, as her anxiety levels grow during the film, this reflected image becomes less and less a source of security and more an intimidating visual field that she fears to confront. This suggests that the understanding of the self as fragmented, knowledge which is located in the Real, is threatening to pierce the boundary and enter her conscious mind. Nina has spent her entire life gazing into the mirror for confirmation of her identity as a White Swan, her idealized imago. She can't embrace her own body because her understanding of it remains pre-mirror phase. That is to say, while striving for the White Swan imago, Nina undergoes a reversal of the mirror phrase, subconsciously interpreting herself as fractured and incomplete, which is represented cinematically with the corporeal reality of a grotesque and malevolent Black Swan.

Nina's greatest fear is a reflection of herself in fragments because that would reveal her internal state (Easthope *The Unconscious* 163). The ideal ego of the mirror image thus becomes the horrific double, which manifests onscreen with the increasingly emerging presence of the Black Swan (portrayed both in mirror reflections and changes to her physical body), which are representative of her internal fragmentation and the knowledge that primal repression has failed (Žižek *Enjoy Your Symptom* 25). These moments also represent the converging of two registers – the Real (represented by the Black Swan) and the Imaginary (her image-based, pre-language reality).

Therefore, most abominable for Nina is the moment when the body parts of the Black Swan literally break through the boundaries of her own body, as opposed to remaining in the comparable safety of the glass surface of a mirror. The confines of the mirror (the glass surface) represent the boundary of her unconscious mind. Resultantly the Black Swan's appearances in mirror reflections are less frightening to Nina. So long as the image stays 'behind' the glass wall, the unconscious understanding of her fragmented self has not yet broken through the boundary. By comparison, when the Black Swan transcends glass and enters embodied space, it suggests the divide between unconscious and conscious has been broken; the visual construction of the Imaginary being pierced by the Real and the cinematic depiction of an atemporal conversation between her conscious and unconscious minds. This first occurs half an hour into *Black Swan*, when Nina washes her hands in the bathroom of a concert hall foyer. She notices a small nick in the skin of her middle finger near the nail. She attempts to remove the stray piece of skin but the skin won't detach from her finger and instead she pulls back several centimetres of skin in the direction of her knuckle. Though simplistic, this image is simultaneously fascinating and repulsive. This scene symbolizes Nina's entrance into psychosis as, after blinking several times, she realizes she hasn't removed skin from her finger after all, thereby signalling that her initial perception of reality was impaired. This hallucination is the visual depiction of her unconscious breaking into her conscious, cinematically conveyed by the parallel image of her body breaking apart – indicative of the psychotic individual whose symptoms manifest from a divided subject who is struggling for, but failing at, an integrated identity.

Though it may seem that the Black Swan is the only symbol of the existence of psychosis, the presence of the White Swan (as the mirror image and something she attempts to embody) is as much a manifestation of Nina's psychosis as the Black Swan. The White Swan is also only an image to aspire to (an imago) in the same way that the Black Swan is only an image to cower from. Neither of them is real and the White Swan is no more able to provide Nina with stable selfhood than the Black Swan.

Mother/child libidinal relationship and the Oedipus complex

According to Freud, the trajectory of the development of individual subjectivity traces the child's psychosexual development through a series of stages which begin in early infancy. The child moves systematically through the oral (0–1 year), anal (1–3 years), phallic (3–6 years), latent (6 years to puberty) and, finally, genital (puberty to adulthood) stages. Each stage represents the fixation of libido on a different area of the body which may be simultaneously pleasurable and frustrating.

During the Lacanian mirror phase (which overlaps the oral and anal psychosexual stages) the child, who desires the mother, also seeks to become the mother's desire (Dor *Reading of Lacan* 98). This is what Lacanian feminists call the pre-Oedipal stage. The close bond that mother and child share during infantile years encourages this desire even through essential caretaking of the child's needs such as feeding and changing (Kristeva *Hatred* 86-7). This bond makes the child feel that it can be the thing which the mother lacks (a phallus) and become a maternal phallus for her. The child may not necessarily *have* a phallus, but, as this is before the gender differentiation stage, the infant (male or female) will always strive to *be* the phallus (ibid).

This intimate dialectic between mother and child works during these early years so long as it seems there is no other mediating element or agency (such as a father) to interfere (ibid 99). The mother's erotic complicity in the relationship is manifested through maternal seduction, 'expressed through the way in which she responds to the child's sexual overtures' (Dor *Clinical Lacan* 55). The child experiences this as encouragement and continues the libidinal relations.

While the pre-Oedipal child strives to be the phallus for the mother, the phase also contains enough room for some ambiguity around phallic identification. In part this ambiguity stems from the aforementioned mother's erotic complicity. Phallic ambiguity may also be generated by the father's silent complacency during this phase. In *Black Swan*, although Nina is an adult rather than a pre-Oedipal child, both of these elements are present with an overbearing mother figure and an entirely absent father. Furthermore, the initial infantile sense of bodily fragmentation (prior to the mirror stage) remains and the resulting subject is an adult whose infantile sense of self oscillates between an alienated but unified image and the real fragmented self, portrayed onscreen, respectively, by the White Swan imago and Black Swan spectre, two physical manifestations of the subject's psychological state. This suggests that, even though psychological development proceeds in stages, it remains possible for subjects to become fixated or to return in endless loops to earlier unresolved stages, as Freud argues.

The shift from the pre-Oedipal phase to the Oedipus complex (which takes place during the phallic period of psychosexual development) is marked by the entry of the father into the mother-child phallus relationship. The addition of the father into this close relationship is initially seen as an intrusion (Dor *Reading of Lacan* 100), as he presents himself as the 'rightful claimant to the mother', which the child finds frustrating (ibid 103). Within the Oedipus complex the castration complex arises where the paternal metaphor called the Name-of-the-Father creates castration anxiety (ibid 108). The complex is resolved in the male child when his castration anxiety provokes an identification *with* the male parent. Female children move on from the desire for their father by first developing penis envy and secondly repressing this envy and swapping it with desire for a baby. The female child represses feelings of libidinal tension towards her mother and identifies *with* her instead. Either way the child must acknowledge it is not the maternal phallus and relinquish its position as the object of the mother's desire. Resultantly the libidinal bonds between mother and child are repressed and the child is able to move forward into the next development stages.

The Oedipus complex follows on from the mirror phase, so while the fear of castration usually stems from the paternal function, the alienation and body fragmentation an infant endures prior to the mirror phase is related to the mother (Dor *Reading of Lacan* 95). Resultantly the development of the subject's identity is affected by both male and female roles. Lacan emphasizes the importance of acknowledging the triadic Oedipal family, particularly in the understanding of psychosis. Psychosis, as a psychological mechanism, has several parts (in this case people) involved in it; it is not a sudden or singular shift from one point to another (Grigg *Mechanism of Psychosis* 64). It should be noted the paternal function is not the same thing as the actual presence of a male figure: the father figure is a metaphor; therefore, should the presence of a literal father be absent, the child will still theoretically go through the Oedipus complex (ibid 94). However, there are circumstances where the dissolution of the Oedipus complex is not achieved. *Black Swan* puts forward such a scenario where, in the absence of the father figure, the mother-child libidinal bonds aren't broken after Nina's infancy. While Lacan suggests that the child deeply enjoys being the maternal phallus as an infant, it takes a reciprocal enjoyment on the part of the mother for this relationship to continue beyond infancy. Most often, such desire is repressed by the mother as the child grows, making continuation of this intimacy unusual.

In addition to attending to her child's bodily needs (Nina is after all an athlete), Nina's mother Erica sustains the child's erotic pleasures usually constrained to infancy. However, this pleasure is complementary because Erica also receives pleasure from doing so. As desire is by nature never sated, Erica is never satisfied – either sexually or professionally. Her own failings as a dancer amount to anxiety for Nina's career and she receives pleasure only vicariously through Nina. Nina and Erica share a common desire, a common anxiety and therefore a common pleasure. They are bound together through her mother's obsession (which becomes Nina's obsession) and yet this binding, based in a libidinal connection, is both terrible and pleasurable – jouissance. Jouissance is the term used extensively by Lacan to denote a pleasure which is both transgressive and excessive in nature. Jouissance straddles the boundary of pleasure and pain to provide the subject with an experience that is explicitly intense at a psychological and/or physical level.

Erica's domineering presence engulfs her daughter (Ouweneel 201), preventing Nina from moving successfully beyond the mirror phase into the Symbolic order. Consequentially the viewer witnesses an almost erotic closeness between the mother and daughter as two adult women. Nina and Erica live together in a small New York apartment. Upon returning home from work each day Nina is greeted at the door by Erica, who enquires into how training, auditions and rehearsals went. They talk about other dancers in the company, discuss technical skills and share identical ambitions for Nina's career. As part of their close co-habitation they eat together, celebrate together and grieve together when things aren't going well. The intimate connection between them is particularly emphasized in the scene where they celebrate Nina being given the role of Swan Queen. As they stand together in the kitchen, Nina is reluctant to indulge in a slice of celebratory cake. A series of tight mid-shots and close-ups emphasizes the small space and limited physical distance between Erica and Nina. As a symbol of Erica's mutual enjoyment of the pre-Oedipal intimate dyad between mother and child, Erica coaxes Nina into having some cake by extending an icing-covered finger in her direction and encouraging Nina to lick the icing off in a pseudo-erotic gesture. This moment features a close-up shot capturing both Erica's iced finger and Nina's reluctant expression. These tight visual frames promote an increasingly claustrophobic sense, as if Nina is caught between closing walls. Eventually Nina complies with her mother's demand, licking the icing from the finger and feigning pleasure.

Foreclosure, the Name-of-the-Father and psychosis

Psychoanalysis maintains that the individual's development of identity is based on repression and the very nature of repressed material is that it always returns in an attempt to be un-repressed (Lacan *The Psychoses* 12). This process emerges in various human behaviours, some of which can be considered symptoms of pathology. These are the experiences which manifest as neurotic behaviours. There are some events, however, which are not experienced in the Symbolic order to begin with and therefore can't be repressed. These events are 'foreclosed' and remain in the order of the atemporal Real, unavailable to language and symbolization, until such time as they erupt as hallucinations. This is the case when Nina experiences the morphing of her physical body into swan body parts or when she hallucinates the tearing of skin back from her fingernail; the foreclosed is manifesting in these moments as something unspeakable, something not representable in the Symbolic, something from the Real.

Lacan's concept of foreclosure is based on Jacques Damouretts and Edouard Pichon's use of the term (Grigg *Mechanism of Psychosis* 49). As structural linguists, Damouretts and Pichon held that once a speaker has uttered a word, it then prevents certain possibilities from occurring because the utterance forecloses future events. However, for Lacan, rather than the utterance preventing the possibility of an event taking place, foreclosure refers to the 'fact that the speaker lacks the very linguistic resources for making the statement at all' because the experience never made it into the Symbolic order and therefore can't be represented with language (ibid). Put another away, the word (the signifier) is absent. Herein lies a key difference between repression and foreclosure; repression is linguistic in nature because for something to be repressed in the unconscious (which is structured like a language) it has to be first registered in the Symbolic (the realm of language) (Wright 74). If the repressed element has been registered in the Symbolic, then it has already been recognized by the subject. However, in psychosis the 'necessary signifiers' (ibid) (the words and the language) are absent so the subject can't recognize and then repress, but forecloses instead: 'foreclosure is a mechanism that simply treats the foreclosed as if it did not exist' (Grigg *Lacan, Language and Philosophy* 7). It follows, then, that Nina's psychotic hallucinations are events in the domain of the Real – she doesn't have the linguistic resources for these 'unspeakable' symptoms to manifest within the Symbolic.

In order for the child to successfully navigate the full trajectory of the pre-Oedipal stage and the Oedipus complex, it must be able to differentiate itself as a subject and hence as a separate individual from the mother. This differentiation, which aligns with entry into the Symbolic order, requires the ability to substitute a representation of experience for experience itself. In other words, symbolization must occur through language. However, the foundation for symbolization occurs during primal repression, a process which secures the primordial signifier, referred to by Lacan as the Name-of-the-Father (Dor *Reading of Lacan* 113). Given that Nina does not have a single paternal figure but rather a very over-bearing maternal figure in her life, primal repression fails, the Name-of-the-Father paternal metaphor is foreclosed, and Nina does not gain entry into the Symbolic, but continues to exist instead within the Imaginary for most of her adult life. Foreclosure (*verwerfung*) is the action which prevents primal repression from occurring in some cases (ibid 121). As foreclosure doesn't necessarily lead to psychosis, it is important to recognize that it is only Name-of-the-Father foreclosure which creates psychosis, because the Name-of-the-Father is the primordial signifier.

During the process of foreclosure, the subject banishes the possibility of castration threatened by the Name-of-the-Father from the register of language and symbolization; it is sent to 'another place'. This place is external to the subject (and the subject's world); the foreclosed is expelled into the alien domain of the Real. The Real differs from reality as reality can be represented and consciously perceived (Grigg *Lacan, Language and Philosophy* 7), although interestingly the Real can manifest in physical reality for the psychotic subject. As previously discussed, this is the case in *Black Swan* where the psychotic experiences of Nina are cinematically conveyed to the viewer as they present themselves visually in her reality – and specifically through her own corporeal reality, highlighting the connection between the subject's corporeal reality and psychological state. Only through this manifestation of the Real emerging in reality can the viewer understand the way that Nina experiences her psychosis (hallucinations and paranoia primarily) (Ouweneel 199).

As foreclosure of the Name-of-the-Father creates psychosis (Restuccia 203), it is logical that Nina's psychosis in *Black Swan* emerges not only at the climax of her career (and therefore an emotionally stress filled time), but also at the time in her life she first comes under the control of a male choreographer, Thomas (Vincent Cassel), who functions as both the object of her sexual desire and the governor of her career. While Nina's childhood is lacking a father figure and is overly endowed with the maternal presence, it could be argued that she does not escape the primordial signifier altogether; rather, it appears in a deferred form as Thomas. Thomas has an influential position in Nina's life; he wields significant power and his actions have considerable effect on her physically, mentally and emotionally, indicating his role as the master phallus. Thomas may be seen as governing the ballet world, where his opinion is law, and he regulates the desire of his dancers. It is during her interactions with Thomas that it becomes apparent that Nina's Oedipal trajectory is incomplete: she simultaneously fears him (she cowers before his criticism), rebels against him (resists his advice) and desires him (attempts to sexually seduce him in order to get the role of Swan Queen). Two decades after it was meant to occur, a male figure (Thomas) enters Nina's life and fulfils the paternal metaphor; Thomas enters the position of Name-of-the-Father for Nina. Resultantly Nina resumes the trajectory of her Oedipal complex, although in delayed form, and far too late to prevent the foreclosure which leads to her psychosis. As the Name-of-the-Father is a paternal metaphor which replaces desire for the mother (and the mother's desire) and puts in its place phallic meaning (Grigg *Lacan, Language and Philosophy* 7), this explains the hostile tension between Erica and Thomas, who are fighting for control over, and intimacy with, Nina. If we view Thomas as a belated primordial signifier for Nina, perhaps this is why he has even more effect on her than her mother during the timeframe of *Black Swan*. As the father figure he outranks the mother in the same way that the paternal metaphor (Name-of-the-Father) is a primordial signifier because it holds a particularly powerful position in the 'subject's symbolic universe', where it governs order, including regulating laws and rules surrounding desire of both the child and mother (Dor *Reading of Lacan* 93).

According to Lacan the onset of a psychotic episode can't be predicted, although the elements required for the onset are present all along, existing dormant within the subject since childhood (Grigg *Mechanism of Psychosis* 60). The trigger is an event where the Name-of-the-Father is called into 'symbolic opposition to the subject', meaning the subject is called into a position, through language, that illuminates the lack of the primordial signifier (ibid), which has been foreclosed. This outcome is somewhat more significant than neurosis, which occurs if the resolution of the Oedipus complex merely suffers a disruption.

Having said this, Lacan considers that in subjects with an underlying psychotic structure who are yet to enter into a full-blown psychosis there is a degree of 'suppletion' (*suppleance*). Suppletion is the pre-psychosis attempt to find an alternative substitute for what is absent at the level of the Symbolic register. In other words, the subject finds a 'stand-in', another person who can temporarily cover for the absence of the Name-of-the-Father. The substitute is adequate until an enigma occurs and the lack of meaning beneath is revealed. Grigg states that it is not uncommon for this series of events to occur at the beginning of adulthood, where previously the libidinal relationship between mother and child wasn't challenged (ibid). Although *Black Swan* casts Nina in her mid-late 20s, the foreclosure on the Name-of-the-Father and absence of primal repression in her childhood enable the continuation of her infantile relation well into her adult years. Resultantly, until the time frame in which *Black Swan* is set, the Nina-Erica libidinal relationship thrived. With her new role as the prima ballerina, this relationship is challenged for the first time by Thomas, who makes Nina aware of her own ambitions and desires beyond the ones she shares with Erica. Erica views Thomas as a threat, having endangered the intimacy she had previously shared unspoiled with Nina in their pre-Oedipal dyad; however, once Thomas activates the position of Name-of-the-Father for Nina, anyone else can theoretically occupy this function too – Erica included.

One such example of suppletion and Erica fulfilling this role emerges in the scene where Nina awakens one morning in her bed. Assuming she is alone in her bedroom, she begins to masturbate. As her erotic pleasure builds towards sexual climax, she turns her head to the side and notices Erica sitting in a chair beside the bed. Although Erica is asleep in the chair, and therefore hasn't directly witnessed Nina's masturbation, her very presence in the same room is an encroachment on the literal and metaphorical space of independence that post-Oedipal adult subjects usually enjoy (Pheasant-Kelly *Abject Spaces* 30). Therefore, this scene can be interpreted as a filmic portrayal of the castration threat where Erica functions as an authoritarian figure over Nina's sexuality. As Nina has not fully moved beyond the Imaginary into the Symbolic, she continues to exist in the infantile state which indulges in frequent masturbation. Castration threat occurs when the parental figure acknowledges this masturbation and discourages it by implicitly threatening to remove (in other words, castrate) the genitalia. The parent's threat is authoritative, and in most cases, is enough to shift the child into the next developmental stage beyond the maternal phallus intimacy with the mother. In *Black Swan* Erica's presence in the room suggests she attempts to wield the authoritative power of a parent restricting masturbation and threatening castration. However, in this instance the threat is empty, given that Erica does not actually wish Nina to move beyond her role as maternal phallus in the pre-Oedipal phase and, moreover, that she herself is asleep. This scene suggests that, while Erica embodies the role of an authoritarian presence, she continues to have erotic complicity in the outdated libidinal relationship between herself and her child.

Lacan further suggests that during an episode of psychosis a phenomenon occurs that he calls *pousse à la femme* (which means a 'push towards woman'). *Pousse à la femme* is an attempt by the psychotic subject to gain 'endorsement and consent from the father' (Grigg *Lacan, Language and Philosophy* 14) through a process of feminization. Again, Nina's desperate need to please Thomas may be interpreted as her attempt at gaining endorsement and consent from the closest thing she's ever had to a father figure. The process of feminization can be observed in Nina's subservient demeanour towards Thomas and her physical embodiment of feminine delicacy. This physical feminization is exacerbated by her thinness, her grace on stage and her wardrobe off-stage, which entirely consists of soft pinks and whites. Most importantly, the *pousse à la femme*, in Nina's case, indicates her increasingly ambiguous relation to the Imaginary register of pre-Oedipal intimacy.

The conscious unconscious and the breaking of boundaries

Given that Nina suffers a gradual banishment from the Imaginary and has also been prevented from entering the Symbolic, she is theoretically left nowhere to exist besides Lacan's third register – the Real. In other words, it seems logical that she experiences foreclosure of the Name-of-the-Father in such a traumatic way and psychologically suffers because of this. During psychosis the unconscious is (unusually) at the surface of the subject and becomes conscious (Lacan *The Psychoses* 11). Take, for example, Nina's unconscious understanding of herself as fragmented and incomplete – a knowledge so horrific it is located in the Real, manifests visually through the depiction of a Black Swan appearing at certain moments at the boundaries of her own body, revealing the connection between psychological state and corporeal reality. However, articulating the unconscious through certain (psychotic) behaviours doesn't necessarily mean that the unconscious recognizes itself. Lacan also states, 'The subject speaks to himself with his ego' (ibid 14) in an atemporal conversation, although, ironically, it would seem the subject is unaware this conversation is going on. Lacan then argues that the intrigue is not in the way that the unconscious manifests behaviourally in the subject while remaining out of reach of the subject's comprehension (although this is remarkable), but rather why the unconscious manifests in the realm of the Real.

Psychosis is marked by the subject reacting to seemingly insignificant signs and investing them with meaning and significance (Lacan *The Psychoses* 9). Lacan uses the example of the subject who sees a red car in the street. If the subject is psychotic they will conceive that the red car went past deliberately at that moment, that its presence is significant; they imbue it with meaning. Similarly, everything becomes a sign for the psychotic individual (Kristeva *Desire in Language* 139). The whole world is full of attributed meanings, many of them negative and sinister, making the psychotic subject alienated and often afraid. Nina's decline into psychosis is highlighted by her investment of meaning into events which are insignificant. For example, she perceives that a single glance from a rival dancer, Lily (Mila Kunis), is evidence of Lily attempting to usurp Nina's position in the company. Similarly, fleeting shadows in the dance studio are interpreted by Nina as Lily and Thomas erotically embracing. These insignificant things are imbued with significance because the absence of a primordial signifier in Nina's childhood and hence the absence of primal repression means that signifying chains remain unanchored to the Symbolic. Those signifying chains float freely so signification occurs anywhere at any time or, as Lacan calls it 'the emergence in reality of an enormous meaning that has the appearance of being nothing at all' (Lacan *The Psychoses* 85). The meaning the psychotic garners from these experiences (elements, objects, events or people) is understandable to them, yet totally unnatural to others, making paranoia a difficult phenomenon for the non-paranoid to comprehend. Essentially each psychotic subject reinvents a Symbolic realm, where they alone exist. The difficulty for the analyst is that the signifiers are random, so the problem lies in understanding the mechanism the subject (unknowingly) employs. In other words, the psychoanalyst needs to consider structural traits and patterns rather than a mere observing of symptoms (Dor *The Clinical Lacan* 16). In the case of Nina there is a definite persecution paranoia occurring, although even the viewer is not in a position to know whether this paranoia is justified.

The central clinical characteristic of psychosis is an altered relationship with reality (DSM-V; Lacan *The Psychoses* 44). This altered relationship with reality is called 'delusion' and functions as a defence mechanism for the subject (ibid 79). Interestingly, for the psychotic, an alternative connection with reality isn't necessarily problematic, given that those experiences may not negatively affect the subject (ibid 75). The problem lies in the psychotic's certainty of that reality, that they believe what they are experiencing to be real regardless of what that entails – even the extraordinary. It is the psychotic's utter conviction of the truth of signifying events that makes them delusional. So while it is unlikely that Lily wishes to usurp Nina's prima ballerina position, Nina is not in a frame of mind where she can view the situation objectively. She is certain that Lily slipped drugs into her drink so that she would be late for rehearsal the following day, despite this being an extraordinary accusation. Lacan claims the psychotic's 'certainty is radical' (ibid), meaning that others who aren't psychotic may experience the same things but have significant doubt surrounding the truth or reality of the experience. Indeed, the truly deluded subject will become increasingly certain of their beliefs (ibid 77). In addition to this, the deeper the psychotic enters into the conviction of their delusion, the more of their world the delusion will encapsulate. In *Black Swan* for example, Nina's suspicion of Lily as a sabotaging force grows to also include Thomas, her mother and some of the other dances in the company. In theory, left untreated, the psychotic subject's whole existence will be pulled into the delusion.

Mirrors are an appropriate cinematic prop for the depiction of psychosis given that they provide an image which functions as the visual manifestation of the emergence of the Real in reality, and they convey the relationship between corporeal reality and psychological state. In other words, the viewer is able to see what Nina is experiencing through her own meaning generation. Further to that, since the subject's ego identity is based on a reflective image, Nina continues to look to the image for confirmation of the ideal ego (her imago). Nonetheless, the mirror is also the object which exposes the subconscious understanding of the body as fragmented and incomplete, and in turn the Oedipus complex as unresolved. Yet, the mirror also serves as an aesthetic representative of subjective destitution – the eventual realization that the supposed 'reflection' is actually not reliable in its depiction of 'reality' (Pile 124). Ultimately, it is precisely the authenticity of the mirror image that *Black Swan* throws into doubt; the reflection cannot be trusted.

Not surprisingly, then, given the constant presence of mirrors in *Black Swan*, and the link between corporeal reality and psychological state, the three most crucial moments of psychosis take place in front of full-length dance studio mirrors. The psychotic deterioration of Nina's psyche is depicted in a costume-measuring scene where she senses a shift in the reflected image in front of her, though she herself doesn't move. When she tries to scrutinize this movement, the mirror image 'behaves' and whatever she thought she saw disappears. A second key scene shows Nina rehearsing by herself in the studio late at night. Her body and the image in the reflection are framed simultaneously through a series of long shots and extreme long shots. As she rotates *en pointe* before the mirror the reflected image loses synchronization with her real-world self. The mirror image is slightly behind her timing, completing the rotation a second after her. When she attempts to eradicate her suspicions (as in the previous costume-measuring scene), the mirror image doesn't conform this time but instead refuses to move even when Nina lifts an arm. It is at this moment that the malevolent Black Swan Nina fears, which is the visual representation of the fragmented self, is explicitly shown and the effect is horrifying for both Nina and the viewer.

This moment indicates the emergence of Nina's pathology, a psychosis which is based on the realization that she is fragmented and incomplete. As previously stated, the confines of the mirror's glass surface function as something of a safety barrier – a boundary between Nina's subconscious and conscious mind. So long as Nina's real body and mirror image remain synchronized, the horrific understanding of the self as fragmented and incomplete remains undisturbed. These two images falling out of synch visually signifies that Nina's conscious and subconscious are out of synch; they contain different information and they 'talk' to each other in an atemporal conversation. Her conscious contains the White Swan imago while the subconscious contains the Black Swan reality. Terrified, Nina takes several steps backwards, reversing into another studio mirror. Now the reflection, still representative of the Black Swan, turns independently to look malevolently at the real Nina. This moment of turning and confronting the image is the first visual representation of outright rivalry between the ideal ego gained in the mirror phase (the White Swan imago) and the actual fragmented self (the Black Swan).

These 'mirror moments' in *Black Swan* are visual hallucinations, part of the set of symptoms that occur with psychosis. Lacan refers to a number of 'elementary phenomena' which manifest during psychosis (Grigg *Mechanism of Psychosis* 57). Such phenomena can specifically include thought-echoes, verbal enunciations and hallucinations. Hallucinations exist within the realm of the Real but appear as if in reality to the psychotic subject (ibid 53) because, whereas the repressed returns as a neurotic symptom, the foreclosed returns in a form 'outside the subject' by reappearing in the Real (ibid 56). Hallucinations may be verbal, visual or tactile in nature (Lacan *The Psychoses* 14) and are 'located at both the symbolic and imaginary levels', meaning symptoms of psychosis may contain language and image and manifest in the form of hallucination (Grigg *Mechanism of Psychosis* 53). In Nina's case her psychosis reveals itself insidiously through the increasingly frightening visual depiction of body malformations, which are entirely appropriate given that her psychosis is based on the realization of the self as fragmented and incomplete. In contrast to the grace of her body on the dance floor, her psychosis initially manifests in the form of her body encountering monstrous phenomena such as her skin peeling back from her nail, the emergence of black feathers through her skin and eventually the snapping of her shin bone which reforms into a swan's leg (Grosz 45; Laine *Bodies in Pain* 127–31). These grotesque events are the horrific Real erupting into Nina's reality, pushing at the seams of her conscious.

Nina's psychological deterioration manifests visually and physically in the image of a Swan for a particular reason. Not only is the Black Swan representative of horrific knowledge, but the White Swan is Nina's imago. The emergence of separated swan body parts, pushed through her skin, suggest that her fragmented self is literalized onscreen as dissected pieces of her imago. This suggests that both the illusion of the White Swan imago and the Black Swan spectre of foreclosure must be shattered if she is to regain psychological health. It is also reconfirmation that the White Swan is as much a symbol of her psychosis as the Black Swan, thereby reinforcing the subjective destitution function of the mirror within *Black Swan*: the mirror is an aestheticized version of subjective destitution, the realization that the reflection is actually not a depiction of reality, and the mirror image is untrustworthy.

Black Swan's climax involves a physically aggressive altercation on opening night of Swan Lake. Interestingly Nina and Lily (the supposed rival dancer) look similar, though Lily is a better embodiment of the seductive Black Swan. When Nina looks in her dressing room mirror during the interval, she (being in a paranoid psychosis) sees Lily in the reflection, dressed and ready to go on stage as the Black Swan. Mistaking the reflection for the real thing, in a moment of physical aggression Nina (as the White Swan) fights with the reflection and shatters the mirror. The shattering of the mirror is symbolic of the moment that the barrier surrounding Nina's conscious mind is fully punctured by the traumatic subconscious knowledge. The breaking of the glass surface indicates the walls are down, and the conscious is being flooded with the psychosis that is based on her traumatic understanding of her fragmented self. As she fights, the image of Lily morphs slightly to reveal that it was Nina was in the reflection all along and what the viewer sees is an image of Nina fighting her absolute replica – herself – thus suggesting a very palpable struggle between the imago White Swan and the fragmented self, the Black Swan. This physical altercation indicates that Nina is struggling desperately to maintain the ideal ego she aspires to whilst the foreclosed significance of her infantile relation with her mother attempts to push through to the conscious. Although she has already succumbed to psychosis, any acknowledgement of her libidinal connection with her mother and her incomplete self is horrific, and this physical fight is the last-ditch attempt to avoid acknowledging those traumatic truths. Accordingly, the White-Swan-Nina stabs the reflection-Nina with a shard of glass from the shattered mirror.

As the Black-Swan-reflection lies unconscious in a pool of her own blood, Nina goes out to perform the role of the Black Swan. During the performance the skin on her arms gradually develops black feathers. This is a visual symbol that, despite her attempts to silence the truth (by stabbing the reflection), with the blurring of the border between reality and the Real, Nina finally recognizes she is fragmented and she *is* the Black Swan. By the end of the performance the feathers have grown into huge, fully developed black wings. Previously the emergence of Black Swan body parts through Nina's own skin was grotesque and rebelled against. The uninhibited growth of the wings and their ethereal beauty in this moment suggests Nina is no longer attempting to fight the appearance of the Black Swan and acknowledges herself as fragmentary. The presence of those wings represents her fragmentation and fixity in an ever-recurring mirror phase with her mother, deprived of the paternal metaphor and resulting in maldevelopment that has plagued her since.

When Nina returns to the dressing room, she discovers that the body she stabbed has disappeared. At this moment she emerges from her psychotic episode, reconnecting with reality and understanding that she didn't stab another dancer but her own mirror image – and in stabbing her mirror image she has, of course, stabbed herself. This newfound clarity signifies not only her emergence out of psychosis but the realization that she is neither her White Swan imago or her fearsome Black Swan doppelgänger; she is Nina Sayers, who lives in the real world, in a physical body that is separate from her reflection image and from her mother.

Nina manages to dance the final scene, but upon landing her last jump, she reveals her abdominal wound and (ironically) whispers the words, 'I was perfect', a long overdue acknowledgement of her own ability as a dancer and her acceptability as an individual. Up to this point Nina was still heavily reliant on the reassurance of the mirror imago and yet had been prevented from entering the Symbolic by Erica. Resultantly she never properly used the term 'I' in reference to the self and hadn't claimed full ownership of herself as separate from others (and in particular her mother). The use of the term 'I' at this moment suggests her psychotic break actually assisted her in moving into the realm of the Symbolic where she can utilize language to distinguish herself for the first time, although it is important to note that this moment comes at the point of her death. However, an alternative reading is that the words 'I was perfect' are actually an indication of Nina's understanding, not of her perfection as a dancer and individual, but that her identity as a subject who is both fragmented Black Swan and imago White Swan, is a normal and genuine state of the human condition; that clarity, truth and even 'perfection' can be found in combinations, inconsistencies and imperfections.

Agony and ecstasy: Jouissance

Jouissance is a 'fundamental cornerstone of Lacan's thought' (Braunstein 102). It is a difficult word to translate into English (arguably there is no singular equivalent) and as such has remained written in French. Some suggest that jouissance may be compared with a combination of the terms 'lust' and 'enjoyment', although it is not correct to say that jouissance is solely pleasurable. In accordance with this Lacan also stated that an element of jouissance exists at the point where pain appears, suggesting that jouissance is both non-pleasurable and pleasurable, or pleasurable in a masochistic way. Yet it is also not accurate to say that jouissance is satisfaction or satiety that comes after pleasure. Rather, jouissance is beyond satisfaction; it's what the subject encounters on the return trip from satisfaction, the result of the death drive (ibid 106). The law (Name-of-the-Father) is closely linked with desire (the mother-child libidinal relation). Therefore, jouissance is also linked to the law through the act of transgressing it. This simple formula would also suggest that jouissance is the utter breaking of boundaries rather than the pushing of their limits (ibid 108).

For Lacan the body is the location of jouissance and involves the process of tension and release (Nasio 106), reiterating again the link between corporeal reality and psychological state. According to Braunstein, 'Jouissance is alien to speech, a bodily hieroglyphic that can only be deciphered after the incorporation of the subject in the world of language' (109). It is not surprising then that a film which focuses on the aesthetic profession of ballet incorporates the transgressive pleasure of jouissance. In the course of *Black Swan* jouissance is present in several instances. The impossible perfectionism demanded of ballet dancers requires hours of excruciating practice, which only the very dedicated (or the psychotic) will maintain into professional careers. So while the love of dance and the pleasure that comes from dancing drives Nina, this pleasure is also met by an equally painful amount of suffering (both physical and mental), which is required to attain that pleasure. In a less physical but similar psychological sense, the emergence of the Black Swan provides both agony and ecstasy for Nina, who longs to embrace this darker side of her creative ability yet suffers for every second the Black Swan occupies her being (given the Black Swan represents such a painful truth). Nina is the epitome of the cliché of the tortured artist who suffers through terrible pain for her art, yet masochistically enjoys the suffering.

The moment in the dressing room when Nina stabs her reflection/herself with a shard of glass is particularly meaningful. The destabilization of her imago happens as an internal process. As the Black Swan erupts from the Real and pushes increasingly at her conscious boundaries during the course of the film, she doesn't so much unravel as implode. This self-destructive process is symbolized in a finale by the shattering of her reflection in the mirror and the stabbing of her torso. She is so engulfed by the psychosis and yet so desperately afraid of acknowledging the truth that she uses a fragment (the shard of mirror) of her fragmented self (the Black Swan reflection) to avoid acknowledging the truth (that she is fragmented). It is important to recognize that she uses a shard of her former Black Swan reflection to stab her White Swan self, suggesting (again) the subconscious attempt to 'free' the truth by breaking the shell of the White Swan imago. While for the majority of the film the Black Swan has appeared to be a malevolent force, this scene turns this perception on its head and reinforces the notion that the White Swan imago is as much a symbol of Nina's psychosis as the Black Swan. This inversion occurs when one considers the Black Swan is actually trying to 'help' Nina recognize her underlying fragmented self in order to repair it, to move beyond the mother-child libidinal relationship and to become a better functioning adult. So although the insertion of a piece of glass into her own torso is physically painful, the action may simultaneously be driven by pleasure – the pleasure of revealing the painful truth.

Finally, the erotic mother-child relationship Nina shares with her mother is also a basis of jouissance in *Black Swan*. While Nina derives pleasure from the closeness she has with her mother, the comfort of her pink bedroom, her childhood toys and the support her mother provides, it is also painful for her to be caught at the juncture of childhood and adulthood. She is an adult living a child's life, straining to have her independence and her freedom whilst simultaneously fearing those things. In this respect her unique relationship with Erica is both wonderful and terrible, and she experiences a painful pleasure from it. Given Thomas's role as the late-arriving Law of the Father that attempts to shut down the libidinal relationship between Nina and Erica, their ongoing pre-Oedipal relations are certainly transgressive, from which jouissance is derived. Yet, eventually Nina chooses to move beyond this relationship, declaring to Erica that she wants to move out and have her own space as an adult. In response to Erica's upset question, 'Where's my sweet girl?', Nina triumphantly replies, 'She's gone!'

Conclusion: The agency of the reflection

The mirror phase has long been acknowledged as an important stage in the development of the subject. Lacan in particular theorized that recognizing one's reflection was a crucial moment in the psychological progression of the infant. Engaging with the mirror and recognizing the reflection indicates the infant subject understands the self as a person separate from the mother and with physical autonomy. Although I acknowledge the importance of this psychoanalytic work and concur that the subject initially conceptualizes itself through image, I also argue that a prolonged and intense relationship with the reflection of one's image can be ultimately damaging, a confirmation that the subject's corporeal reality and psychological state are linked. *Black Swan* suggests that for an infant, the image is informative. For an adult, the image is destructive.

Beyond the early infancy years the mirror ceases to be a neutral zone which placidly reflects colour and movement. For people such as dancers, gymnasts and models who engage with the mirror for sustained periods of time, the reflection gains significantly more meaning. In these instances, the reflection first becomes a confirmation of identity – a reassurance that the subject exists so long as the reflection is there. Secondly, the individual in the aesthetic professions returns to that image again and again to solidify a sense of self. Eventually, the identity of these individuals comes to depend on the mirror image rather than be solidified by it. These professions are notorious for their demand of aesthetic perfection. Consequentially the ballerina (Nina in this case) is no longer able to turn to the image for self-confirmation: neither confirmation of identity or of perfection can be reliably found in the mirror.

This analysis has sought to formally identify the link between the image and psychosis in *Black Swan*. The psychoanalytic reading of this text revealed that the mirror wields more power than usually attributed to it; the mirror isn't benign and the reflection has agency. Those whose identity relies on the mirror image become tormented by the desire to first make the image flawless and then to embody the image and the perfection that comes with it at all times. The attempt to embody and sustain perfection in one's corporeal reality is impossible, and the drive to do so can cause immense emotional, psychological and physical stress.

Despite the Black Swan appearing in the mirror image as malevolent and representative of her psychological disorder, *Black Swan* suggests that the greater damage is inflicted on Nina not through the haunting psychosis of the Black Swan, but through the taunting perfectionism of the White Swan and *untruth* of the imago reflection. This finding appears unique within the current literature about the film, which generally focuses on the Black Swan's negative positioning as a symbol of disease, inequality and Otherness (Marston 695–711; Sandino 305–17), or a horrific indicator of madness and distress (Bignall 121–38; Clover 7–9; Fisher and Jacobs 58–62; Smith et al. 97–101), or a sign of repressed female sexuality within the patriarchy (Corpus 157–60; Subramanian and Lagerwey 1–20). These readings of *Black Swan* tend to avoid acknowledging that the obsessive striving for perfectionism, presented onscreen by the mirror imago and the ethereal White Swan, is an aspect of Nina's identity which is just as dangerous and damaging in the subject's diegetic trajectory through psychosis.

While in the instance of *Black Swan* the central character Nina faces several confrontations with other characters, it is the relationship with her reflection that takes centre stage in this film. Arguably, this is because the relationship with her reflection is the nodal point for all of her struggles, such as her intense relationship with her mother, her rivalry with other dancers and her emerging sexual desires. Nina's declining psychological health is appropriately depicted through that mirror image and the harder she tries to *be* her imago through the embodiment of perfection, the further into psychological disorder she progresses. In the end the most horrific fear for Nina, that she be taken over by the grotesque Black Swan, is actually the event which breaks the cycle of perfectionist delusion, albeit this belated movement into the Symbolic comes at the point of her death, and allows her to identify as something other than an image.

2

The Machinist (2004)

Introduction to insomnia and *The Machinist*

The DSM-V recognizes a state of chronic sleeplessness as a psychiatric condition commonly called 'insomnia' (APA). Insomnia sits within the 'Sleep-Wake Disorders' of the DSM-V, amongst hyper-somnolence, narcolepsy and nightmare disorder. Individuals suffering from these disorders typically experience impairment to daytime functioning, including difficulties with concentration, memory or performance of manual tasks. Most relevant to this chapter's psychoanalysis of the 2004 film *The Machinist* (Anderson), is the DSM-V's statement that persistent sleep problems 'present a prodromal expression of an episode of mental illness' (APA), meaning the sleep disruption is a sign of other psychological disturbance to come. This corresponds to the fact that disturbances to sleep are more likely to begin during a period of acute emotional and psychological stress and that people who generally repress emotions or are anxious are more vulnerable to insomnia. Eluned Summers-Bremner, who specializes in trauma, cultural memory and clinical psychoanalysis, points out that, ironically, when sleep becomes particularly necessary, anxiety about not getting enough sleep makes the process of getting to sleep even more difficult (Summers-Bremner 65). Consequently, the individual who is lacking sleep often encounters an exponential decrease in sleep due to the growing anxiety surrounding the lack (ibid). Keeping these DSM-V criteria in mind, Reznik from *The Machinist* sits comfortably within the insomniac category of Sleep-Wake Disorders. For a period of one year he experiences consistent difficulty achieving a deep state of unconsciousness conducive to rest. Reznik's sleep disturbance has particularly large repercussions, as it generates subsequent psychological symptoms with severely destructive indications.

The Machinist is a psychological thriller about Trevor Reznik (Christian Bale), who becomes convinced he is the target of a plot to harm him. The film documents his progression from an initial sense that something is amiss in his life into a full-blown paranoid state which severely impacts on his ability to function normally. The crux of *The Machinist* is that, despite Reznik's increasing suspicion of the people around him, he is actually the guilty party. It is this guilt which causes his insomnia and creates disorder in multiple aspects of his life; in tracking this disorder, this film analysis will confirm the destructive power of guilt, shedding particular light on how the subject physically responds to guilt, and highlighting the links between psychological state and corporeal reality, as well as psychological state and death.

The Machinist includes a series of cinematic 'red herrings' in the form of a group of psychological symptoms which function as stepping stones, eventually leading to the truth. At the start of the film the viewer is first made aware that Reznik can't sleep, followed by revealing that he is also physically emaciated, that he is pathologically writing notes to himself, that he is suffering from paranoia and finally, that he is having hallucinations. Reznik's insomnia, which at first seems so central to the diegetic mystery, is therefore just the initial symptom of his guilt which facilitates the onset of his other symptoms; it is what Lacan and Žižek refer to as a 'cyphered message' for what he is 'not able to confront' (Žižek *Enjoy Your Symptom* 175). Individually the symptoms depict a suffering subject and instantiate a confusing diegesis, but when analysed together, they reveal a diegetic truth; as Žižek explains, 'one can only arrive at the final truth though the path of errors, so these errors are not simply discarded, but "sublated" in the final truth' (*Event* 98). The final truth arrived at is that one year prior to the setting of the film Reznik was the driver in a hit-and-run accident which killed a child; it is his killing of an 'Other' which triggers his disordered psychological state. He spends the duration of this film feeling suspicious of the people around him, but eventually acknowledges his own guilt, and consequently, gets to sleep, the psychological (guilt) functioning as a gateway to the neurological (insomnia). Unfortunately for Reznik, the acknowledgement of his guilt only comes after it has generated some very negative experiences – insomnia, emaciation, paranoia, hallucinations and his ostracism from mainstream society.

Most scholarship regarding *The Machinist* is provoked by Christian Bale's physical weight loss for the role of Reznik (Fielding 2). Quinlivan suggests the film 'explores a kind of metamorphosis of the mind and body … embodied by his wasting body which comes to stand for his desire to repent and punish himself' (34); Steward argues that Reznik's emaciation is indicative of suffering (81) which the director 'magnifies and accentuates' through lingering shots illuminating bones beneath skin (79); Bould and Vint argue that Reznik's emaciation is a model of capitalist subjectivity; and Fouz-Hernandez suggests that Reznik's anorexic physique pushes him into a liminal zone of masculinity, challenging traditional socio-cultural ideals of hegemonic gender identity.

Few pieces of literature look beyond Reznik's emaciation but several scholars also consider the link between insomnia and guilt (Fristanty; Wolf-Meyer; Quinlivan; Wedding and McCrae), Andrade acknowledges the role of the double or doppelgänger as a representation of both threat and desire in *The Machinist*, and Potter and Rey argue that Reznik suffers from PTSD. Potter and Rey's reading of *The Machinist* is problematic because Reznik's insomnia prevents the heightened neurological alertness and nightmares that are characteristic of PTSD, nor does he engage in PTSD avoidant behaviours or develop the psychological disorder from a perceived threat to his own life. Regardless of the interpretation of Reznik's physicality, almost all the literature published about *The Machinist* concurs that the film sits within the genre of psychological thriller (Fielding; Kimber; Panek; Taubin; Wedding and McCrae; Wolf-Meyer).

Reznik's memory: The unknown known

One of the key questions regarding *The Machinist* concerns why and how Reznik committed a hit-and-run crime and forgot about it for a period of a year. In order to approach this, the relationship between emotion and memory needs to be briefly considered.

Chris Brewin, Professor of Clinical Psychology specializing in memory and PTSD, argues that intense emotion at a particular moment in time has significant effects on the functionality of memory (Brewin 88). The most extreme example of altered memory due to emotional intensity is total memory loss (amnesia) regarding the event (ibid 98). Over time the memory begins to return to the individual but this process may take days or it may take years, meaning Reznik's year-long amnesia of the car accident is certainly possible. Psychoanalytic thinking suggests this post-trauma amnesia can occur because repression functions as a defence mechanism which pushes uncomfortable experiences into the unconscious mind (ibid). With regard to Reznik, Brewin argues that the extreme negative emotions (shock, despair, disgust, fear) involved in the hit-and-run accident affected not only the accuracy of his memory (in terms of details), but also the conscious accessibility to this memory. The event was simply too awful and therefore repressed in the unconscious to become what Žižek refers to as 'unknown knowns': things which the subject knows about, but doesn't realize they know consciously (*Event* 11).

Elisabeth Bronfen, Professor of Cultural Studies and Literature, suggests Reznik's various psychological issues (insomnia, emaciation, paranoia and hallucinations) are therefore expressions of the return of the repressed (Bronfen *Night Passages* 87), entering into the conscious as symptoms, which themselves function as metaphors for the trauma of the car accident (Belau *Trauma, Repetition* 153). Because the origin of these symptoms is mysterious (due to the amnesia) they appear to the subject as being external to him. As a film full of red herrings, *The Machinist* encourages the viewer and Reznik to believe this, before eventually revealing that, of course, symptoms originate from an internal space (Dor *Clinical Lacan* 14) – Reznik's own guilty conscience – and failure to resolve the original guilt only results in further psychological suffering, such is its destructive nature.

For the duration of *The Machinist* the viewer is no more aware of the truth than Reznik. The audience learns he is guilty piece by piece, only as he himself recalls the traumatic event of hitting a child (called Nicholas) with his car. The effect of this gradual unfolding storyline is twofold; initially the nonlinear narrative and the mysterious driver of the plot cement *The Machinist* in the psychological thriller film genre. Additionally, because the viewer's knowledge of the diegesis is directly tied to Reznik's knowledge, his subjectivity informs the basis of the text. In other words, we 'read' this film solely through Reznik's experiences.

The restriction of the viewer's knowledge is evident from the outset, and what *The Machinist* excludes from its narrative 'proves just as significant' as what it includes (McSweeney 39). For example, the opening scene of *The Machinist* captures Reznik, with a long shot, through the dark glass of his apartment window. The viewer, positioned outside the window, looks in on him rolling something long and heavy in a carpet. Reznik then drives to the seaside at night-time and heaves the rolled carpet into the ocean. It is not certain that the carpet contains a dead body, but Reznik's suspicious behaviour (driving to the seaside at night) and the length and weight of the object suggest he is disposing of a corpse; a signposting that Reznik's story is linked with death. Reznik is observed doing this by a man who, standing a few metres away in the darkness, holds a flashlight in his direction and asks, 'Who are you?' Neither Reznik nor the viewer can see the identity of the man, hidden from view by the brightness of his torch beam. Reznik doesn't answer the question, and the following scene shows

Reznik scrubbing his hands with bleach in his apartment. However, a large flashlight sits on the table behind him, signalling that the anonymous man who 'catches' Reznik with the body is actually himself, and the voice he hears is the voice of his own conscience (his superego), although this much is not obvious to the viewer upon first watching the film. This indication of his guilty conscience is re-iterated by the post-it note stuck to the wall behind Reznik, which also says, 'Who are you?' The opening sequence asks a variety of questions to which the film provides no answers until the closing scenes, with only Reznik's insomnia approached in the film as an obvious psychological disorder.

Insomnia as a psychological and social issue

Simon Williams, who specializes in the sociology and politics of sleep, states that historically insomnia has been approached with a variety of treatments including prayer and meditation, blood-letting, exercise and diet, music, herbal remedies and acupuncture, psychological therapy and, in more recent times, prescribed pharmaceutical substances (Williams 21). At one point during *The Machinist* Reznik confides to his lover Stevie (Jennifer Jason Leigh) that 'nothing helps' in reference to the ways he has tried to get to sleep. Many practitioners of Western medicine prescribe sleeping medication on a temporary basis with the proviso that the patient consider what else may be causing the insomnia and attempt to resolve this deeper issue. In other words, the genesis of the insomnia must be approached in order to be resolved, and *The Machinist* suggests it is for this reason that Reznik finds 'nothing helps' his chronic insomnia other than resolving the deeper issue – his guilt, thereby further cementing the link between the subject's psychological state and corporeal reality. However, rather than simply developing a worsening sleep disorder, *The Machinist* conveys that the guilty subject goes down an increasingly destructive path which manifests through multiple symptoms.

In the past century sleep has played second fiddle to the apparently more interesting discussion of dreams (ibid 27). Dreams have received increased intellectual and philosophical attention (arguably due to Freud), although sleep in itself remains as misunderstood and as central to the subject's psychological state. According to Williams, sleep has a mysterious role in society as it is not a particularly well understood facet of physiology, yet (almost) every human sleeps on a daily basis for a significant length of time (ibid 9). Some of the earliest civilizations (including the Greeks, Egyptians and Chinese) were fascinated by sleep, and yet 3,000 years later many of their original questions remain unanswered (ibid).

The inexplicable nature of sleep extends to Reznik's insomnia in *The Machinist* as well. For the duration of a year he hasn't been able to sleep and yet, in all that time (and despite the significant effect it has on his life), he is no closer to understanding his insomnia. Reznik perceives both the onset and the continuation of the insomnia to be a random phenomenon and this misrecognition prevents him from attributing it as a psychological illness and, moreover, an illness with significant meaning. The lack of meaning tied to his insomnia inhibits him from resolving it, and in addition to this, he is also oblivious to the effect the insomnia is having on other aspects of his life and the destructive ramifications that unresolved guilt causes. He knows he feels tired but he has little awareness of the impact his insomnia is having on his capacity to successfully work as a machinist, to interact with the people around him (either professionally or personally) and to live within a healthy, functioning body. The ancient mysteriousness surrounding sleep therefore seeps into this filmic text and even contributes to its position in the thriller genre, through a narrative which is based on 'not-knowing' until the final scenes of the film. The eventual revelation of Reznik's guilt is somewhat ironic, given that those who are awake while others sleep have a long history of association with virtue. The individual who remains vigilantly awake suggests a righteous protection of those who sleep (Summers-Bremner 129) and in the early stages of the film *The Machinist* reinforces this ancient notion, representing Reznik as the protagonist who, along with exhibiting the chronic exhaustion detailed in the DSM-V, is both a righteous vigilante and an innocent victim of some unusual events. At the start of *The Machinist* the viewer does not perceive that the role of death within the plot is caused by Reznik. Only at the end of the film, when he remembers his moral and legal transgression (a hit-and-run incident), does he sleep, alluding to the idea that he is no longer the vigilante who upholds the law.

In addition to his psychological reasons for insomnia, the urban setting of *The Machinist* also problematizes Reznik's environment. Dense urban spaces have a particular filmic connection with insomnia given the sound and light that emits from large numbers of people living in close confines. Various urban anxieties regarding crime and conflict also contribute to the prevalence of insomnia amongst the millions of people who live in cities (ibid 110), where such anxieties and locations lend themselves well to dramatic narratives. While on the one hand the notion of the eternal city or the city that never sleeps is romantic, the constant buzz of nocturnal activity can become nightmarish for those who seek a haven of near silence and complete darkness in order to sleep (ibid 111). In addition to this, dense urban settings provide their own set of problems for central characters such as Reznik who struggle with issues of personal identity (Dryden 19). Amid the 'labyrinth metropolis' of a large city, themes of split personality, doubles and mistaken identities are commonly used (ibid), including *The Machinist* which visualizes Reznik's hallucination, caused by exhaustion, as a doppelgänger named Ivan (John Sharian).

Some medical investigations have attempted to understand sleep better by creating environments in which the amount of sleep is reduced or completely removed. For example, a 1989 study found that rats, which were deprived entirely of sleep for four weeks, suffered serious physical problems and resultantly died (Williams 19). While no documented cases of similar experiments being conducted on humans exist, sleep deprivation is a well-known form of torture (Summers-Bremner 133) due to its disorientating effects, which include visual and aural hallucinations, cognitive impairment, paranoia and changes to personality (Dryden 20). Reznik experiences all of these symptoms during *The Machinist* at some point, and often simultaneously; the doppelgänger Ivan is both a visual and aural hallucination, his inability to concentrate at work signals cognitive impairment, and his suspicious and antagonistic interactions with his colleagues and his lover suggest both paranoia and personality changes. Sleep norms vary hugely between cultures and ages[1] (Summers-Bremner 108) and are affected by climate, local customs and socio-economic conditions. Amid the wide variation of sleeping norms and the little that is understood about sleeping, it is evident that individuals who exist with consistent disturbances to their sleep norm experience negative physical and psychological side effects, which may feasibly eventuate in death if not treated (96).

---

[1] Children and teenagers need up to twelve hours each night but many adults can function effectively on 6–8 hours each night (Williams 198). Certain African tribes are said to be able to sleep while standing, some South American groups favour the hammock over the mattress and various European societies embrace a polyphasic sleeping pattern which includes a daytime siesta and a longer night-time sleep (ibid 108).

Sleep and the (living) death of insomnia

Sleeping involves an alteration to the individual's conscious state; however, the space between deep sleep and alert wakefulness is a wide spectrum. Someone who is lightly asleep or 'dozing' may also be restless and 'wired', while someone who is awake may be slow to respond and be unaware of surroundings (ibid). Although Reznik is constantly awake, he is rarely alert; his speech and movements are slowed by tiredness, and his energy levels only seem to rise when confronted by paranoid delusions, in the heat of survival instinct. Reznik moves through his day as if he were sleep-walking, with eyes open and limbs moving (albeit slowly) but cognitively deficient – in other words, awake but not awake. Interestingly this constant wakefulness renders Reznik zombie-like, the subject who, after 'a traumatic intrusion', exists as 'the empty form of the "living-dead" subject' (Žižek *Event* 88) – a deduction supported by his emaciated physical form which, like a zombie, indicates that he is also in a state of decay. This is not to argue that Reznik *is* a zombie in the virally infected, flesh-eating sense or that *The Machinist* contains elements of the zombie genre, but to highlight that he exhibits some similarities to the mindless creatures who move as physically tortured bodies through the diegesis, blind to the misery of their decaying state and the incident that generated it. Bronfen and Webster Goodwin argue that the 'cadaverous presence is such that it simultaneously occupies two places, the here and the nowhere' (12), which suggests that Reznik is literally present but also somehow metaphysically removed, his insomnia generating a spectral quality which aligns his psychological disorder with a sense of atemporality. *The Machinist* therefore presents the unusual possibility of an individual who is conscious without being alive, seemingly impossible in most circumstances, but theoretically applicable when one of the essential human needs (sleep) is fundamentally affected. This is another confirmation of how destructive unresolved guilt can be on the human subject, and further evidence of the link between psychological and physical state.

However, running parallel to the idea that Reznik is the 'living-dead' is the notion that he is the 'already dead' (Žižek *Enjoy Your Symptom* 171). *The Machinist* is not film noir although it contains certain noir elements; the nonlinear narrative structure, the driving mystery of the plot, the grim male protagonist and the dark visual quality are all reminiscent of classic noir cinema. Film noir, unlike the classic detective novel, does not reinstate a sense of universal balance and order, when the story's events are revealed in full at the end (ibid). Instead, the text's (usually male) hero unravels a series of linear events which often culminate in his own death. In other words, at the moment when the subject finally becomes integrated into the overarching truth, the big Other, 'the narrativization of his fate becomes possible only when the subject is in a sense already dead, although still alive' (ibid). So it is with Reznik in *The Machinist*, who although still breathing at the film's end, is condemned to a considerable sentence (both through the judicial system and through having to live with the guilt of killing a child). He is dead in an equivalent sense to film noir endings – it is the death of his freedom, it is the death of his life, if not of him.

But as Reznik was guilty of the crime all along, according to Žižek he was, 'already dead' – he (and the viewer) just didn't know it because death is a signifier with 'an incessantly receding, ungraspable signified, always pointing to other signifiers' (Bronfen and Webster Goodwin 4). In other words, every time Reznik unravels some of the mystery he gets closer, not to revealing the truth about another person (as he suspects he will), but to another symptom, another level of suffering under guilt, and to his own metaphorical death. So although it takes 101 minutes of screen time to reveal Reznik ends up autonomously dead, right from the very first scene in *The Machinist* 'the game is already over' (Žižek *Enjoy Your Symptom* 171). As a series of sinister events unfold around Reznik, each attempt to understand what or who is behind them is actually a perilous step towards 'killing' himself, or as Žižek says, 'a deadly menace looms over his endeavor' to tell a story about himself (171), and to convey the connection between being responsible for the death of an Other and being psychologically disordered.

As Reznik's insomnia induces a living-death of suboptimal physical and cognitive functioning, and he is also doomed from the beginning to meet his metaphorical death at the end, *The Machinist* overturns what being 'alive' actually means. He breathes, he walks, he talks and he feels, but Reznik is a spectre in the diegesis who barely exists in the real world, moving through it with an atemporal quality that can only be altered through an acknowledgement of his disordered psychological state. *The Machinist* suggests that guilt-fuelled insomnia can render a person inhuman, paradoxically ensuring he is always conscious, always suffering, but never alive. This notion is supported by two female characters, Stevie and Marie (Aitana Sanchez-Gijon), both commenting that 'If you were any thinner you wouldn't exist', a reference to his diminishing presence in the living world. Such references to Reznik's 'living-dead' status confirm that sleep is not only essential for optimum functioning, but is part of what constitutes being human, reaffirming that severe disruption of sleeping patterns dehumanizes the individual and that the physical and the psychological are intimately linked.

Emaciation: Reznik's body as canvas

Reznik's emaciation is the physical illustration of his psychological suffering, the visual suggestion that he is being destroyed from the inside out. Bronfen (*Night Passages* 138) claims that dreams are the place in which the subject can 'give free rein to all forbidden desires' and essentially 'vent', but as Reznik doesn't dream in the traditional sense, I interpret that Reznik vents through the emaciation symptom instead. Therefore, while at a denotative level his emaciation stems from a combination of no sleep, an active job and a disinterest in food, his bodily state connotes decay as if his physical deterioration were brought on by a disease in his mind, what French psychoanalyst Didier Anzieu, who focuses on the body rather than language (as per Lacan), refers to as the displacement of 'violent archaic affects … from the psyche into the body' (6). This disease ironically feeds on his increasing guilt, as the more Reznik avoids acknowledging the truth, the thinner he becomes, further confirming the connection between his psychological state and his corporeal reality. His body functions as the literal place at which the guilt is aimed. However, Reznik has repressed memory of the hit-and-run accident and is therefore yet to acknowledge his subsequent guilt on a conscious level. This means that, as his body is the literal location his guilt is displayed on, he doesn't identify with this underweight version of himself and frequently doesn't recognize himself in the mirror.

The immediate scenes following the opening sequence (with the carpet and the body) depict how physically thin Reznik is. He stands in his bathroom examining his protruding clavicle, while the shot also captures all the knobs of his spine. As he pulls baggy jeans and a belt on, his lover Stevie comments, 'If you were any thinner you wouldn't exist.' While this is a direct reference to his diminishing physical frame, it also connects with the film's theme of illusive identity; the film makes the viewer unsure of which characters are real and which are imagined, suggesting that Reznik's insomnia triggers his 'fading out' from the living world. Similarly, Reznik's fading emaciated form signals his presence as what Bronfen and Webster Goodwin (7) refer to as a 'figure of liminality', who remains awake while others sleep, who has no 'regular' friendships or family, and who lives in an increasing state of persecution paranoia on the edge of mainstream society. Essentially, Reznik's emaciation is a visual display of the destructiveness of guilt – it eats the subject from the inside out, highlighting the link between the psychological and physical in a visually grotesque manner.

Judith Halberstam, whose work largely focuses on gender and sexuality (with specific interest in gender binarism, masculinity and tomboys) states that Reznik's emaciated reaction to his unconscious guilt is in fact a typically male reaction, whereby a 'monomaniacal system' draws all attention onto the male body (112). As Reznik's physical state is aesthetically shocking, this physicality visually detracts from (a) the insomnia that contributes to the indifference to food and subsequent emaciation and (b) the guilt that lies beneath the insomnia. Both the viewer and Reznik become preoccupied with his deteriorating physical health, rather than recognizing his emaciation as another symptom in a line of knock-on effects from guilt.

Over the duration of the film Reznik's weight continues to drop and his general physical health also goes into decline. The film depicts Reznik drowsily reading a book late at night. He nearly falls asleep but is woken when the book drops to the floor with a crash. The book is *The Idiot* by Fyodor Dostoyevsky and its presence in the film suggests Reznik can learn something from its moral. *The Idiot* is a story about a young man who, despite being an honourable character, goes mad with grief and lives out the remainder of his days in a psychiatric hospital. This scene takes place with Reznik wearing only a pair of boxer shorts, meaning his emaciated physique is highly visible at all times, whether sitting or standing. Placing the book back on the table, Reznik steps on his scales in the bathroom and records his weight on a post-it note. He places the note below a selection of others – thereby documenting his lowest weight yet (121 pounds). As a reminder that Reznik's plummeting weight (his corporeal reality) is connected with his guilt (his psychological state), he looks towards a bottle of bleach sitting atop the toilet. He used this bleach to wash his hands in the opening scene, after attempting to dispose of a body.

At one point Reznik runs from the police in a paranoid panic and turns to Stevie, his lover, for help as he's now injured, bleeding, emaciated and sleep-deprived. Stevie cleans him up in her bath and his bones are again plainly visible. He appears to be having trouble holding his torso upright or walking straight – although admittedly these symptoms could be due to the injuries of the hit-and-run. Either way the serious decrepitude of his physical state symbolically suggests that he is moving into increasingly desperate psychological territory, with the weight of unacknowledged guilt paradoxically conveyed through the stripping back of his flesh. Furthermore, following an accident at Reznik's workplace where his colleague loses an arm, Reznik scrubs his hands over his sink using bleach, re-establishing that this prop is linked to his guilt. He looks cautiously in the bathroom mirror while doing so and immediately vomits in the toilet – a visceral reaction to his own skeletal reflection. To reinforce the connection between guilt and weight, the lowest post-it note on the wall next to the bathroom mirror now reads '119' (pounds).

Lacan's mirror stage theory has particular relevance to *The Machinist* given Reznik's relationship with his literal mirror image. Indeed, arguably the film's most memorable feature is Reznik's emaciated figure – revealed through nude or semi-nude scenes, using various wide frames and visually enhanced through the use of mirrors; the viewer has no choice but to observe two sets of bones and skin as they each fill the frame. Reznik's character trajectory involves a gradual recognition of himself, the final marker of which is understanding that he and Ivan are the same person. However, leading up to this point Reznik doesn't recall his past; he doesn't understand why he can't sleep and why he is losing weight. Given his inability to grasp his own identity, it makes sense that in moments of interaction with a mirror, he stares back at his emaciated reflection in surprise, barely recognizing the man looking back at him. These moments suggest that after the trauma of the hit-and-run accident Reznik experiences a psychical splitting akin to the pre-mirror-stage infant who is yet to understand itself as one with its reflection. Reznik looks into the mirror and doesn't recognize his own reflection; he can't 'appropriate the image as oneself', as infants do during the mirror stage (Ruddell 39) because he doesn't know himself, another negative effect of repressed guilt, and another example of the link between the subject's corporeal reality and psychological state.

Dual meanings: Repetition and obsession

In addition to the reflection of multiple mirror surfaces, doubling also occurs through the process of repetition in *The Machinist*. Repetition can be seen in Reznik's frequent handwashing activities and in his weighing of himself on the scales, but it is the handwashing which is reminiscent of obsessive compulsive disorder. Obsessive subjects take pleasure in isolation and ritualization (Dor *Clinical Lacan* 113) and they often exhibit defiance in an attempt to be a 'champion of legality' (ibid 45). These traits are all attributable to Reznik; his insomnia isolates him by placing him in the liminal zone of society, he engages in handwashing and weighing rituals, and he spends the duration of the film accusing other people of wrong-doing while attempting to be the righteous upholder of moral behaviour. This final trait is due to the obsessive subject always being haunted by the Law-of-the-Father and constantly made to feel guilty about desire (ibid 119). This generates an 'inner tug of war' which torments the obsessive subject, where on the one hand he attempts to uphold the law and on the other hand he evades it (ibid 120).

The desire to compulsively repeat an occurrence suggests there is some pleasure to be gained through this repetition and may 'seem to guarantee self-preservation, self-assertion, and mastery' (Slethaug 14). For example, Reznik routinely washes his hands in bleach after an emotionally difficult moment. This repeated handwashing appears to function as a soothing ritual, whilst confirming the bleach as a prop connected to his guilt. Repetition is also part of the process a traumatized subject goes through, performing the moment of trauma over and over again, reproducing it as an action rather than a memory (Belau *Introduction: Remembering* xv). In the case of Reznik, who has repressed the traumatic incident, he is unaware that he is engaging in such repetitive handwashing behaviour – it's an instinctive action he engages in to gain pleasure from literally and symbolically cleansing himself. However, until Reznik consciously acknowledges his guilt, the repeated attempt to cleanse himself of guilt through self-assertion and mastery proves futile.

Reznik's repeated weighing of himself is less an attempt to sooth himself and more motivated by a desire for mastery (or at least monitoring) of his physical state. Such monitoring connects with the paranoid subject who constantly keeps an eye on 'every sign'. This attempt at mastery is also futile, given that Reznik's emaciation is connected to his insomnia (and therefore his guilt) and won't be understood or resolved until knowledge of his crime enters his conscious mind. In other words, he can obsessively monitor his weight as much as he wants but it will continue to decline while he remains in denial.

Dual meanings: Written language

Written words (on post-it notes) also have a significant part in *The Machinist*, as does the minimalist dialogue which is thick with double meaning. The truth of the diegesis (that Reznik is guilty of killing a child) exists inside a language-based web, the Symbolic, and Reznik's guilt is hinted at linguistically because language functions as a gateway to the unconscious, yet trauma (of killing a child in this instance) is located in the Real. The Real is unrepresentable in nature but Ellie Ragland (who practices Lacanian psychoanalysis) states, it 'never ceases not writing itself' (*Lacan, The Death Drive* 86). This is literally true in *The Machinist* when Reznik's unconscious mind writes notes attempting to trigger Reznik's conscious mind into remembering. For example, Reznik finds a note stuck to his fridge which depicts a game of hangman with the outline of a noose already drawn and space for six letters, and he believes it to have been drawn and put there by someone else. At a later date he sees two letters have been filled out on the hangman game and the drawing has been added to. Reznik confides in Stevie about what is happening and when she asks what he is worried about he replies, 'I don't know yet.' This line is an indication that his conscious mind is aware there is something wrong and something to be concerned about but he doesn't yet know what it is, or at least, he is unable to articulate it as the knowledge is still a repressed memory in his unconscious.

There are also numerous examples in *The Machinist* where verbal communications between characters allude to a conversation between Reznik's conscious and unconscious mind. However, as these instances occur with the characters Ivan and Marie (who are both figments of Reznik's imagination), an analysis of their use of language will be covered in later sections which look specifically at these characters as hallucinatory figures.

Paranoia and persecution

Bronfen claims that 'the insomniac imagines curious things, confusing all kinds of issues ... [and] fabricates relations between objects and events that are in fact unrelated' (*Night Passages* 160). This description of insomnia is similar to the Lacanian definition of paranoia as a subject who invests random signs with a great deal of meaning which are natural and logical to them but baffling to other non-paranoid subjects (Dor *The Clinical Lacan* 16). It is hardly surprising then that Reznik's insomnia declines into paranoia as it progresses through *The Machinist*. During paranoia the subject finds meaning in everything, in order to avoid the truth that their universe (the Symbolic order) is disintegrating. Freud perceived that Daniel Schreber's paranoia was not so much indicative of madness, as indicative of an attempt to escape madness (Žižek *Event* 84).² Freud believed that Schreber's paranoia was brought on by repressed homosexual desire and deduced that Schreber resisted 'his desire for men by expressing a fear of persecution by other men' (Halberstam 108), thereby implying that paranoia and persecution go hand-in-hand. While there is no evidence to suggest that Reznik has homosexual desires, a similar mechanism is employed in the process of his paranoia. The repression of his memory of the car accident and subsequent guilt facilitates the development of a paranoia in which he is the innocent victim of a conspiracy, as opposed to the guilty party. In this position he becomes preoccupied by the belief that another man (Ivan) is 'out to get him'; but this perception of Ivan as someone to be feared, someone who can't be trusted and someone who is guilty, is an unconscious projection of how Reznik feels about himself.

At one point in his paranoia Schreber imagined he was becoming physically female (109). In his delusional state where he believed himself the centre of the universe, he accepted this physical transformation as part of the network which connected him with God. Reznik doesn't perceive himself to go through any gender transformations in *The Machinist*, but again there are parallels between the structure of Schreber's and Reznik's paranoid delusions. For example, Reznik goes through a physical change when he loses a huge amount of weight in the space of a year. In an emaciated state Reznik arguably commands less of a masculine presence, but the real concern here is that he begins to believe, like Schreber, that this new physical state is part of some greater pattern where he is also prevented from sleeping. This sense of conspiracy is part of the widening effect of unresolved guilt, and is contributed to further by Ivan's entrance.

Ivan is introduced in *The Machinist* relatively early, presented as an intriguing character from the outset. At fourteen minutes into the film Reznik sits in his parked car and nearly falls asleep before a man's voice wakes him, saying, 'Looks like rain. Radio says there's a storm on the way.' When Reznik essentially ignores the man, he goes on, 'I'd say it's already here.' As unconscious fantasies (which hallucinations are part of) can depict 'concerns about annihilation' (Razinsky 20), these lines allude to Reznik's oncoming psychological breakdown. The man introduces himself as Ivan, another worker at the factory. A few days later

---

[2] Dr Daniel Schreber was a German judge who suffered from several episodes of mental illness between the late nineteenth and early twentieth centuries. Although Freud did not treat Schreber himself, he studied Schreber's book, *Memoirs of My Nervous Illness*, closely.

Reznik finds out that there isn't a man called Ivan employed at the factory and at this point he begins to develop persecution paranoia, believing that someone is setting him up to be framed. He becomes suspicious of his coworkers, who in turn become hostile towards him. Ivan is a hallucinatory figure of Reznik's paranoia, developed out of fear of persecution stemming from guilt that is unresolved. Contemporary of Freud and fellow Austrian psychoanalyst Otto Rank (76) claims that when the protagonist of the text is unable to accept his own guilt on a conscious level he relocates it from his own ego and places it onto another ego – in this instance, the character Ivan. Ivan is therefore the physical manifestation of Reznik's superego, the internalization of the paternal metaphor; Ivan *is* Reznik, and therefore fulfils two functions: as a doppelgänger about whom Reznik hallucinates in his sleep-deprived state, and as the version of Reznik who lays down the law and represents authority, indicated through his statement, '*I'd* say it's already here.'

Ivan's characterization in *The Machinist*, as a person of intrigue who is inherently but not explicitly threatening, aligns with what Žižek refers to as the 'traditional father', whose 'fundamental feature is not an open display of power but the threat of potential power' (*Enjoy Your Symptom* 180). For this type of figure 'there are no limits; yet, simultaneously, he possesses an insight into the very kernel of our (subject's) being, our desire has no secret for him' (ibid). Again, this describes Ivan's unique ability to appear illogically in any space, starting with the car park next to Reznik ('there are no limits'), and to have inherent and powerful knowledge of Reznik's guilt and crime ('no secret for him'), thereby reaffirming that Ivan functions as the internalized Name-of-the-Father, the superego. Freud claims that with the establishment of the superego the distinction 'between doing something bad and wishing to do it disappears entirely' because thoughts can't be hidden from the superego (*Civilisation* 62). Because Ivan is the visual depiction of Reznik's superego, Reznik experiences him as his 'chief pursuer' (Rank 74). The internalized Name-of-the-Father is therefore not the literal presence of the father (nor does Ivan function as a 'father figure'), but the representative presence who mediates desire (Dor *The Clinical Lacan* 23) and functions as the law.

Halfway through *The Machinist* Reznik finds a photograph of Ivan and another of his co-workers, Reynolds. He takes this as proof that he is being set up at work and from there his paranoia exponentially progresses. Reznik is at the factory one day when the machine he is working on self-activates and pulls his arm into the mechanism (much like his colleague's prior accident). Reznik pulls free with the help of a coworker but he turns on all of them, suspecting one of them rigged the machine to hurt him. He gets physically aggressive and the foreman fires him. He tries to find the photo of Ivan and Reynolds in his wallet but it has disappeared. Later that night he searches his apartment for the photo but can't find it, calling himself an 'idiot' as he looks, and thus recalling the Dostoyevsky novel he was previously reading.

Reznik's paranoia comes to a climax when he sees the photograph of Ivan and Reynolds again, but this time in his lover Stevie's bedroom. He confronts her about it and she responds by pointing out that it's a photo of him and Reynolds, reaffirming that Ivan is the paranoid projection of his own superego (himself). He refuses to look at the photo or accept what she is saying and Stevie kicks him out of her apartment, telling him their relationship is over. While Reznik ransacks his own apartment looking for the photo of Reynolds and Ivan, trickles of blood start to run down the outside of the fridge, although Reznik is so preoccupied with looking for the photo he doesn't notice. This is symbolic of the fact that while Reznik focuses his energy on what he perceives to be the threat to him (Ivan), he doesn't acknowledge his own guilt (the blood), and, accordingly, his paranoia continues to grow while his destructive insomnia continues.

Hallucinations: Marie, the superego and the 'dream'

The viewer is introduced to Ivan and Marie as two real people, but the film eventually reveals they are both a figment of Reznik's insomnia-induced hallucinations, functioning as the visual representation of Reznik's superego. As the voice of his conscience they both attempt to get Reznik to acknowledge his guilt on a conscious level, although Ivan represents the authority figure to be feared, the internalized Name-of-the-Father of the superego, while Marie exists in a less frightening entity, as a gentle coaxing force, encouraging Reznik to 'come clean'. Ivan and Marie have two additional functions in *The Machinist*, however; Marie works as a 'dream-state' alternative and Ivan is also the cinematic doppelgänger.

It's significant that at times when Reznik is close to falling asleep he is symbolically woken by his own guilt – either a book falling off the table or by another character engaging him in a conversation. This suggests that whatever, or whoever, prevents Reznik from attaining sleep is linked in with his guilt. Interestingly the only central character who doesn't prevent Reznik from falling asleep is prostitute-turned-girlfriend Stevie. In fact, Stevie encourages Reznik to go to sleep in her bed, but despite Stevie's encouragement, he is totally unable to relax and confides in her that he hasn't slept 'in a year'. But Stevie is not alone in encouraging Reznik to sleep – Marie also makes similar comments.

It is not a coincidence that Reznik hallucinates this particular woman as his superego or that her demeanour is warm and motherly; in real life Marie was the mother of the child (Nicholas) whom Reznik killed. He did not speak to her at the scene of the accident, her real name possibly isn't Marie, but this is the female hallucination through whom his superego speaks.

Reznik hallucinates that Marie works the late-night shift at an airport diner – a place he frequents in lieu of sleeping. They exchange simple but friendly dialogue, which eventually leads to Reznik meeting Marie (and her son Nicholas) at places other than the diner, such as a fairground and the beach. On one occasion Marie tells Reznik that he's tired and that he needs to sleep, to which, crucially, she states, 'You don't fool me Trevor Reznik. I have you all figured out.' As Marie is later revealed to be an embodiment of his superego, her response 'I have you all figured out' is an attempt to get him to admit to his wrongdoing in order to get the release he needs – sleep. In another scene at the airport diner Marie asks Reznik, 'Is someone chasing you?', which resonates as another attempt of his superego to have him acknowledge his guilt on a conscious level.

Because Reznik doesn't sleep in the traditional sense, his interactions (hallucinations) with Marie may be interpreted as the insomniac's alternative to dreams, what I will refer to as 'hallucination-dreams'. This interpretation is supported by Freud's reading of the content of dreams as wish fulfilment; on an unconscious level Reznik wishes that Nicholas were still alive and that Marie were happy, but this wish can't be observed consciously because Reznik has repressed knowledge of Nicholas' death and Marie's mourning along with his own guilt. This reaffirms that the dream world is what Bronfen (*Night Passages* 17) refers to as 'a stage for nocturnal psychic theatre' where the censorship of the 'daytime' consciousness is skirted. Yet Reznik's desire to believe that Nicholas and Marie are well is not psychologically unusual; as Noll Zimmerman suggests, it is human nature to embrace an alternative reality 'whether knowingly or not ... rather than face reality' (21).

For the duration of the film neither Reznik nor the viewer perceives these hallucination-dreams to be part of Reznik's unconscious mind; they see them play out in the real world. For this reason it becomes increasingly difficult for Reznik to locate the source of his psychological disturbance, because the real-life event (the hit-and-run of a child) becomes part of an unreal dream world while the dream world (hallucinations about Maria) becomes part of his reality. In psychoanalytic terms the frame that regulates access to reality is called the fantasy (Žižek *Event* 24), but 'the disintegration of a fantasy can have disastrous consequences' (ibid 26). *The Machinist* uses hallucination-dreams as a cinematic device to portray Reznik's fantasy so that the psychological impact of Reznik's crime is accessible to the viewer and eventually also to Reznik (when it is revealed that a seemingly normal character is a hallucination produced by repressed guilt). Ironically then, this film, which centres around a character who can't sleep, ends up incorporating the dream (albeit in a non-traditional sense) as a significant aspect of the narrative, confirming Sharon Packer's argument that dreams 'add a metanarrative, and tell a story within a story' (Packer 38–9).

Hallucinations: Ivan, the superego and the doppelgänger

Caroline Ruddell, who researches in the area of horror and witchcraft in film and television, argues that Lacanian psychoanalysis lends itself particularly well to the double cinematic image as it accepts that human identity isn't always coherent and embraces the psychical split as part of human experience (Ruddell 35). As far as screenplays go, doppelgängers make interesting plot devices across a variety of cinematic genres, although a deeper reading of these texts finds psychological meaning beneath the sheer aesthetic interest of the double image (124). The narrative is often driven by the relationship between the central character and the doppelgänger, who is frequently a visual projection of the protagonist's psychological status, such as Nina's Black Swan in *Black Swan* or, in *The Machinist*, Ivan as the result of an exhaustion-induced hallucination facilitated by paranoia and repressed guilt.

Ruddell refers to how the frequent presence of mirrors in *Dr Jekyll and Mr Hyde* allude to the internal struggle occurring between two characters for one body – a common plot device used in films employing the double (57). Notably, though, while *The Machinist* also uses mirrors in a variety of scenes, these reflective surfaces don't portray a struggle for one body. While Reznik's psyche has been split (represented onscreen by the characters Reznik and Ivan), Ivan always commands a separate physicality to Reznik, allowing them to interact with each other in conversations. This suggests that the battle occurring in *The Machinist* is not between two people for one body, but for a divided subjectivity to re-merge back into one body, representing the reunification of his psyche through the acknowledgement of his guilt.

Literary scholar Gordon Slethaug, working in the area of interdisciplinary methodology, traces the role of the double in literature as far back as Plato, whereas in the Victorian era the artistic double involved not only matter (the body) but spirit, thereby embracing binaries between good and evil, mortality and immortality, poetry and science, or the individual and society (Slethaug 10). There was a suggestion at that time, emerging out of religious beliefs, that 'each thing was divided against itself', with one half emerging as a protagonist (signifying the church and holiness) and the other as antagonist (signifying sin) (ibid). The rise of Freudian theory brought a new understanding to internal dualism (ibid 13). Generally speaking the introduction of psychoanalysis turned the dualistic individual into a conflict between the conscious and unconscious minds with Freud suggesting that antagonistic doubles represent an internal opposition (as opposed to peaceful doubles, which suggest well-being) (ibid 14). Indeed, Ivan embodies the role of Reznik's superego, one half of the cinematic representation of the battle between Reznik's conscious and conscience (or ego and superego).

The reasons for the appearance of a double include psychological hallucinations, illusions, delusions or vivid imagining (Schneider 107), while other possible interpretations suggest that the double is a figure who signifies the oncoming destruction of the self or an 'agent of persecution' (Bronfen *Night Passages* 225). Whatever the reason for the appearance, when a viewer sees the double onscreen, the double is granted an 'extra-diegetic reality' (Schneider 108), meaning they exist within the world of the film but are not restricted by the temporal confines of other characters. For example, they may appear in locations that other characters don't have access to such as mirror surfaces, bathrooms or car interiors and they may appear there suddenly and illogically. Indeed, the double in cinema is a transient, otherworldly creature, sometimes aware of their own presence, other times not (Rank xiii). Ivan, for example, seems to be aware of his own status and function, relayed through his immediate and consistent smugness, as if he knows something that Reznik doesn't. While Reznik initially interprets this to mean Ivan is antagonistic and dangerous, it actually means that Ivan understands he is the hidden truth of Reznik's repressed guilt. In *The Machinist* while the double may not be visible to all characters, he is fully visible to the viewer and to the protagonist and, because of this, the viewer does not perceive the double as a hallucinatory figure. Resultantly, when

Reznik is initially prevented from falling asleep in the car park by the voice of Ivan ('Looks like rain'), the viewer receives this information in the form of a physical male character, because when viewers identify with a character through their cinematic subjectivity, as is the case in *The Machinist*, they are also made to 'experience the power of intrapsychic fantasy, indeed to experience fantasy as reality' (Sexeny 57).

Doubles can be divided into types based on whether they are a product of abnormal psychology, induced substances, supernatural events, alien life forms or technological engineering (Schneider 110–11). As Ivan is a product of Reznik's psychological instability, he comes under the 'mental doubles' category and can be subcategorized as a 'projection', given he is part of the same personality in different bodies (ibid 112). Given that the bodies are 'spatially as opposed to temporally distinct from one another', this allows Reznik and Ivan to engage in conversation (ibid), as depicted in Ivan's first scene in the car park. Making Ivan this type of double allows *The Machinist* to visually and aurally depict interaction between Reznik's ego (Reznik) and Reznik's superego (Ivan), the friction which drives the narrative of the film. Yet Ruddell also suggests that doubles can be used as representations of 'tensions between the past and present' (Ruddell 66). In *The Machinist* for example, Ivan represents the Reznik of the past, who one year prior committed a terrible crime and avoided taking responsibility. In this sense Ivan functions as a ghost who is there to remind Reznik that he is guilty. As a hallucinatory figure, he is a fantasy and 'it may be recalled that fantasy is, according to Lacan, a screen masking the Real' (Begin 54), in which trauma (such as killing a child) is situated. On the other hand, Reznik represents the Reznik of the present, where his modern state (sleep-deprived, emaciated and paranoid) is suffering physically and psychologically from the guilt he has repressed. The friction between these two time zones can therefore be illustrated by the friction between these two characters. Rank interprets this meeting of past and present circumstances as uncanny, with the subject's attempts to ignore or forget the past only succeeding in cementing the past into the subject's present and future (6).

Therefore, the double is 'uncanny', a broad term that can apply to phenomena that are somewhat disturbing but not necessarily horrific (Freeland 88). According to Cynthia Freeland, whose area of expertise is aesthetics and horror, the uncanny may seem 'creepy' yet also 'enticing' and what makes the uncanny so odd is that a seemingly normal element from daily life appears in a way which is unusual, making something familiar also seem inherently strange (90). *Unheimlich* (the original Freudian term and German translation of 'uncanny') is a word comprised of two parts: the prefix '*un*' signals a negation, a repression, and '*heimlich*' means 'familiar'. Therefore, when the two parts combine, the term means 'something that was familiar has become not-familiar, strange, and threatening' (Harari 62). Freud had an interest in the uncanny in so far as it related to psychology and he took particular interest in doubling (Freeland 89). Freeland states that to Freud, the double is an 'idea the infant employs to ward off fear of death' (91), perhaps because by doubling himself the child believes it has security and a greater chance of survival. But this belief recedes upon growing up, so that when a double does reappear to the adult subject the effect is reversed and the double can signal death by alluding to the self being built on fragmentation and incompleteness, which makes its very presence frightening.

Notably, Reznik doesn't recognize Ivan's true identity as his own superego until the end of the film. The reason for this is twofold. At the more obvious level Ivan looks physically different to Reznik. Why would anyone (Reznik or the film viewer) suspect two people who look different are actually the same person? Secondly, Reznik doesn't recognize Ivan because Ivan represents Reznik's guilt, and for most of the film, Reznik does not acknowledge the part of himself that is guilty (because guilt has been repressed along with traumatic memory so exists in the unconscious). The image of Ivan therefore *will* look different to the image of Reznik (despite the connotations of the double being an identical image), because Reznik isn't ready to recognize the truth and, therefore, himself.

The doppelgänger often refers to the 'good twin' and 'bad twin' model, or may be viewed as a 'figure of death' (Bronfen *Night Passages* 97) or a representation of the monster from within (Ruddell 55). Ruddell suggests that in films which employ the double, the viewer is encouraged to sympathize with one 'twin' over the other. Even if the personality or characterization of both characters is similar, cinema tends to demonize one (ibid). In such cases the 'malevolent' image is frequently read as a representation of 'the monster within or the return of the repressed' (ibid). Ivan initially appears as an antagonist but is later revealed to be the embodiment of Reznik's internal angst, confirming Ruddell's conclusion that the use of doubles 'sheds light on what it means to be human … hybrids of good and bad' (127). The dichotomy between good and bad twins often lends itself particularly well to films from a horror or fantasy genre where the fight between good and evil can be personified by the two characters. Although *The Machinist* is a psychological thriller, the film includes various elements from the gothic horror genre, such as a plot which includes mystery and questionable identity and an aesthetic which is predominantly shadowy and frightening. Part of the encapsulating thematic darkness of this text is the eventual realization that Ivan, who appears as such an abhorrent, monstrous figure, is actually the protagonist; that the evil which manifests physically in Ivan's form, which the viewer is encouraged to fear and hate, is actually Reznik, the character whom the viewer trusted. Part of the duping of the viewer is that the film has suggested, through a narrative which revolves around suspicion of others and the characterization of Reznik as righteous victim, that Reznik is morally opposed to whatever monstrous actions Ivan has partaken in, only to reveal that Reznik has equal capacity for monstrosity.

It's somewhat ironic that the protagonist, who views the double as an evil force, also has the propensity for ruthlessness and frequently resorts to violence against the double (Bronfen *Night Passages* 225), playing with Dolgopolov's suggestion that the doppelgänger relates to the notion of 'the hunter and the hunted' (55). One such example of this occurs towards the end of *The Machinist*, when Reznik sees Ivan break into his apartment with Marie's young son Nicholas in tow. When Reznik confronts Ivan in his bathroom and asks Ivan where Nicholas is, Ivan gestures towards the shower curtain and says, 'You know he's dead' before commenting on Reznik's 'faulty memory'. Both lines identify that Reznik's superego is prodding at his conscious mind; he is 'waking up' to the paranoid hallucination finally. But not ready to confront his guilt, Reznik responds by brutally cutting Ivan's throat. He attempts to dispose of the body by rolling it in carpet and heaving it into the sea (depicted in the opening scene of the film). Whatever Ivan's crimes are, Reznik is revealed in this interaction as ruthless and a killer. Both Bronfen and Rank claim that because the doppelgänger and protagonist are intimately linked, killing the double is an act of symbolic suicide (Bronfen *Night Passages* 225; Rank 79). However, as Ivan is a projection of Reznik's superego onto a hallucinatory figure, he can't be killed, and reappears in a later scene. I posit then that Reznik's attempt to murder Ivan is not a symbolic suicide, but rather symbolic of repudiation of his guilt.

Later that night, while Reznik washes his hands in bleach after trying to dispose of Ivan's body, Ivan reappears in Reznik's vision as he stares in the mirror. Ivan's 'resurrection' reasserts that he is a character constituted by guilt. In other words, he can't be killed off – the only way for him to cease is for Reznik to kill his actual self or to confess his crime, alleviating his guilt and allowing Ivan to re-merge into Reznik. Understanding it's impossible for a murdered man to come back to life, the unconscious knowledge of Reznik's crime finally makes its way into Reznik's conscious mind. Reznik repeats the words 'I know who you are' over and over as the viewer is shown flashbacks of the hit-and-run he committed a year before, 'signaling trauma's return' (de Bruyn 16) and visually conveying Reznik's 'wounded psyche' (ibid).

Gregory Dolgopolov, who writes extensively about identity across national borders in cinema, argues that the double becomes an omen of destruction, given the protagonist's inability to transform (59). However, if the protagonist is willing to 'reevaluate' the situation and transform, the double will no longer represent death (ibid). Such is the case with Reznik, who, while not willing to confront Ivan's true identity and function, experiences his double as sinister and dangerous. When Reznik embraces the truth, he transforms himself into a more self-aware subject who is initiating the process of psychological reparation and Ivan is no longer a menacing or threatening figure. Yet, as Ivan is Reznik's superego, he is not appeased with the mere acknowledgement of truth and guilt; the superego calls for punishment and Ivan therefore remains visible (to Reznik and the viewer) until Reznik confesses to his crime by handing himself over to the police. In the final scene of the film Reznik goes to the police station to hand himself in and Ivan stays outside the building, suggesting the re-merging of Reznik's psyche has already begun as he acknowledges his crime and leaves the physical representation of his guilt at the doorway. The viewer understands that Ivan will fade from Reznik's perception as the legal proceedings against him get underway.

The notion that Reznik has repressed something horrific and is living with a split psyche is present from the outset of the film when the question 'Who are you?' is initially asked. *The Machinist* spends 101 minutes trying to answer, only to find out in the last ten minutes that Reznik is defined by his guilt. Thus, if the central question is 'Who are you?', then the answer is 'I am Guilty' as opposed to 'I am Reznik'. It is not a coincidence that the moment of this realization occurs (for Reznik and for the viewer) in front of a mirror. Ivan appears in the bathroom behind Reznik, signifying that as the superego he exists beneath Reznik's consciousness as a fundamental guiding moral force. For the first time he is visible to Reznik and the viewer in a reflected surface; this signals that, by looking in a mirror and seeing a reflection of his guilt-inducing superego, Reznik is now ready to acknowledge that Ivan is a part of him, and therefore, that he is guilty. Staring into his own face he says the words, 'I know who you are', a verbal confirmation that claims himself and Ivan as one person, and moreover as a person who ran over a child and fled the scene.

While the doppelgänger is for the most part a menacing character, in *The Machinist* Ivan's final moments are spent encouraging Reznik to hand himself in. This detail asserts two things. Firstly, Ivan as a (usually) sinister man is a subjective hallucination from Reznik's point of view. Ivan appears to Reznik as a sinister character because he is a representation of Reznik's guilt, which has only negative emotions attached to it. Secondly, Ivan's final act of encouraging Reznik to 'do the right thing' suggests he, as the superego, can actually facilitate psychological reparation through a sense of reciprocal punishment, not just psychological destruction through suffering. Furthermore, as he is the visual manifestation of Reznik's superego, it's not that Ivan *has* the capacity to act with moral integrity after all; rather, he *is* the capacity for moral integrity, who has simply been misunderstood and misrecognized for most of the film while his corresponding ego – Reznik – denied culpability and encountered the effects of unresolved guilt. In the final scene Reznik drives to the police station, with Ivan sitting alongside, and reports himself at the front desk. He is accompanied to a cell by two officers and mutters the words, 'I just want to sleep' before he collapses onto the cell bench and finally closes his eyes. These final moments convey that guilt was the key to Reznik's insomnia, a confirmation of the relationship between psychological state and physical state, but also been psychological state and death (in this particular case, the death of a child). Now that he has admitted his guilt, his mind and his body allow him the small but not insignificant relief in the form of sleep.

Conclusion: Destructive guilt and the stepping stone symptoms

The DSM-V argues that persistent sleeping problems, such as insomnia, indicate underlying or forthcoming mental illness (APA). *The Machinist* employs its central character Reznik to confirm this notion, while the application of a psychoanalytic approach unpacks the origin and mechanism of his psychological disorder. The central mystery of *The Machinist* as a cinematic text is that, in accordance with the DSM-V, Reznik's insomnia is generated out of psychological suffering (the guilt of killing) and leads onto further psychological symptoms such as paranoid hallucinations.

The knowledge that Reznik killed a child and then fled the scene is too traumatic for his conscious mind to acknowledge; hence the event exists in the unrepresentable realm of the Real. As he is 'not able to confront' it (Žižek *Enjoy Your Symptom* 175), Reznik represses the memory of the incident in his unconscious, where it exists as an 'unknown known' (Žižek *Event* 11) for most of the narrative. Reznik's insomnia, emaciation, notes to himself and hallucinations of Marie and Ivan are each an example of a 'cyphered message' (Žižek *Enjoy Your Symptom* 175), a symptom through which Reznik's unconscious attempts to provoke him into acknowledging the incident on a conscious level. These diegetic elements are initially construed as signs of conspiracy, but later revealed to be stepping stones towards the acknowledgement of guilt.

Insomnia takes a visible toll on Reznik's physicality; he moves languidly and speaks slowly, revealing the extent of his exhaustion, and cinematically suggesting a connection between physicality and psychological state. His bodily emaciation reinforces the notion that he is a 'living-corpse', moving through the diegesis torturously, while aesthetically documenting his internal destruction under the stress of unresolved guilt. He begins to write conscious notes documenting his plummeting weight, and unconscious notes of a game of hangman which insinuates he is a killer. As these symptoms contribute to his growing suspicion that something is awry, he hallucinates two characters, Marie and Ivan.

Marie functions as a projection of Reznik's superego; a warm and caring woman who works in a late night diner, Marie is an exhaustion-induced hallucination, but she is also the image of the mother of the child who Reznik killed. Her embodiment of this particular image and gentle coaxing of Reznik to acknowledge the truth suggests that the superego need not necessarily be characterized as harsh, disciplinary or disapproving. As Freud points out, the superego can arise from internalization of either the mother or father, or indeed both parents, as ego ideal. In Marie, this projection of his superego seems genuinely concerned with his unresolved guilt and subsequent psychological suffering. Alternatively, Ivan's characterization of Reznik's superego is as a dangerous and untrustworthy person – a reflection of how Reznik feels unconsciously about himself. When Ivan finally pushes Reznik into acknowledging his guilt on a conscious level, his role as a supposedly sinister character is overturned in revelation that he, as Reznik's superego, is the facilitator of psychological progression. With Reznik's guilt finally acknowledged and formally admitted, and the link between the child's death and psychological disorder confirmed, the doppelgänger-superego (Ivan) and the dream-hallucination superego (Marie) cease to appear, signifying the reunification of Reznik's psyche and allowing him the sleep he desperately sought.

3

The Girl with the Dragon Tattoo (2009)

Introduction to PTSD and *The Girl with the Dragon Tattoo*

The word 'trauma' originates from the Greek *trauma*, which means to pierce the skin and cause damage to bodily tissue. Freud was among the first who used the term metaphorically to explain how the mind can also be wounded (Garland 9), and was interested in the way that a memory could become a devastating psychological wound (Roth *Memory, Trauma and History* 81). With contemporary psychological clinicians Jean-Martin Charcot and Pierre Janet, Freud began to apply psychoanalytic theory to trauma studies (ibid 79). His goal was to help the subject make sense of the past so that they would incur less suffering in the present (ibid). More recent trauma theorists have also worked to establish the ways in which trauma has a significant impact on the post-trauma subject – often to the extent that subjectivity is fundamentally changed.

However, while society now perceives that trauma's impact on the victim can be psychological and/or physical, this was not officially recognized by the American Psychiatric Association until as late as 1980, when it added diagnostic criteria for post-traumatic stress disorder [PTSD] to its Diagnostic and Statistical Manual [DSM-III] (Caruth *Recapturing* 3). As the medically recognized categorization of what had been commonly referred to as 'shell shock' and 'battle fatigue', this initial listing implied that PTSD was suffered by people who had been in warzones or natural disasters. It was another fourteen years before the DSM-IV acknowledged that PTSD is also experienced by victims of child abuse, domestic violence and sexual assault (ibid), which itself reflects the fact that rape was only categorized as a traumatic event in the late twentieth century (Žižek *Event* 86). Lisbeth Salander is a cinematic character who develops PTSD following rape as a young adult. These events change Lisbeth by redirecting the trajectory of her identity, establishing her as a person who suffers mentally and manifests her trauma physically – a girl with a dragon tattoo.

The traumatized subject lives two lives: the person before the trauma and the person after the trauma. As the individual's identity is fundamentally altered by trauma (or their response to trauma), their subjectivity becomes rooted in the Real (as opposed to the Imaginary). The traumatized subject lacks a sense of self and this lack pushes at the boundaries of their existence (Kristeva *Hatred* 185). This aligns with the modern psychological notion that the subject with particularly severe PTSD[1] may, rather than feeling like a damaged person, acknowledge that they don't feel like a person at all. Trauma, therefore, whether viewed psychoanalytically or through modern psychology, is understood to be so powerful that it can obliterate the basic understanding of the self as human. It amounts to the most fundamental change to subjectivity an individual can endure.

The first in a trilogy of films about a crime-fighting duo, Lisbeth (Noomi Rapace) is the female protagonist in *The Girl with the Dragon Tattoo* [*Män som hatar kvinnor*] (Oplev, 2009). *Dragon Tattoo* received substantial critical acclaim and had a successful run at both the Swedish and international box office. Adapted from a series of novels by the late Swedish author Stieg Larsson, these films explore the history of Scandinavian Nazism, state corruption and an implicit misogynist attitude in Swedish society. While the trilogy covers a time span of several years, *Dragon Tattoo* plays out within the space of about one year, primarily in Sweden. At twenty-four years old Lisbeth lives on the fringe of Swedish society, working as a freelance researcher for Milton Security who hacks the internet to retrieve sensitive information. She has a photographic memory, a genius-level IQ and difficulty interacting with other people. At twelve years old, essentially orphaned, she was placed into public custody, spending several years in a state psychiatric paediatric institute. At twenty-four she still legally exists as a ward of the state under her appointed guardian Holger Palmgren. When Holger suffers a sudden stroke, he is replaced by another man, Nils Erik Bjurman, a successful Stockholm lawyer. Bjurman, incorrectly believing his new ward to be powerless and unintelligent, physically assaults and rapes Lisbeth in the early stages of the film. Lisbeth survives the rape but develops PTSD as a result. She finds retaliation by physically and sexually attacking Bjurman in a revenge assault some time later.

Meanwhile, the film's male protagonist Mikael Blomkvist (Michael Nyqvist), with his professional reputation as a journalist in disarray, takes an extended

---

[1] Also known as C-PTSD, to be defined later in the chapter.

break from Stockholm and works as an independent researcher for elderly business tycoon Erik Vanger. Vanger employs Mikael to solve the crime of his missing niece Harriet, who mysteriously disappeared from the fictional town of Hedestad forty years prior. Mikael enlists the help of Lisbeth and together they unravel the Hedestad mystery; Harriet Vanger is not dead, but fled to Australia at aged sixteen to escape her father and brother, who were both physically and sexually abusing her. Her father, Gottfried, died many years ago but Harriet's brother, Martin, is still alive. In the years since Gottfried's death, Martin continued his father's work as a serial rapist, torturer and murderer of dozens of women over four decades. When Martin suspects that the truth is about to be exposed, he attempts to kill Mikael but is interrupted by Lisbeth, who attacks him with a golf club and then chases him to his death in an explosive car crash. Lisbeth's difficult adolescence, rape at twenty-four and subsequent PTSD, inform much of her characterization in *Dragon Tattoo*. She is an example of living *with* trauma, in contrast to Martin's dead victims, while also illustrating the subject who is fundamentally changed by trauma.

The existing scholarship regarding *The Girl with the Dragon Tattoo* is most often based on the process of adaptation (Archer; Berger; Bergman 2014; Choudbury; Gates; Rose) between book and screen, or between the original Swedish version and the Hollywood remake. Archer argues that literature which compares the Swedish and American versions tends to 'occlude a more nuanced analysis of the films themselves', focusing instead on industry and geo-political space (3), while Gates suggests that Lisbeth's reimagining in different versions is deliberately based on the target audience; the Hollywood version of Lisbeth, for example is more hetero-normative than the 'Othered' Swedish version. The 'Othering' of Lisbeth is broadly acknowledged and usually attributed to trauma (Rose; Sari), although some authors identify that her Othering comes from a perceived neuro-diversity (Marinan 119) or systemic networks of ideological power such as race, gender and class (Johnston 2016).

Schorn argues that *Dragon Tattoo* offers an alternative to the typical depiction of a passive rape victim by having the victim reclaim agency through a rape-revenge narrative (1). Henry and Nesselhauf identify *Dragon Tattoo* as a rape-revenge film as well, but Henry suggests that both Lisbeth and supporting character Harriet Vanger (whose rape story of forty years previous is shown in flashback) contribute to this classification. Henry points out that the inclusion of Harriet and Lisbeth's sexual assaults adds a multi-generational temporality to the text which is not seen in other classic rape-revenge films.

Lisbeth's aesthetic is frequently discussed in other literature, although rather than interpreting her physicality through a Kristevan lens (as I do), various scholars perceive her body as symbolic of the Swedish state (Gregersdotter), as a 'social text and vehicle of resistance' (Choudbury 5), as a visual expression of identity (Bergman 2019), or a compensatory surface for traumatic events (Bergman 2019). Similarly to Reznik in *The Machinist*, it is also commonly acknowledged that Lisbeth's physicality cuts across gender norms (Choudbury; Reitz).

The mental impact of trauma: Repetition

The most recent addition of the DSM suggests that PTSD can potentially afflict anyone who has 'exposure to actual or threatened death, serious injury or sexual violation' (APA), a clear and specific link between death and psychological state. Previous to the publication of the DSM-V, PTSD was listed as an anxiety disorder, though it has now been shifted into a new category called 'Trauma and Stress-Related Disorders', which helps in aligning PTSD specifically with the occurrence of an external event. In order to be diagnosed with PTSD the event must be 'outside the range of human experience' (Brown 100). This broad criterion is problematic as human experience is, of course, so varied that what constitutes the range of human experience is highly contestable. Symptoms span several components, including 're-experiencing' (intrusive thoughts, nightmares and flashbacks), 'avoidance behaviours' (evading people, places or thoughts connected with the event), 'mood alterations' (memory problems, self-blame, reduced interest in activities and detachment from others) and 'increased arousal' (difficulty concentrating and sleeping, increased startle response, hypervigilance and irritability) (APA).

Practising British psychotherapist Caroline Garland refers to the repetition symptoms of PTSD as the mind's attempt to process, or what Freud refers to as 'discharge' (13). Despite the DSM-V's recognition of PTSD as one outcome of a significant external event, Cathy Caruth, who is best known for her immense contribution to the modern understanding of trauma with specialist knowledge in memory studies, also claims that the pathology of PTSD cannot be anchored in the event itself (which may be traumatizing to some people, but not to others) (*Recapturing* 4). Instead the pathological structure of PTSD is best understood by the subject's experience of and response to the event, which commonly involves re-experiencing the event. The event is not completely absorbed by the subject at the time that it occurs, which is the key reason it reappears belatedly, lending the DSM-V categorization the name '*Post*-Traumatic Stress Disorder'.

As part of the process of repetition that the traumatized subject goes through, they will 'act out' the traumatic moment again and again, thereby reproducing it, as an action, rather than a memory (Belau *Remembering, Repeating and Working Through* xv). Although repetition, like other PTSD symptoms, is literal, there is still a symbolism in it because the repetition itself is a sign that something is wrong. Therefore, although the content of the repetition is experienced as literal, the phenomenon of repetition is symbolic – signalling an unprocessed memory wriggling to get free. The sheer number of times Lisbeth has a re-experiencing PTSD symptom indicates two things. First, it shows Lisbeth has not psychologically processed the rape, but secondly it also alludes to the extent of her trauma. Because, although each repetition is a small movement towards an attempt at processing, this small movement is almost futile in the face of such a horrific attack. Arguably what may assist in making these small increments more productive is the sharing of her experience and her resultant psychological pain. However, later sections of this chapter will explain why giving voice to traumatic experiences brings problems of its own.

The re-experiencing and increased arousal symptoms of PTSD are agitated by a hyper-stimulated central nervous system (Van Der Kolk and Van Der Hart 173), which during an episode of re-experience makes the PTSD sufferer feel as if they are in the same physiological and psychological state they were in during the original traumatic event (ibid 174). For example, when they have a nightmare or flashback they may begin to hyperventilate, shake, sweat, feel physical pain and suffer involuntary muscle spasms, all indicative of the link between psychological state and physical experience. Lisbeth suffers a variety of repetition symptoms after the rape, including repeated flashbacks, intrusive thoughts and nightmares. The flashbacks and intrusive thoughts are cinematically conveyed through quick inter-cutting of imagery from the rape scene, simulating the intrusive 'flash' of another temporality into the current moment and demonstrating the 'functioning of the wounded psyche' (de Bruyn 16). This editing technique also cements *Dragon Tattoo* as a film constructed through Lisbeth's subjectivity, with the viewer experiencing a visual and aural disorientation not unlike the flashback symptom of Lisbeth's disorder. Nightmares are also portrayed through fragmented snippets, although the dream world is defined by a soft focus along the edges of the screen.

In addition to this, *Dragon Tattoo* draws further attention to Lisbeth's suffering by showing her asleep while she has a nightmare. These particular shots illustrate the hyperarousal symptoms Lisbeth suffers after trauma (even while sleeping) and the physicality of PTSD. Trauma is often remembered at a physical level, through the body, in what is known as 'muscle memory' (Laine *Feeling Cinema* 50). Lisbeth's muscle memory of her rape trauma is evident when she has a nightmare while sleeping in the passenger seat of Mikael's car. Her eyes, her shoulders and her hands twitch and she moans in fear while reliving the trauma in her dream. When they reach a hotel and Mikael touches her shoulder to wake her, she literally jumps awake, strikes his hand away from her body aggressively and changes breathing patterns. This startle response is typical of someone with PTSD and, combined with the twitching muscles, signifies her body is recalling the trauma along with her mind – further cementing the link between the subject's psychological state and corporeal reality.

PTSD has very literal symptoms and, unlike other pathologies of the mind such as psychosis and hysteria, does not manipulate or displace original meanings with symbols (Garland 17). Instead, PTSD sufferers simply replay moments of history as they actually happened, or in Caruth's own words, 'It is not so much a symptom of the unconscious, as it is a symptom of history' (Caruth *Recapturing* 5). Stimulation of certain senses can evoke recall in the traumatized subject, although such triggers are unpredictable (Rutherford 84); for instance, the smell of lighter fluid, the sound of a gunshot on the television or the feel of certain fabrics on the skin can elicit an immediate 'return' to the traumatic event, a transcendence of temporality common to several psychological disorders, but particularly painful and acute in PTSD sufferers. PTSD then is not a pathology which provides warnings; each re-experiencing symptom reinforces the event for the subject: '*This* is it; it's happening – *now!*' The reappearance of the traumatic event emerges seemingly randomly, 'against the will of the one it inhabits' (Caruth *Recapturing* 5). This re-experiencing of the event, unexpected and unbidden, contributes to the traumatic-ness of the trauma, with the 'inserting, knocking, shattering' of the memory re-traumatizing the subject (de Bruyn 135). This is why, when Lisbeth is touched lightly but unexpectedly on the shoulder by Mikael, it is enough to trigger panic in her mind and in her body. It is instinctual for Lisbeth to defend her corporeal space because the PTSD informs her that '*it's happening*'. Or, as Dirk de Bruyn, who publishes in the area of memory, imagination and trauma, says, re-experiencing symptoms themselves are re-traumatizing, 'delivering back the trauma rather than the memory' (135). With Mikael, there is no need for Lisbeth to defend her corporeal space, but re-experiencing triggers don't differentiate between the presence of the perpetrator and a 'safe person', and part of the calamity of PTSD is that, to the victim, there are no 'safe people' left in the world. Resultantly the post-trauma subject is triggered into re-experiencing symptoms frequently, unexpectedly and with the full impact of the original event 'unchanged and frozen' (de Bruyn 54); the literalness of the symptom ensures that each 're-experience' is accompanied by the sense that the event '*is happening to me now*', rather than the sense that '*I am re-experiencing something that has passed*'. In other words, certain sensory elements may evoke recall, but the subject with PTSD doesn't *recognize* they are *re*-calling; the subject with PTSD both transcends temporal confines and experiences threat within their corporeal reality.

The mental impact of trauma: Belatedness and latency

The time between the occurrence of the event and the first experience of symptoms is what Freud refers to as an 'incubation period', terminology which alludes to the process of physically infectious diseases (Caruth *Recapturing* 7). In the space of the incubation period, when post-traumatic symptoms are yet to manifest, a period of 'latency' exists. Therefore, the name post-traumatic stress disorder has a dual meaning; the name refers both to the emergence of symptoms after (a) the original event and (b) the period of latency. Some sufferers may experience this latency period as symptom-free but are able to remember the event, while others enter a post-traumatic amnesia during the latent period (ibid). *Dragon Tattoo* doesn't suggest Lisbeth has any post-traumatic amnesia, but we are left to infer that a period of latency occurs because, after Lisbeth's rape scene, *Dragon Tattoo* focuses exclusively on Mikael's storyline for a time. This implies the passing of time before the narrative returns to Lisbeth and portrays the onset of her PTSD symptoms.

Lisbeth's rape is an unwavering, graphic and realistic depiction of sexual assault, which occurs at Bjurman's home address. As Lisbeth's new legal guardian, Bjurman exercises control over her finances, and he insists she approach him personally to apply for payment of all 'non-essential items'. This restriction of her financial autonomy is the method Bjurman uses to ensure Lisbeth is vulnerable to his rules, and the reason she visits him at his apartment (to ask for money for a new computer). The beginning of the rape scene does not signal the oncoming brutality; the natural camera movement achieved with steadycam, the quiet dialogue between them, the classical music playing and the warmth of Bjurman's apartment lighting lull both Lisbeth and the viewer into a sense of security. It is this cinematic depiction of normalcy that makes Bjurman's sudden fist in Lisbeth's face so shocking. She is stunned into passivity for a few moments (he has knocked her unconscious) and it is within these seconds that he handcuffs her to the headboard of his bed and stuffs fabric into her mouth. Her return to consciousness is portrayed through the slightly blurred frames of Bjurman moving around the room, conveying that the image is from Lisbeth's point of view. Yet as he begins to undress her, to tie her ankles to the bottom of the bed and to beat her ferociously with the end of an electrical cable, the lighting in the room remains warm and Bjurman's voice maintains its formal tone.

This situation casts Lisbeth and the viewer into a psychological space which is founded on both the real and the surreal. The moment is real in its maintenance of normalcy, its representation of sounds and images that are naturalistic and realistic. However, the scene is also surreal because those normal surrounds are the location of a traumatic event occurring at that moment. It seems absurd that something so horrific may be occurring in such banal circumstances, and this absurdity makes the moment surreal. Physically restrained and aware of what is about to happen to her, Lisbeth is psychologically overthrown. The inescapable reality of the situation leaves her only one option – the psychical dissociative splitting that Freud argues occurs in the face of a traumatic event. While Lisbeth understands and experiences what is happening, she is not fully psychologically processing it and this is why her rape returns at later dates in the form of repetition symptoms. The revisiting of this moment is what Caruth refers to as 'belatedness' (Caruth *An Interview* 104) and it is the belatedness which constitutes the essence of trauma, and contributes to the temporal transcendence she experiences as a symptom of her PTSD. Freud argues therefore that trauma is perpetuated through 'an inherent latency within the experience itself' (Caruth *Recapturing* 8). In other words, trauma is characterized by an absence in the original moment.

According to Michael Roth, who researches in the area of psychology, memory and history, trauma can't be integrated into the 'normal world' through words, because recounting the event will be limited by symbolic systems of communication which inevitably sanitize the experience of something which is 'beyond words' (Roth *Memory, Trauma and History* 91). Yet, this doesn't stop filmic texts from attempting to depict trauma through a series of stylistic choices regarding mise-en-scène, editing and soundtrack (Pheasant-Kelly *Abject Spaces* 10–11). For example, when Bjurman is beginning to enter Lisbeth's body, the sound of her cries and his voice are faded out and replaced by the sound of static. On the one hand, this ambiguous buzz reinforces that Lisbeth's subjectivity cements the narrative, as the viewer hears what is happening inside her head (which is static, as during overwhelming psychical experience 'no internal dialogue operates') (de Bruyn 56). On the other hand, the static is also employed to convey that there are no aural representations which can adequately capture the horror of the rape occurring on screen. This de-synchronization of image and sound confirms that the static, which replaces the actual sounds of the event (Lisbeth's cries, Bjurman's words and the classical music playing in the apartment), functions as an aural porthole to the Real. The entire rape is not shown visually either; after Bjurman has physically entered Lisbeth, the scene ends on a close-up image of Lisbeth screaming as she is pulled backwards by her hair. The fade-to-black at this moment announces that what the audience have just witnessed is only the beginning of the assault, which lasts two hours.[2] Both the static and the premature truncation confirm that trauma transcends a system of representation – aural or visual.

Freud argues that rather than the subject forgetting details of the event during the latent period, it's actually that the subject wasn't fully conscious during the event itself because of the psychical dissociative splitting. This 'defense against overwhelming experience' (ibid 47) allows the event to be experienced in the moment but not processed in the moment. Therefore, despite the disintegrated memory that trauma survivors often exhibit (ibid 54), the problem is not that the subject didn't have enough cognitive access to the traumatic event, but that they had too much access (Caruth *Recapturing* 6). In the face of excessive access to something horrific, the subject's mind is unable to absorb all of it; hence it returns at later moments (in the form of the repetition symptoms of flashbacks, nightmares and intrusive thoughts) to be processed belatedly. Lisbeth, for example, is psychically overwhelmed by the rape (and its associated physical assault) so her mind fails to experience and process it all at the time. This 'splitting' creates traumatic memories (de Bruyn 93) which are consequently stored as 'inaccessible fragments' (ibid 47) and re-emerge as 'marooned episodic events' (ibid) during future moments when she is still unprepared and unwilling to experience and process it fully. However, because the Real can't

---

[2] The audience learns this when Lisbeth later attacks Bjurman in retaliation.

be directly represented, trauma is perhaps best witnessed by the carnage it leaves behind, what Dominick LaCapra, whose work integrates psychoanalysis, post-structuralism and critical theory, refers to as a 'haunting presence or symptomatic revenant' (49). Therefore, Lisbeth's PTSD symptoms can be viewed as the flotsam and jetsam left in trauma's wake – the residue of the Real.

The ongoing impact of Lisbeth's repetition and re-experiencing symptoms confirm that while atrocity is a 'one-off', an 'act', trauma is 'an experience' to be processed and re-encountered (Rutherford 85), adding further weight to the notion that trauma fundamentally changes the subject. Yet, while Lisbeth's PTSD symptoms have a huge impact on her lived experience, there is a more nuanced diagnosis which suggests she is even more deeply defined by the trauma she experiences – the notion of *Complex* PTSD.

The mental impact of trauma: Complex PTSD

Lisbeth suffers a clear case of PTSD as a result of her rape, but it is also important to examine her history prior to this event. In addition to the basic DSM-V criterion for PTSD, Garland (11) also refers to trauma as the event responsible for the fundamental alteration of the subject's world view into a realization that the world is unpredictable and that the self is vulnerable. While the DSM-V criterion acknowledges trauma as the disruption of the mind after certain events, this fails to include a deeper level of impact, what Garland refers to as 'the collapse of meaning' the subject endures, and the long-term effect this has on personality (11). Similarly, Ronnie Janoff-Bulman, whose early writing focused on victimization and trauma, cites three 'core assumptions' about the world that are overturned after a violent attack: a belief (1) that the world is essentially benevolent, (2) that events which happen in life are meaningful in some way and (3) that the self has intrinsic worth (77). Unpredictable violence or events which are seemingly meaningless throw this basic belief triad into chaos (Brewin 72). The individual who is raped may experience a challenge to one of these things or a complete ripping down of all three.[3] Lisbeth, for example, believes the world is closer to malevolent than benevolent and distrusts everyone she comes into

---

[3] Not surprisingly then, research suggests that rape victims suffer psychologically long after the event, with many encountering symptoms of depression or PTSD one year post-assault, and some reporting minimal recovery 4–6 years afterwards (Janoff-Bulman 74).

contact with. She does not find meaningfulness in her negative life events and struggles to conceive of herself as a productive member of society.

Throughout *Dragon Tattoo* (and in the two sequels which follow) the narrative reveals that Bjurman's rape of Lisbeth is not her first trauma. When she was a child, her father, Alexander Zalachenko, was absent for long periods of time. When he returned home Zalachenko beat her mother fiercely, eventually leaving her with irreversible brain damage, which placed her in a permanent care facility until she died there as a relatively young woman. Witnessing this domestic abuse over a period of years was the first sustained traumatic experience for Lisbeth. Immediately following the final assault which caused the brain injury, Lisbeth (who was twelve years old) avenged her mother and sought to safeguard herself by dousing her father with petrol and setting him on fire. This act was the second traumatic event in her life. The petrol attack didn't kill Zalachenko, as Lisbeth had hoped, and instead she was institutionalized in a paediatric psychiatric hospital long term. In the hospital she was subjected to inhumane treatment under the care of Doctor Peter Teleborian (who had his own corrupt connection with Zalachenko). For a continual period of several months Lisbeth was physically restrained under Teleborian's instruction, and treated without regard for the basic human rights of dignity and freedom. These three traumatic sequences in Lisbeth's life don't amount to a clear diagnosis of PTSD, as *Dragon Tattoo* indicates her re-experiencing and increased arousal symptoms only appear after the rape by Bjurman, not before. Yet Lisbeth is undeniably affected by these earlier traumatic experiences; they inform the person she is before the rape, at the beginning of *Dragon Tattoo*, depicting her as a sufferer of the more nebulous complex-post traumatic stress disorder [C-PTSD]. C-PTSD, like PTSD, is still a contestable diagnosis and is sometimes referred to in medical literature as DESNOS [Disorders of Extreme Distress Not Otherwise Specified] (Lewis Herman 88). C-PTSD is primarily differentiated from PTSD by the development of changes to the individual's personality, as opposed to behaviours (ibid 89). Individuals with C-PTSD frequently find it difficult to relate to other people or to develop a functioning self-identity as adults; they demonstrate increased vulnerability to self-harm and to being repeatedly hurt by others (ibid). Theorists and clinicians who advocate for the classification of C-PTSD argue that regular PTSD criteria do not accommodate the distinct response individuals have when subjected to *prolonged* and *repeated* trauma, such as in a concentration camp, prison, sex slavery or religious cult (ibid 73).

From a young age Lisbeth's life has been one series of traumatic hurdles after another and she is made vulnerable by each of these. For example, the domestic abuse she witnessed as a child made her want to kill her own father. This attempt resulted in her wrongful confinement in a psychiatric hospital, where her father's relationship with Teleborian made her especially vulnerable to his transgressions. When she was released it was under legal guardianship which restricted her autonomy. These restrictions made her vulnerable to Bjurman, who took advantage of this and raped her. The rape makes her vulnerable to every 'Other' she comes into contact with and on it goes. Aside from increasing her vulnerability, Lisbeth responds to each of these 'hurdles' by getting less and less sociable, each turn of events changing her at the level of her identity.

People with C-PTSD may also be more aware of their own altered state than those with PTSD (ibid 95). Many show an understanding that they have been monumentally and permanently changed by their trauma, as opposed to acknowledging that they are suffering from symptoms, as is the case of a self-aware PTSD sufferer (ibid). For example, when Mikael and Lisbeth are in Hedestad, he complains that he doesn't know anything about her because she is so emotionally closed off. She responds flatly and definitively, 'That's the way it is.' These words indicate Lisbeth has accepted the permanence of her identity as a survivor of sustained periods of trauma. Mikael asks her, 'How did you turn out like this?' rather than, 'Why are you behaving like this?' signalling his own growing conception of Lisbeth as fundamentally *different* from other people. Lisbeth is a person who has not been 'the same' since the first trauma, who develops a rigid personality salvaged from a sustained traumatic injury and who exists distanced from the rest of society. Fully intellectually capable but not socially functional, Lisbeth is a fundamentally altered C-PTSD sufferer. Her childhood experiences and her captivity as a teenager make her stringently hostile and weary of everyone she meets. She is a darker person, a sadder person because of those early, sustained traumas, and as an adult she has not worked out how to 'be' in the world. Her rape at twenty-four, and the subsequent PTSD, reinforces her C-PTSD-formed suspicions that she is justified in her hostility towards others. Therefore, as her symptoms escalate, the PTSD and C-PTSD compound one another, mutually reinforcing each other in a dark tangle of fear and anger.

Yet Kristeva states that paranoid anger is actually a useful symptom for the traumatized subject, as it gives them some distraction from the trauma (Kristeva *Hatred* 191). Hostility and anger are so firmly set in Lisbeth that many viewers of *Dragon Tattoo* may assume this is an inherent part of her persona, but I argue that it is a symptom, perhaps not reversible, of C-PTSD. I acknowledge that it may be part of her personality, but it has not come there organically and such a trait is further confirmation of the way in which trauma changes the subject. While her anger prevents Lisbeth from forming connections with other people, it also assists in keeping her alive, for 'the armor of the hateful warrior' can be used by the traumatized subject to hide behind (ibid), as they negotiate their way through an unknown landscape to survive in a dangerous world.

The mental impact of trauma: Memory and the honorary silence

The domestic abuse witnessed in childhood, the brain damage to her mother and the incarceration in a psychiatric hospital have made survival a central aspect of Lisbeth's identity. Those challenges and her rape at twenty-four ultimately strengthen her, after nearly destroying her. However, the PTSD she endures post-rape makes her even more solitary and more attached to an existence which is based on a sense of 'enduring', rather than 'living'. Lisbeth's endurance is abetted by her isolation and her withdrawal; thus, her trauma becomes central not only to her identity but also to her survival. Therefore, the notion of 'letting go of' or 'moving on from' her trauma in any way represents a twofold potential death to Lisbeth. Firstly, this is because being emotionally cold and distanced has assisted Lisbeth in staying alive, and a softening of those qualities will make her more vulnerable to attack. Secondly, as Lisbeth witnessed her mother's domestic abuse from a very young age and her list of traumatic life experiences extends into adolescence and the present, she is a subject who has never been 'without' trauma. Lisbeth has never known an existence other than the one which is a fight for survival and, if she 'lets go' of her identity as a survivor, she symbolically kills herself, for 'she' does not exist beyond her trauma.

Film theorist Tarja Laine, who writes predominantly in the area of affect and emotions, suggests that trauma, ironically, can be 'remembered but not memorized', provided it remains a traumatic memory rather than a narrative memory (Laine *Feeling Cinema* 50). To elaborate, if during PTSD the subject begins to recall accurate details of the traumatic event and piece together a narrative for the first time, it means that the event becomes memorable and hence extends to consciousness (Caruth *Recapturing* 154). A narrative memory is also able to be talked about; it is 'utterable', and therefore reducible to language (Caruth ibid), whereas 'a traumatic memory's compartmentalization and fragmentation produces unspeakability' (de Bruyn 56). So narrative memory can be disclosed, and if trauma can be 'told' it can also fade (Roth *Ironists Cage* 208). Roth argues that if the subject speaks about the event, translating traumatic memory into narrative memory, this breaches the pact that the subject can form with the event – a pact which attempts to signify the magnitude of the event's impact on the subject by remaining 'unutterable' (ibid 207). If trauma becomes part of narrative memory, if it moves fully into the Symbolic and is represented through language, the traumatized subject may have concerns that the event will become reduced and 'relativized' (ibid 205) through a system of mere representation (language), which fails to convey the horror of the trauma or its resounding impact on the subject's identity.[4] While a 'reduction' may seem like a positive move towards recovery, the traumatized subject needs to feel first that the scope of the trauma is understood, before attempting to 'work through' it, and while a move towards narrative memory may seem a logical defence mechanism against an overwhelming psychical experience, the continuation of the event within traumatic memory signifies the behemoth impact the trauma had on the subject's identity; narrative memory is viewed as a detraction, not a coping mechanism, in this regard.

Lisbeth is a prime example of someone who holds onto her trauma by not talking about it, lest it become reduced through the process of recounting it. Lisbeth lives on the fringe of society and has few people to confide in; however, she does develop a relationship with Mikael during their investigation in Hedestad and has several opportunities to disclose her story to him. The most overt of these is when, lying in bed together, Mikael wants to sleep next to Lisbeth, but although she has just had sex with him, she doesn't want to engage in any behaviour (like sharing a bed) that may strengthen the emotional connection with him; she thus literally turns her back on him. In response Mikael asks, 'What has happened to you?' At this point Lisbeth could tell Mikael about

---

[4] Ellie Ragland argues that representations of trauma in linguistic or artistic formation may appear to be potentially helpful for the traumatized, but the use of words and imagery in painting and prose, for example, reduce the severity of the trauma and the severity of the effect by distancing both the creator and the consumer with representative symbols (Ragland *Psychical Nature* 81). She posits that this is why so many Jewish Holocaust survivors were reluctant to speak about their experiences in concentration camps – because the narrating of it could never accurately convey the abjection of it (ibid). The only people who will be able to know the horror of a traumatic event are the people who were there; everything else is a lighter grey shade of the original black.

her past, but she does not. Instead, she upholds a silence which signifies her reluctance to bring the trauma into the Symbolic, and maintains its position as something so impactful on her subjectivity that it is unspeakable.

For the subject who has based an identity and survival on clinging to the sacred, untouchable horror of the event, the idea of 'letting go' brings new problems forth: Who am I without this event so central in my life? Could I have let go sooner and suffered less? Traumatic memory (which is not integrated into the life of the subject) therefore functions as an anchor which roots the individual to a familiar, albeit painful, subjectivity. Turning traumatic memory into narrative memory through recall and through language cuts loose the anchor, but for some, the familiar restriction of the anchor is preferable to the freedom of the new. Given that Lisbeth's subjectivity has been fostered by the traumatic circumstances of her life, she is a subject who remains chronically attached to identifying with her trauma.

Holding on to her trauma is not Lisbeth's only post-trauma survival tactic, however; Melanie Klein's identification theory suggests she also employs the image of the Other to displace her internalized trauma onto an external entity.

The mental impact of trauma: Identification and unexpected agency

Early identification (the mirror stage) is a process which contributes to the subject's basic development and understanding of the self. However, identification can also be employed as a tool for trauma sufferers by influencing 'how survivors react to their sense of inner fragmentation and dislocation and attempt to reintegrate their experiences' (Srinath 139). In other words, identification with another can assist the psychologically traumatized subject with understanding their own trauma and the person they've become as a result of the trauma. To illustrate how identification can work in the adult subject, Srinath refers to the moment allied soldiers entered the German concentration camp, Buchenwald, in April of 1945. When an inmate and a liberating solider look at each other, the inmate sees the horror of his own traumatized face mirrored in the expression of the soldier looking back at him. In this sense identification is similar to the mirror stage encountered during infancy, only in place of the actual mirror surface is another person, and that person functions as a reflection of the subject, re-informing, and then reinforcing, understanding of the self.

The renowned Austrian-British child psychoanalyst Melanie Klein takes this concept further by talking about 'projective identification' (Srinath 140). In this case the traumatized subject seemingly cuts away the part of the self that is most heavily affected by psychical pain, and projects it outward into the external world, away from the self. Projective identification is a way of displacing an intolerable internal state through the isolation and containment of a specific psychological experience. However, projective identification can work subversively when the subject identifies with the perpetrator of their trauma, a process Anna Freud claimed to be an alternative defence mechanism for the traumatized subject (ibid 142). During perpetrator projective identification the victim attempts to reduce the object or person it most fears by identifying with it or as 'one of them'. For example, the child who is afraid of the dark may choose to scare other siblings by posing as a night-time threat. If they are the monster, how can they also fear the monster? Perpetrator identification therefore is 'a person's attempt at control or mastery over a traumatic or threatening situation by turning the passive role into an active role' (ibid). While it may seem that Lisbeth's [C]PTSD-induced hostility and aggression is evidence of her projective perpetrator identification (a mirroring of the violence of Zalachenko, Teleborian, Bjurman and Martin Vanger), her agency comes from identification with other abused women rather than with the abusers. Lisbeth's mastery is gained not through malicious violence on another, but through the realization that as a living subject she still has options; she has the choice to act or to not act. For example, her reciprocal assault of Bjurman signifies her choice to act (and her agency), and her treatment of Martin Vanger also signifies her agency through her choice to remain passive.

A clear moment of projective identification occurs in *Dragon Tattoo* when Lisbeth looks at a huge display board of Martin Vanger's murder victims. Each of those faces is a grisly corpse, some discoloured through strangulation, some disfigured through his torture of them, some covered by the plastic bag that suffocated them, but all of them rape victims as well. Most of these women also came from challenging backgrounds, such as prostitution or illegal immigration, and were 'Othered' by society like Lisbeth. Martin chose these women because they were less likely to be reported missing, and some of their deaths went entirely unnoticed in much the same way that the domestic abuse in Lisbeth's family, and her wrongful imprisonment in a locked ward, went unnoticed and unpunished by mainstream Swedish society.

As Lisbeth looks at that board, her own face reflects the horror on theirs, eternally captured in their last moments with the experience of rape and murder etched in their expressions. Herein lies the only difference between them and Lisbeth: she is not dead – irrefutably changed, yes, but still living. The moment of projective identification is depicted through Lisbeth's point-of-view shot which slowly pans over the display, simulating her gaze rolling past each face. The reverse shot depicts a tight close-up of her face, a focus on her eyes digesting the images in front of her. Both of these frames are underpinned by the consistent sound of her breath, the aural confirmation of the difference between herself and the victims – life. This acknowledgement of her own trauma through the faces of others is the first step towards bringing her experience into the Symbolic order – a pre-step before engaging in the bigger move of talking about it with another person. So while identification with a number of raped murder victims appears utterly negative, it actually generates a shift in Lisbeth, allowing her to conceptualize herself as a survivor, and therefore as the only one in that large group of women left with any agency.

Lisbeth's understanding of her agency as a living victim is heavily informed by the previous scene when, having chased Martin down the road and initiated his car crash, Lisbeth simply watches as he burns alive. Martin cries out to her for help, but Lisbeth chooses instead to do nothing; the camera lingers on her face as she stares unblinking into the flames, calmly observing his gruesome death. *Dragon Tattoo* therefore depicts the paradoxical scenario where a character who identifies with those who are powerless embraces her own agency as a living subject through deliberate passivity. When later questioned by Mikael about whether she could have saved him, Lisbeth shows no remorse, unleashing a diatribe at Mikael in justification of her choice: 'Don't make him into a fucking victim … He was a killer and rapist and he enjoyed it … He wasn't a victim. He was an evil motherfucker who hated women.'

The point to be drawn out here is that trauma changes the subject hugely, but not necessarily with total negativity. Lisbeth suffers the re-experiencing symptoms, increased arousal symptoms and mood alterations of PTSD; she suffers the personality changes and transformed world views of C-PTSD, but she eventually gains understanding that, in being alive, she has an agency denied to the dead. Most importantly, Lisbeth's agency develops, not in spite of her encounter with the trauma, but because of it – a notion to be substantiated on in the following section on abjection.

The physical effect of trauma: The raped body, abjection and temporality

The abject exists in the space between Lacan's Imaginary and Symbolic orders. It exists in this anti-place, 'on the edge of non-existence and hallucination, of a reality that, if I acknowledge it, annihilates me' (Kristeva *Powers of Horror* 2). The abject stands in opposition to the subject; it is a huge, unwieldy burden, although it weighs nothing at all and 'yet it crushes me' (Kristeva *Hatred* 184). Kristeva refers to the abject as 'imaginary uncanniness and real threat' (*Powers of Horror* 4), yet abjection is also different from uncanniness in that it is 'more violent' and can be defined by its inability to 'know' its surrounds (*Hatred* 185). Kristeva illustrates the concept of the abject by referring to the children's shoes at Auschwitz or the smell of a decaying corpse (*Powers of Horror* 3–4), both horrific things which go beyond the perimeter of 'normal human experience' and cannot be 'done justice' to through retelling or representation (as per Ellie Ragland's argument regarding Jewish Holocaust survivors' reluctance to talk about their experience [*see previous footnote*]). Bodily fluids such as blood, pus and sweat are not signifiers of death, but signifiers of the edge of life. These unpleasant aspects of physicality are the last stop, the last boundary of the subject before death is reached and the cadaver, the dead body, is the step beyond that last boundary (Kristeva *Powers of Horror* 3–4). Kristeva believes that 'death is wholly abject' (Pheasant-Kelly *Abject Spaces* 192) because biologically 'life and death are mutually exclusive; where life is present, death shall not be, and where death is, life is no longer' (Razinsky 135). Therefore, the decaying cadaver, as a previously living thing, transgresses the life-death divide and renders the corpse abject (Kristeva *Powers of Horror* 3–4). Abjection is precisely a horror not consciously encountered before, yet repeatedly experienced on a corporeal level via the disgust reflexes of the body (Pile 90).

Abjection is horrific precisely because it 'does not respect borders, positions or rules' (Kristeva *Powers of Horror* 4). The zone without boundaries is the place where Garland suggests 'meaning collapses' for the traumatized subject, yet the more the subject attempts to define the zone, the more the boundaries recede into vagueness and ambiguity. The subject who encounters the abject beholds 'the breaking down of a world that has erased its borders' (Kristeva *Powers of Horror* 4). While the abject is 'banished' to the non-space between the Imaginary and Symbolic orders, it continues 'challenging its master' (the subject) from that position (ibid 2), signifying abjection's ability to transcend normal boundaries.

Abjection is therefore a post-apocalyptic, hostile wasteland where 'nothing is familiar, not even the shadow of a memory' (ibid 5). Acknowledgement of the abject is perilous to the subject but, akin to the Žižekian Real, the abject has a seductive pull which engages the subject in a simultaneous movement towards and away from it. Therefore, although Lisbeth responds to the trauma of her rape with anger and resentment, her identity as a PTSD-suffering traumatized survivor is also informed by it. Kristeva describes this pull as an 'inescapable boomerang', which 'places the one haunted by it literally beside himself' (ibid 1). The pull of the abject 'simultaneously beseeches and pulverizes the subject' (ibid 5), who, feeling dislocated from everything and everybody else, turns inwards and discovers the abject has left its mark on them. In *Dragon Tattoo*, Lisbeth isolates herself only to realize, amid the silence of her seclusion, that she can't ever escape or avoid the primary signifier of her rape – her own body.

The relationship that *Dragon Tattoo* establishes between abjection and the body is appropriate, given that the most basic form of abjection is 'food loathing' (ibid 2). Kristeva uses the example of the repulsed subject who reacts viscerally and gags in response to skin forming on the surface of milk to illustrate this loathing. The gag reflex is the body's attempt to regurgitate the subject's encounter with the abject – to expel it from the stomach, out through the throat and beyond the lips (the perimeter of the body), where it will no longer contaminate the subject. In attempting to physically expel the abject from the body (vomiting), the subject transcends its own corporeal boundaries – what was inside it is now outside of it in a previously detached and separate space. The subject's integral identification of the self as 'I' is now partly within the bounds of corporeal reality and partly outside of it. With 'guts sprawling', Kristeva states the vomiting subject is 'in the process of becoming an other' (ibid 3-4). The transitioning subject, having fallen into the gap between the Imaginary and the Symbolic, gives birth to itself, to the new self that emerges from the old (which was a combination of I and m[other]), and whose new identification is founded on the encounter with the abject. She states, 'I expel *myself*, I spit *myself* out, I abject *myself* within the same motion through which "I" claim to establish *myself*' (ibid 3). Therefore, corporeal boundaries mark the understanding of the self as subject and as separate from the other, and challenges to, or violations of, those corporeal boundaries have deep implications for the subject's psychological state. Kristeva claims, 'abjection is one of those violent and obscure revolts of the being against what is menacing it and what appears to come from an outside as well as an exorbitant inside' (*Hatred* 184). This duplicitous presence correlates with the effect rape has on the subject – an abused body which dehumanizes the subject internally, causing a sense of being repulsed by one's own corporeal reality; rape renders the body abject. The physical line separating 'self' from 'other' and defining corporeal reality is crossed when a rapist penetrates the bodily orifices of the victim, and as abjection is characterized by the transgressing of boundaries, the victim's body becomes a site of abjection. Lisbeth's rape is an encounter with the Real which renders her body abject because multiple (physical, emotional, ethical, legal and moral) boundaries are crossed when Bjurman assaults and penetrates her; it is the clearest demonstration of the link between a subject's psychological state and corporeal reality.

Because the traumatic event, situated in the realm of the Real, is unspeakable, Lisbeth displays it instead through her appearance. Lisbeth can't speak about her trauma, but she performs it – and every day she presents herself in this way she engages in a typically Kristevan attempt to expel the abject, actively reinforcing the connection between disordered psychological state and corporeal reality. She displays her traumatic history through several aspects of her physical presence. Lisbeth has tattoos on her body (the largest of which is the iconic dragon on her back); she has a multitude of piercings in both ears, eyebrows, nose and nipples; she dyes her hair jet black and shaves the underside of one section; she frequently wears black lipstick and eyeshadow; and she dresses in predominantly black clothes and shoes which are gender ambiguous. In addition to these presentation choices Lisbeth displays her trauma through hostile body language (arms crossed, stiff back, angry facial expression and erratic eye contact) and antagonistic behaviour (her dialogue with others is blunt and delivered in acidic tones and she doesn't bother with common niceties). All of these elements, aesthetic and behavioural, are Lisbeth's attempt at depicting herself as dangerous, brutal and inhuman, the visual manifestation of what was done to her, and the closest representation she can find for depicting abjection (which, being abject, is not representable). This visual display of trauma, stemming from her abject physicality, depicts what Žižek refers to as the subject who 'lives death as a form of life' (*Event* 86), for it is her encounter with trauma in the domain of the Real (where she feared for her life) which is embodied, even embraced, in her psychological disorder PTSD. Similarly to Klein's theories on projective identification, this is Lisbeth's attempt at cutting away the part of herself which is most affected by psychical pain and placing it outside, by displacing an intolerable internal state onto an external surface. However, Lisbeth's attempt at expelling abjection only succeeds in visually depicting it; she thereby further embodies the abject she is trying to cleanse herself of. This illustrates Laine's assertion that the target of the traumatized subject's anger can also be inadvertently adapted as 'an intimate part of the self' (*Feeling Cinema* 115) and reconfirms the argument that the subject is deeply changed by trauma.

Abjection transcends both meta-spatial and temporal boundaries. Kristeva claims that the abject is 'a *land of oblivion* that is constantly remembered' (*Powers of Horror* 8) and that the 'time of abjection is double: a time of oblivion and thunder, of veiled infinity and the moment when revelation bursts forth' (ibid 9). Kristeva's references to the transcendent qualities of the abject can be linked with the nature of traumatic memory. The 'land of oblivion' is a remote, dislocated and horrific space, far removed from all others, banished from the representable realm of the Symbolic, yet constantly present in the subject's psyche through a series of PTSD symptoms; it also acts as confirmation of the link between a subject's disordered psychological state and an altered relationship with temporality.

The 'double time' Kristeva refers to is trauma's unique ability to transcend normal temporal restrictions. The subject is unable to fully process the traumatic event as it happens (creating traumatic memory, rather than narrative memory), yet the subject re-experiences the event afterwards (post-trauma). In this sense the abject body exists in two temporal zones, or 'double time'; in the original moment (the 'time of oblivion and thunder', which is also a place of oblivion) and in each moment after the event when the subject encounters any of the re-experiencing symptoms of PTSD ('the moment when revelation bursts forth'). Trauma's 'veiled infinity', pulls the abjected subject into the same temporal ambiguity, reaffirming that the sufferer of PTSD lives neither in the present or in the past, but in the non-space and non-time of the abject, another example of the link between psychological disorder and unusual experiences of temporality. It is not surprising then that Roth concurs with the notion that trauma fundamentally changes the subject by asking, 'What kind of life can be built from a past that refuses translation or assimilation into the present but that will not be forgotten?' (*Ironist's Cage* 206).

Indeed, Caruth points out that part of the traumatic-ness of trauma is the fact it is not reducible to a singular event or moment in time (*Trauma: Explorations* 9) because trauma transcends the confines of normal temporalities through repetition. The abject's 'challenging' of the subject from a 'banished non-space' that Kristeva refers to can be witnessed in the re-experiencing and increased arousal symptoms of PTSD. Each time Lisbeth has a nightmare or a flashback about the rape, each time she jumps at a noise or movement, it is the unprocessed trauma calling out from the encounter with the abject, reaching out beyond its banished location, as well as additional confirmation that psychological state has clear links with both the subject's corporeal reality and sense of temporality. This unusual ability to emerge at different times and locations provides some insight into the lived experience of trauma victims; survival beyond the event itself can be harrowing, and even arguably a more difficult path than the event's threatened alternative – death. And yet, as Kristeva states (*Powers of Horror* 6), 'he is not mad, he through whom the abject exists', but he is suffering, and he is changed.

The physical effect of trauma: Boundaries and behaviours

Although Kristeva's theory of abjection and discussion of boundaries focuses on the body (Pheasant-Kelly *Abject Spaces* 12), it's also important to look at the various social, legal and ethical lines that are transgressed in *Dragon Tattoo*.

Firstly, adding to the suffering of those who have PTSD is the unsympathetic social response towards them. Lisbeth's [C]PTSD impacts upon her identity and interactions with others to the extent that she appears dysfunctional to the rest of society; in other words, she exemplifies a disability. The disabled subject presents the frightening possibility that anyone who is not disabled may become disabled too (Kristeva *Hatred* 29). Resultantly the suffering subject is commonly marginalized at the borders of mainstream society, for they are the living reminder of vulnerability, evoking the 'horror of narcissistic injury' (ibid 43) for others.

Lisbeth has almost no friends[5] and almost no family[6] and people at her workplace avoid her.[7] Living at the margins of the social world, she sleeps during the day, works at night, has minimal physical interaction with others and lives a very solitary existence in a liminal social zone. In fact, the time she spends with

---

[5] In *Dragon Tattoo*'s sequel *The Girl Who Played with Fire*, Lisbeth has a friendship with a woman called Miriam Wu, but as Miriam is not part of *Dragon Tattoo*, Mikael Blomkvist and a hacker called 'Plague' are the only characters who are 'friends' with Lisbeth.

[6] Lisbeth's mother, Agneta Salander, is technically alive in *Dragon Tattoo* but is brain damaged, living in a nursing home and hasn't seen Lisbeth in many years. Her father, Alexander Zalachenko, is alive but has also not seen Lisbeth since she attacked him with petrol at twelve years old.

[7] Lisbeth is only on speaking terms with one person at Milton Security – her boss Dragan Armanskij, who understands she is an excellent researcher but also socially challenged.

Mikael in Hedestad is the most social interaction she's had in years. Kristeva's utopic vision is a world in which the vulnerability of the disabled person, such as Lisbeth, rather than being feared is 'shared' by all (*Hatred* 30). While I won't argue that cyberspace is a utopia, the exception to Lisbeth's general marginalization is in her online presence, where she goes by the alias 'Wasp'. The internet's ability to mask appearances and social skills works in Lisbeth's favour, and in cyberspace Lisbeth has regular contact with other hackers. In the real world, though, for vulnerability to be shared, physical interaction is also required between the disabled person and others (ibid 31). The inability to share contributes further to the traumatized subject's suffering in what Kristeva refers to as the 'malaise of the isolated world of disability' (ibid 32), perceiving that those who have disabilities live in an 'antiworld' (ibid). Therefore, while Lisbeth has some social connection with people online, this doesn't challenge the reality of her real-world isolation beyond the border of mainstream society. Additionally, so long as Lisbeth is unable to speak about her trauma with Mikael (despite his attempts to know), the 'abyss' that separates her 'world of disability from [his] world of the able' remains in place (ibid 39), deepening her identification as a traumatized *and* isolated subject.

The second crossing of non-corporeal boundaries revolves around the act of assault in regards to legal and ethical lines. Premeditated crime purposely ignores the law, involves conscious scheming and reveals the flimsiness of the judicial rules imposed on society to prevent anarchy from emerging (Kristeva *Powers of Horror* 4). Bjurman is not an 'opportunity rapist'; he didn't take spontaneous advantage of unforeseen events, but purposely put Lisbeth into a position of financial vulnerability so that she is coerced into meeting him at his own home. Other than these manipulative behaviours, Bjurman's level of premeditative engagement in raping Lisbeth is obvious; handcuffs, ropes, electrical cable and sex toys were prepared and placed close to the bed, signifying he had planned the attack carefully. What makes Bjurman's act particularly reprehensible is that, as Lisbeth's state-appointed guardian, his legal and ethical responsibility is to *protect* his ward from harm and to ensure she functions successfully in society. His choice not to assist with Lisbeth's well-being makes Bjurman a negligent guardian, but his choice to actively harm Lisbeth is the crossing of a boundary which renders his actions abhorrent. In addition to his moral transgression, Bjurman's standing as a respected Stockholm lawyer means he is even less likely to be held accountable for his crime or to be suspected in the first place of planning and committing it. While he crosses boundaries in order to commit his crime, these same boundaries protect him from retribution, because (ironically) society is unlikely to believe he would cross them. Knowing this, Lisbeth is forced to react and resolve the situation in her own way, without the help of a legal system which has previously ignored her.

In retaliation Lisbeth plans an attack on Bjurman – and she prepares as well as he did. Engaging in an equally premeditated crime places Lisbeth in contestable moral territory; *Dragon Tattoo* has the protagonist cross some of the same boundaries as the antagonist. Lisbeth tricks Bjurman into thinking that she is in need of more money and goes to his apartment one night to ask for it. Bjurman, believing Lisbeth to be of low intelligence, doesn't consider she might return for revenge and lets her inside. She pulls a hand Taser from her bag, turns quickly and renders Bjurman unconscious before physically and sexually assaulting him. Lisbeth's retaliation is also illegal, yet, given the act was committed in retaliation, the viewer feels less inclined to view her actions as a transgression of moral boundaries and more as a legitimate (albeit brutal) act of warrantable revenge. Kenny suggests that a childhood full of abuse assists in fuelling Lisbeth's fury at Bjurman and informs her decision to respond in a violent manner (145). Kristeva would argue it is her hatred for the man and the act he committed which mitigates her revenge; this hatred is informed by the trauma of her own rape, given that abjection is 'the "degree zero" of hatred' (*Hatred* 185). Lisbeth also attacks Bjurman from a position of less power (physically, socially and financially) and without the legal obligation and authority to care for him (as he does for her as her legal guardian). This is not to say that what Lisbeth does to Bjurman is morally acceptable, but in the context of *Dragon Tattoo* the viewer understands she has crossed fewer boundaries than he. Importantly, the attack allows Lisbeth to renegotiate the power imbalance, achieved through a reciprocal transgression of boundaries centred around the physical body.

The physical effect of trauma: The second skin and tattooing

In his major works Anzieu maps a relationship between the mind and the body previously untouched by psychoanalytic theory (Ng 120), given the Lacanian tendency to use language rather than the body as the primary canvas for analysis (Tarrab, cited in Anzieu and Tarrab 61). Anzieu perceives the surface of the body (the skin) as a significant component of the structure of the mind (Lafrance 16), believing that bodies are sites where 'multiple meanings can be mapped' (Pile 185) and 'where there are invariable resonances of past experience' (Gusain 42).

Anzieu considers that subjectivity is always-already embodied (Lafrance 18), emphasizing the importance of skin in the forming of the individual's identity (Anzieu and Tarrab 64; Thomson 215). New-born infants are not able to differentiate between their own skin and the skin of their mother; they seem part of one shared corporeal existence, until the infant begins to comprehend that it has an inside and a distinctive outside (Lafrance 24). This new understanding of the difference between the self and the (m)other defines 'internal and external space' (Failler 171) and signifies the shift from what Anzieu calls the 'shared skin' to the 'skin ego'. Similarly to Kristeva's understanding of corporeal reality, Anzieu argues that the skin ego is an understanding of the body as a container which holds psychic content, and the container and its contents are intimately linked (Lafrance 23). In the same way that the physical skin acts as a trauma boundary for all internal body parts, the skin ego protects the subject against psychical trauma (ibid 28). If something wounds the subject by violating its sense of 'bodily integrity', another secondary psychic skin develops (Failler 171).

However, the traumatic breaching of the original psychic skin boundary can't be seen by the human eye, which encourages the subject to render the wound visible physically (ibid 172). In Lisbeth's case her sense of bodily integrity is violated when she is physically restrained in the children's psychiatric hospital, and when she is raped by Bjurman. In response to these traumas Anzieu argues that she develops a secondary skin, constituted by various visual modifications including piercings, tattoos, heavy black make up and gender-ambiguous black clothing – all visual and physical indicators of her psychological state. Yet, this secondary skin also functions as the visualization of the wound on her original psychic skin boundary that Failler refers to. The creating of a visible 'wound' enables Lisbeth to re-establish a sense of her personal physical autonomy by reasserting control over her corporeal reality. Ruptures to the skin ego and the development of a secondary psychic skin often lead to increased understanding of the structural makeup of subjectivity (Thomson 226). For example, Lisbeth's identity as a traumatized subject and agency as a surviving subject are generated out of the rupturing of her skin-ego (through her pediatric incarceration and her rape); this is another facet that illustrates the close connection between corporeal reality and psychological state.

This reading of Lisbeth's tattooing habit, which supports agency and autonomy, is reinforced by a visual focus on tattoos in scenes where she is empowered. For instance, while in Hedestad investigating the disappearance of Harriet Vanger, Lisbeth initiates sex with Mikael one night. Boldly walking into his room, she straddles Mikael on the bed and begins to undress him. Lisbeth maintains her position 'on top' and as the pair engage in intercourse the frame lingers on her writhing back, capturing from mid-shot and close-up the dragon tattoo inked broadly across her skin. The sound in this moment is predominantly limited to the creaking of the bed and rhythmic inhaling and exhaling. As the visual frame is filled up by the dragon tattoo, the breathing sound appears to come from the dragon itself, giving the impression of a vital living beast. This reinforces the notion that Lisbeth's tattoos, her second skin, signify a subject who is re-made as traumatized but powerful following an encounter with the Real, as opposed to a subject who is re-made as traumatized and self-destructive.

Furthermore, while Failler, who researches in the area of memory and gender studies, acknowledges that the term 'self-harm' usually refers to cutting, burning, scratching and so on, she also concludes that this umbrella term is wider than traditionally described (169) and frequently reduced to being a solely negative activity (ibid 168). Instead, she suggests that self-harm 'is more productively understood as a means of survival in the wake of psychical trauma' (ibid). In other words, self-harm actually has reparative qualities, given its ability to express internal, personal pain that may otherwise have remained stifled. If self-harm is categorized by the way it helps an individual to express psychical trauma, then Lisbeth engages in self-harm through the repeated inking of her skin. Lisbeth's re-building of identity, after the collapse of meaning in the Real, is heavily based on these modifications to her physicality and reasserts the significance of the images on her skin; she *is* the girl with the dragoon tattoo and she *is* changed. She also purposefully and knowingly manipulates her corporeal reality in relation to her psychological state.

When Lisbeth assaults Bjurman in reciprocation for her rape, she also tattoos his body afterwards – an echo of her own behaviour after trauma, when she tattoos her skin to mark the trauma. As part of her premeditated attack Lisbeth purchases a portable tattoo kit and educates herself to use it at a rudimentary level. After assaulting Bjurman anally with his own sex toy and rectifying the terms of her legal guardianship, Lisbeth then inscribes the words 'I am a rapist and a sadistic pig' into his torso. These key elements of her attack visually depict the reversal of power in the relationship by capturing Lisbeth in predominantly low angles which enlarge and empower her presence, and showing Bjurman in high angles, helpless on the floor of the apartment. These camera angles are particularly pronounced when Lisbeth begins to tattoo Bjurman's flesh; the use of slow-motion editing and tight close-ups of her inky hand hovering over his bloody skin also reinforce her agency and control in this moment. This scene reasserts that the tattooing of skin, *anyone's* skin, is an act of empowerment for Lisbeth in *Dragon Tattoo*.

Furthermore, the penetrating of Bjurman's skin with the tattoo needle may be interpreted as a symbolic rape, with his torso functioning as a substitute vaginal site. The reasoning behind this interpretation is twofold. Firstly, as Lisbeth lacks a penis of her own, she can only sexually assault Bjurman with an external object, such as the sex toy or some other substitute for the phallus (a tattoo needle for example). But secondly, and more significantly, the trauma of rape can't be fully depicted in *Dragon Tattoo* because, as previously stated, the Real is not directly representable. During Bjurman's rape of Lisbeth this incapacity is dealt with by using static noise and cutting to the next scene while the rape is still occurring. In Lisbeth's assault on Bjurman, rather than showing Bjurman's bodily orifice being penetrated, the rape is depicted through the forced needling of his torso. As a representation of the vicious vaginal equivalent, gruesome close-up images of Bjurman's damaged and bloody skin are shown.

Lisbeth's retaliation to Bjurman's attack on her is uniquely brutal; few cinematic rape victims manage such ruthlessly and flawlessly executed revenge on their assailant. But Lisbeth is uncommon in her intelligence, in her level of sustained trauma and in her identity which develops out of that trauma – an identity informed by her psychological state and characterized by a hostile secondary psychical skin and a corporeal autonomy embodied through tattooing.

Conclusion: The changed subject – trauma and survival

Lisbeth suffers daily. She physically re-experiences her trauma through nightmares, flashbacks, hypervigilance, increased startle response and irritability; she detaches from individual people and from society as a whole, living on the fringe of community and avoiding contact when possible; her closest interpersonal link is through an identification with the dead victims of similar traumas, yet she maintains a code of silence about her own traumatic experiences. Furthermore, Lisbeth visually conveys her suffering through a failed attempt to expel the abject (which only solidifies her subjectivity as post-traumatic), and the generation of a second psychical skin, which marks her actual skin with emblems of survival – her tattoos. All of these mental and physical effects are the impact of trauma, previously referred to as the 'flotsam and jetsam' left behind in the wake of an encounter with the Real. Lisbeth escapes death multiple times, and in response she suffers a psychological state which both pulls her into unsafe temporalities at random moments and facilitates the embodiment of the violation of her corporeal reality. Yet, as the post-traumatic subject who 'survives its own death' (Žižek *Event* 86), these things are also markers of the new, changed subject who emerges in response: Lisbeth may be damaged, but she is not broken.

Despite the trauma that Lisbeth has witnessed and been subject to, she continues. Constantly struggling but never weakening, she is a terminator in spirit – she just keeps going. In *Hatred and Forgiveness* Kristeva suggests this tenacity is part of being a woman. She states, 'there is a female endurance that is not a phallic, metallic hardness but a suppleness and plasticity' (114). Rather than gendering her endurance, I argue that the 'suppleness and plasticity' Lisbeth possesses is born out of trauma survival, not gender. Her ability to resist defeat is achieved through the unique resilience that develops out of survival after sustained trauma; that resilience is constituted by the psychological and physical changes that make Lisbeth a 'darker, sadder' person than she otherwise would have been. In other words, suffering 'make[s] way toward a constant renewal of the self' (Kristeva *Hatred* 142). This is not to say, by any means, that Lisbeth is a 'better' person for her suffering, just that she is a changed person. Indeed, part of the success of *Dragon Tattoo* is its refusal to 'fix' Lisbeth, to resolve her issues, or have her 'saved' by Mikael. The film unapologetically portrays a very angry, anti-social, wounded female subject and does not attempt to relativize her trauma by mellowing her behaviour as the narrative progresses. In fact, the almost relentlessly hostile characterization that Lisbeth embodies is the film's way of honouring the magnitude of her trauma – by consistently revealing how the subject is so fundamentally effected by it in the long term.

Herein lies one of the key differences between Lisbeth and many other traumatized female characters – she is fundamentally changed, but she ultimately survives. The change in Lisbeth does re-make her into a different person, but she's a person who lives when many don't and she finds agency in this simple but monumental difference. The girl with the dragon tattoo is repeatedly victimized but turns her experience of trauma into the foundation for an identity focused on surviving. While Lisbeth's anti-social behaviours and hostile appearance do isolate her, they also protect her. Therefore, Lisbeth's expressing and embracing of what appears to be her 'destructiveness' is what drives her survival, so that 'the girl with the dragon tattoo' is actually the 'subject who survived'.

4

Brødre (2004)

Introduction to adjustment disorder, emotional detachment and *Brødre*

Adjustment disorder sits within the 'Trauma and Stressor Related Disorders' section of the DSM-V. Similar to PTSD, adjustment disorder develops following 'exposure to catastrophic or aversive events' (APA). However, unlike PTSD, symptoms of adjustment disorder manifest within three months of the stressor event and usually conclude within six months, and sufferers do not typically experience the flashbacks or hallucinations which are common with PTSD. Adjustment disorder is primarily marked by 'significant impairment in social, occupational, or other important areas of functioning' and 'changes in social relationships', and is subdivided into six categories of affect (APA). Michael, the central character of the Danish film *Brødre* (Bier 2004), exhibits 'adjustment disorder with mixed disturbance of emotions and conduct' (the fifth possible variety), which sees him both emotionally detached from his family and prone to eruptions of violent anger. It is his emotional detachment symptom which signifies his traumatized psychical state and informs his characterization in most of this film. Because emotional detachment is linked with moral choices and behaviour in this character, *Brødre* is a text about how the transgressing of boundaries results in the breaking of bonds. Similar to Nina, Reznik and Lisbeth, Michael's psychological state is closely connected to an encounter with death and with his own corporeal reality, with the symptoms of emotional detachment displaying physically on his body.

 Co-written and directed by Susanne Bier, *Brødre* is the story of Michael Lundberg (Ulrich Thomsen), a Danish army officer sent to Afghanistan on an International Security Assistance Force for the United Nations. The film follows Michael as he is captured by local Taliban forces and discovers that a missing Danish radar technician (Niels Peter) is also being held in the camp. Because of his expertise with weaponry, Michael is of use to his captors; however, the Taliban fighters consider Niels Peter to be of no use so they demand that Michael kill him. If Michael does not kill Niels Peter, they threaten to shoot Michael on the spot. To save his own life,[1] Michael beats Niels Peter to death with the metal pipe provided, breaking the protective bond that he has formed with Niels Peter, and shortly afterward he is rescued by allied forces. Michael's disordered psychological state develops directly from this horrific experience of 'kill or be killed'. Upon his return to Denmark, Michael discovers that his wife Sarah, brother Jannik, daughters and parents all believed him to be dead and that during his captivity Jannik (who is typically the outsider of the family) has grown close to his daughters and his wife. Michael keeps the details of his captivity (including Niels Peter's death) to himself, but the strain of his traumatic experience inhibits him from connecting (or re-connecting) with his family, manifesting pathologically as an adjustment disorder with emotional detachment as the main symptom.

Unable to adjust to his life in Denmark, Michael is emotionally disconnected from his family. This symptom is revealed through his inappropriately militaristic demeanour in domestic settings and outbursts of anger which are disproportionate to the immediate trigger. In other words, the emotional attachment which was previously present has become detached, and in its place is an absence of warmth and familiarity. Michael's inability to emotionally resynchronize with his family is common among victims of harsh confinement who have experienced a torture chamber at 'the threshold of humanity' (Bourke 266). Judith Lewis Herman, a practising psychiatrist specializing in incest trauma, violence and recovery, believes that after release from captivity it is not possible for a former captive to 'go back' to the emotional attachments and relationships that existed in his or her life before the imprisonment (94), and therefore some form of adjustment disorder is inevitable. She states this is because, after having such an extreme relationship with the captor, all other relationships are 'viewed through the lens of extremity ... as though questions of life or death are at stake' (ibid). In addition, I posit that the formally captive subject is inhibited from reconnecting with people who have not experienced the horrific limits of human experience, because the tortured subject discerns

---

[1] 'Any animal, regardless of its species, reacts to a life-threatening attack with one of two patterns of behavior: either with flight, or with aggression and violence'. Either of these options are a route to self-preservation – another instinctual response, hundreds of millions of years old and existing deep within the physical brain, in the limbic system of the cerebrum (Mark and Ervin 14).

an unequivocal and unbridgeable difference between himself/herself and others; they feel detached from humanity and Michael suffers the sense of 'being non-human' (Bourke 266).

As a successful military leader, Michael has spent his whole life exercising high levels of self-discipline and dedication, rewarded through his military position as captain and confirmed when Jannik states, 'He's never been in trouble before and has a bag full of medals.' At just under two minutes into the film Michael walks into a locker room full of young soldiers and informs them of their upcoming mission. He reassures them, 'If any of you doubt that we're doing the right thing, wait 'til we get there. Then you'll know we're doing the right thing, okay?' This simple scene, comprised of shot-reverse-shots between captain and soldiers, quickly solidifies Michael's identity as predominantly based on strong leadership and ethics. However, his attempts at military perfectionism and personal rigidity upon returning to Denmark suggest an emotional detachment beyond normal or healthy levels. Michael attempts to embody ethical perfection and overt morality through a series of emotionally detached behavioural traits that include rigid physical posture, unanimated facial expression and refusal to partake in or acknowledge humour, all evidence of the intimate connection between the subject's psychological status and corporeal reality. Such embodiments are emphasized through the film's cinematography and editing, which capture Michael in a series of tight and disjointed frames upon his return to Denmark. He is often depicted in these scenes through close-ups of only his hands, mouth or eyes, which visually separates Michael from others in order to symbolize the emotional distance between him and his family. In contrast Sarah and his two daughters are often shown in a wider shot from the waist up and often within the same frame, illustrating that the emotional connection between the three of them continues to exist.

Michael's emotional detachment stems from a sense of guilt about the events in Afghanistan. Freud observes that 'it is precisely those people who have carried saintliness furthest who reproach themselves with the worst sinfulness'; in other words, the more 'virtuous a man is, the more severe and distrustful' his superego (*Civilisation* 62–3). For example, although Michael was in an impossible predicament, he reproaches himself for his actions and his emotionally detached behaviours are meant to convey his moral purity in an attempt to counteract his guilt. However, Michael's transgression of boundaries and breaking of bonds in Afghanistan *cannot* be resolved by further detachment from others and he only increases his suffering by remaining so emotionally removed through his obsession with ethical perfectionism. This is not surprising, as Grigg states that obsessives tend to be particularly moral subjects and the influence of the superego can be witnessed in the subject's 'indignation at the immorality of others' (*Lacan, Language and Philosophy* 114).[2] The severity of Michael's self-reproach about killing Niels Peter is palpable in his obsession with being an ethical man (or appearing to be). Yet despite his attempt to embody morality and humanity, Michael's emotional disconnection with everyone around him actually renders him inhuman, further increasing the detachment of the broken emotional bond with his family. That being said, such internal emotional frictions and interpersonal confrontations generate dramatic cinema within a genre (war film) which is already popular for its 'epic storytelling' (Stutterheim 133).

Similarly to *The Girl with the Dragon Tattoo*, much of the literature about *Brødre* is motivated by the adaptation of the original Danish version into the Hollywood remake *Brothers* (2009) (Gemzoe; Molloy, Nielson & Shriver-Rice; Shriver-Rice; Sulaberidze; Westerståhl Stenport). Both Gemzoe (285) and Smaill (14) argue that the American adaptation cuts the 'Nordic-ness' from the material, despite being inspired by it (285). Several authors recognize *Brødre* as part of Bier's 'male soujourner trilogy' (Molloy; Shriver-Rice; Smaill), which includes *After the Wedding* (2006) and *In a Better World* (2011). In each film a white, Western male originates in Denmark and travels to somewhere 'exotic' to help non-Western society (Langkjar 20, 22; Shriver-Rice 243).

Many scholars agree on the style of Bier's work, citing her use of close-up frames on eyes and hands (Hojberg; Sulaberidze) as characteristic of a modern melodrama (Langkjar 19; Molloy 193) which conforms to neither art house nor mainstream cinema (Hojberg, Sulaberidze). Perhaps most importantly much of the published literature concurs that *Brødre*'s eminent trait is 'an intimate psychological storyline' (Shriver-Rice 11) that ventures into a deliberately difficult area of ethics (ibid 10), or what Langkjar refers to as 'unsolvable dilemmas, stark contrasts, and extraordinary moral challenges' (19). It is not surprising that such dilemmas occur in combat with various authors (Baughan 13; Gemzoe 288, Hojberg 260), suggesting that *Brødre* offers a

---

[2] Michael, for example, looks down upon Jannik for his transgression of the Danish legal system (Jannik robbed a bank some years prior) and therefore considers himself superior to him. In addition to this, Michael picks Jannik up from prison in the scene immediately following the locker-room talk which paints him as the morally sound and trustworthy captain; the ethics of one brother are juxtaposed against the flailing moral code of the other.

commentary on 'the damage inflicted by war' (White-Stabley 133). Yet amongst these readings of *Brødre* it is only Nielson who approaches the text through an affectual analysis, concurring with my own interpretation that the psychological and the physical are intricately linked. In this sense it is that '[a]ffect remains in the body as a residual intensity' (161) where 'Michael's body retains the very imprint' (162) of his trauma until he finally 'yields stoicism' and shares his story with his wife.

The post-9/11 subgenre and West/Other dichotomy

War, as a topic, lends itself effectively to cinema. The combination of combat sequences and emotional challenges generates an intense narrative, which often takes place in unusual locations (jungles, deserts, abandoned cities) with stimulating aesthetics. Amongst the trademarks of the genre is the pull of the heroic figure (or figures), who are quickly identified as protagonists within the narrative and who may (or may not) survive the conflict. Cinema, in particular, is able to depict combat and conflict 'in ways that can transcend one-dimensional heroic perspectives' (ibid 125) to generate a provocative depiction of the realities of war. Other aspects of the war film genre include large production budgets, a predominantly male cast and a setting within a non-fictitious war such as Europe in the First World War and the Second World War, the Korean war or the Vietnam war.

Following the events of 11 September 2001 (henceforth referred to as '9/11'), a large number of films specifically about the war in Iraq and Afghanistan (the War on Terror) emerged in the Western hemisphere. This cluster of texts formulated a post-9/11 subgenre, of which *Brødre* is a part of the small Scandinavian contingent, which includes *In a Better World* (Bier 2010), *A War* (Lindholm 2015) and *Wolf and Sheep* (Sadat 2016). The blossoming of this subgenre is not surprising, given that in a time of national (and international) anxiety 'representations of destruction' increase through the various facets of popular culture (Nilges 23). Post-9/11 war films appear to be influenced by the Vietnam-era films, which function as 'an effective template' for the more modern combat texts (McSweeney 60), with the ominous 'Other' being Muslim, Arab, Afghani or Iraqi rather than Vietnamese.

As part of the canon of post-9/11 films, *Brødre* is therefore also part of a larger political statement about the emerging binary between East and

West hemispheres, a sociocultural splitting of the world into two parts. This binary is responsible for an increasing divide which depicts people, places and cultures of the West with favourable bias, and translates anything else as a problematic Other (Begin 54). The majority of post-9/11 war films are interested in examining the effects of the War on Terror on (predominantly white) citizens of the United States and of depicting the American soldier as the primary victim in the War on Terror (McSweeney 62; Stutterheim 125). This trend suggests that Western audiences are willing to acknowledge the psychological repercussions of time spent in combat but at the cost of demonizing the Other of the 'West/Other' dichotomy, through perpetuating the myth that the Other is responsible for the suffering of the Western soldier who selflessly serves.

When Arabs and Muslims are depicted in post-9/11 war films, they are often conflated as the same thing and they 'tend to be heavily stereotyped and limited in the spectrum of their characterisations' (McSweeney 34). Although *Brødre* is not a Hollywood film, it is a cultural product of 'the West' and it also makes no attempt to humanize the Afghani characters in any way; in clearly aligning itself as a text on the 'right' side of the divide, *Brødre* presents the Afghani characters as cruel, two-dimensional figures who are part of the 'irrational' Other (Carlsten 158). As part of the post-9/11 war genre, the binary between Michael (as complex, human and variable) and his captors (as brutal) is particularly pronounced and politicized.

Sean Redmond, who frequently publishes in the area of popular culture, whiteness studies and film authorship, refers to this binary as 'power-saturated', where the soldier is a hero and the Other is an 'irregular/hysterical villain' who comes from the 'hidden, leaky and schizophrenic self of the Eastern/Oriental' (*When Planes Fall* 22–3). In addition to the irregularity of the Other, Redmond also argues that in post-9/11 films the 'Other' 'never engages in a fair or legitimate fight' (*Introduction* 149). In *Brødre* the Afghani characters are not only cowardly but sadistic in their 'games'. Notably, rather than shoot Niels Peter themselves, the captors make Michael kill him and to do so with a blunt object (a heavy metal pipe). This barbaric behaviour reinforces Bourke's remark that the captured war body, Niels Peter's in this case, becomes 'undifferentiated flesh – stripped of individuality, even humanity' (267). The use of Michael as a weapon (because the metal pole is only an object until someone wields it) also marks him as 'undifferentiated flesh' rather than a person. This manipulation of Michael and treatment of Niels Peter depicts the Other as sadistic and illogically evil, reinforcing that Michael was left with an impossible choice – the antithesis of the 'fair fight' that Redmond refers to.

The discrepancy between moral righteousness on one side of the hemisphere boundary and sinister illogicality on the Other is reinforced in three ways through the cinematography used in the war camp scenes. Firstly, the Afghani characters are almost exclusively seen in groups of at least two or three people within the frame, confirming their inhumanity as an anonymous mob. Secondly, these frames are generally long shots which reveal that each Afghani character is armed with at least one firearm, worn by the characters in such a way that the arms are prominent and obvious. Finally, in moments of great tension, such as when the captors insist Michael show them how to use a grenade launcher, the camera work uses an on-the-shoulder documentary-style technique. The constant, yet inconsistent, shifting of the frame reflects the unpredictability of the Afghani 'Other' in this moment, and the terrified anxiety of the Danes in response. Such power-saturated binaries continue to perpetuate cycles of violence through a rhetoric which is based on the reductionist dichotomy of good versus evil. *Brødre* is an artefact of this dichotomy, which thrives on the 'twin strategies of decontextualisation and delegitimization' (Carlsten 154). These strategies allow the Western public to continue consuming film texts which reflect their 9/11 trauma through the depiction of an inhuman enemy and the victimization of the West.

Karen Randell, who specializes in film history, world cinema and contemporary cinema, refers to Cathy Caruth's argument that trauma is experienced belatedly and repeatedly over time, and suggests that the post-9/11 war subgenre functions in a similar way (145). Just as Caruth states that traumatic moments are replayed in the subject's mind, Randell posits that this subgenre is society's attempt to process 9/11 and the War on Terror, but rather than repeated involuntary replaying of the event (as per Caruth's theory), the consumer is choosing to replay the trauma through deliberate consumption of the same type of cinematic text; either way it's a process with the aim of 'working through' and 'working out'. I posit that this subgenre, therefore, is both a canon that works through collective trauma and a symptom of mass-societal trauma. These cinematic texts are akin to the flashbacks and intrusive thoughts that the PTSD victim suffers. In this light, other symptoms of post-9/11 mass-societal trauma include the increase of Islamophobia, the rise of right-wing political ideologies (and politicians) and the continued demarcation in popular culture of anything that doesn't conform to Western norms as alien. I do not argue that *Brødre* specifically is a symptom; rather, it is one episode, or one 'attack', of a recurring symptom of disorder, whereby films such as *Stop-Loss* (Pierce 2008), *The Hurt Locker* (Bigelow 2008), *Green Zone* (Greengrass 2010) and *Zero Dark Thirty* (Bigelow 2013) represent other 'attacks' of the same symptom. Yet 22 years has elapsed since the events of 9/11, suggesting that the repeated production and consumption of the post-9/11 war film indicates societal PTSD and an adjustment disorder on a mass scale, as well as an increasingly distinct binary consisting of two hemispheres.

In addition to acknowledging *Brødre*'s function as a symptom in Western society's trauma, this chapter will look to the symptoms which an individual suffers following his traumatic experience during the War on Terror. Just as 9/11 has proven to be an incomparable, fundamentally influential moment on a mass scale, Michael has a similarly monumentally affecting experience in Afghanistan. In fact, the political situation is somewhat eclipsed by the complexity of the impact on the individual in *Brødre* – Michael's disordered response to the situation reflects, but also smothers, any particularly overt clues about the sociopolitical functions of *Brødre* as a post-9/11 war film. Both of these moments (9/11 and Michael's forced killing of Niels Peter) can be defined in Žižekian terms as an 'Event'. For Žižek, an event is a change of frame, a reframing or a destruction of the frame (Žižek *Event* 19).

As a seasoned soldier Michael has previously experienced war, violence and death, so the event which transcends his normal limits in Afghanistan and re-frames his entire lived experience is traumatic to him because of the unexpected emotion he encounters. The event in the prisoner of war camp with Niels Peter exposes the reality that no one wants to admit to – not that warfare is traumatizing (there are countless other texts which reveal this), but that there may be an unforeseen emotion to be found in killing another person – the experience of pleasure. This moment for Michael is what Žižek refers to as the 'meaningless intrusion(s) of the real that destroy the symbolic texture of the subject's identity' (*Event* 85). It is this traumatic transgression which drives Michael's psychological suffering at the deepest level. As this traumatic re-framing occurs because of an overload of emotion, it is a logical reaction for Michael to respond by counteracting with limited emotionality (manifested through the emotional detachment symptom and displayed through his corporeal reality). It also confirms that emotional detachment remains a key trait of the ideal soldier (lest they feel too much and fail to recover from it), and that emotional detachment is the main symptom of Michael's inability to adjust.

Jouissance and the pleasurable pain of transgression

The 'real Real' of Michael's time in Afghanistan is so 'inexpressible' (Begin 54) that guilt about the more palatable aspect of the trauma (the killing of a junior comrade) serves as a sanctuary, a reassuring psychological mechanism that he is still human with moral and ethical boundaries. Michael's unconscious guilt is born out of the unexpected emotion he encounters when killing Niels Peter – the 'freedom in being forced', and the obscene pleasure this generates in him, the agony of jouissance.

In Lacan's early work he used the term 'jouissance' in reference to enjoyment (usually of a sexual nature). However, this definition developed into a more sophisticated understanding, as a concept more complex than pleasure in the 'regular' sense (Wright 69). Lacan came to use 'jouissance' not simply to describe the experience of pleasure, but as something encountered *beyond* pleasure and in fact 'carried back and forth between pleasure and displeasure' (Ragland *Lacan, The Death Drive* 84). This oscillation between the poles of pleasure and displeasure means jouissance can be witnessed both 'in the suffering of a symptom ... as much as in pleasure' (Wright 69), iterating jouissance as the seemingly impossible human phenomenon of agony in moments of great ecstasy, and pleasure within terrible suffering. It comes as no surprise that this disturbing and paradoxical arrangement of emotions is produced in the Real, through the friction between desire (to transgress a boundary) and law (to prevent transgressing that boundary) (Ragland *Lacan, The Death Drive* 87). Therefore 'jouissance and transgression form a couple: There is no jouissance without transgression' (Grigg *Lacan, Language and Philosophy* 111). Jouissance is the pushing *beyond* boundaries, the extra pain and the extra pleasure beyond the limit, something Ragland describes as 'the *more* than us in us' (Ragland *Lacan, The Death Drive* 84). This encroachment which is characteristic of jouissance aligns with a pre-eminent theme in *Brødre* – transgression and intensity.

When Michael kills Niels Peter, he transgresses several boundaries: a legal boundary which prohibits citizens from killing other citizens without judicial punishment, a moral boundary which fosters the notion that as senior officer Michael should be protecting his junior comrade, and an ethical boundary which rests on what Žižek refers to as the restriction of the big Other, *'thou shalt not kill'* (Grigg *Lacan, Language and Philosophy* 121). Therefore, Michael's encounter with the Real in *Brødre* is his experience with jouissance, generated by the transgressing of multiple boundaries when finding the killing of Niels Peter to be abhorrent *and also* liberating – further confirmation that psychological suffering and disorder is frequently linked with the subject's experience with death (either their own or someone else's).

In the few seconds that it takes Michael to beat Niels Peter to death he finds a pleasure that he has never experienced before – the ironic 'freedom in being forced', and the pleasure of transgression which emerges in moments of 'ecstasy and violence' (Bronfen and Webster Goodwin 11). When Michael is given an ultimatum by one of his captors, ('Kill him or you both die'), he takes the metal pole and begins to hit Niels Peter in an act of self-preservation. His killing of another person is forced upon him, yet being forced to commit this atrocity gives him the rare 'permission to kill' and this is where Michael encounters jouissance. The act of being forced to kill someone is what Grigg refers to as a 'redouble renunciation' (or in Žižek's words the 'loss of loss') (*Lacan, Language and Philosophy* 122); Michael can't be 'guilty' of killing Niels Peter in the 'normal' sense because when forced to kill the act loses some of its power to inflict guilt on the surviving subject. Under threat of death, Michael has a moral 'permission' to kill and this sudden requirement to kill another sidesteps the normally crushing imposition of his perfectionist superego which prohibits any legally, ethically and morally questionable acts. That moment in the desert is the only time in Michael's life that his superego is suppressed, although this is done externally through the actions of his Afghani captors. Backed into a metaphorical corner (and with a gun literally pointed at his head), Michael finally unleashes violence on his comrade.

It's important to reiterate here that Michael's jouissance is not founded on realizing some hatred of Niels Peter, some deeply suppressed appetite to kill, or animalistic desire to release violence on a weaker body. Michael's jouissance is the obscene pleasure which surfaces in the moment of horror, upon realizing he is 'getting away with' an act normally prohibited. Killing another human without bearing the responsibility for it appears to give Michael the paradoxical gift of 'freedom while forced'. It is the unexpected positive outcome of dictatorial authority echoed in the statement, 'I can't be held responsible for my own actions'. However, having relished this waiving of culpability is psychologically problematic for Michael, whose ego-ideal is based on rigid adherence to legal, ethical and moral boundaries. What unsettles Michael the most is not the brutality of the event or the transgressing of his own ethical and moral standards, but the unexpected pleasure he finds in 'escaping' his superego (externally suppressed by the captors) and evading the stringent ethics that accompany his existence in the Symbolic. In other words, the most distressing thing for the subject who subsists on adherence to the law is the joy that is found in rebelling against it. This singular moment, this event, is the source of Michael's deepest trauma.

The event and the act

Žižek defines a monumentally traumatic moment in time as an 'Event'. In *Event: A Philosophical Journey Through a Concept* he first defines the term in the following way:

> An event at its purest and most minimal: something shocking, out of joint that appears to happen all of a sudden and interrupts the usual flow of things; something that emerges seemingly out of nowhere, without discernable causes, an appearance without solid being as its foundation. (*Event* 4)

This description solidifies an event as a singular moment which comes into the lived experience of the subject without warning and without explanation, a rupturing of 'normal' lived experience boundaries. However, Žižek develops the concept, further, arguing that an event is 'the effect that seems to exceed its causes' (*Event* 5). This refined definition suggests that an event is not just a singular occurrence but one that interrupts 'the flow of things' and comes out of nowhere. It also reflects the DSM-V diagnostic criteria for adjustment disorder, which states that sufferers will react 'disproportionately' to daily stressors following a catastrophic event. Michael, for example, exhibits sudden explosions of anger in response to minor domestic issues, signifying the original 'event' in Afghanistan exceeds that one moment in time, continuing to affect Michael several months afterwards and repeatedly breaking the boundaries of normal lived experience.

The event has such impact that it changes the 'very frame through which we perceive the world and engage in it' (ibid 12). According to Žižek, a 'violent intrusion of the Real' (an event) resonates with the main trauma of the subject's past – the birth of subjectivity during the shift between Imaginary and Symbolic orders (and the subsequent movement away from the m(other) (ibid 87). He claims that the subject is generated when 'a living individual is deprived of its substantial content' (ibid), such as self-identity (or identity in connection with the (m)other), in other words when a bond is broken. When Michael is forced to kill Niels Peter in *Brødre*, the act strips him of his substantial content (his sense of identity as ethically sound and noble) and his bond with Niels Peter. This 'stripping' forces him to reconstruct an understanding of himself, in the same way that an infant is forced into constructing a new sense of subjectivity upon entrance into the Symbolic.

The power of this event in Michael's life is such that it not only impacts on everything which comes after it, but also appears to open up a gap between itself and everything (including its causes) that came before (ibid 5). The event therefore becomes an island in time, surrounded on either side by experiences from a different world, where the trauma of being forced to kill Niels Peter seems to come suddenly and illogically for both Michael and the viewer. As a prisoner of war Michael's conditions in the camp are dire (insufficient food and water, no access to bathroom facilities, limited exposure to light and no protection from the cold beyond minimal clothing), yet the order to kill his junior comrade exceeds the severity and the cruelty of these experiences; it is the final atrocity which caps a series of human rights violations and it exists in an atemporal sphere characteristic of traumatic experiences, which lead on to psychological suffering and disorder.

During wartime, Russell Grigg, who has published broadly in the field of psychoanalysis with specific focus on Lacan, jouissance and psychosis, believes that those who commit atrocious acts are 'on the whole, otherwise good, decent, and law abiding citizens' who usually have no history of violent crime (*Lacan, Language and Philosophy* 113). While *Brødre* reinforces Grigg's notion of Michael as a decent, law-abiding person who is forced into an act of violence, the film does not allow the same explanation for Michael's Afghani captors. In falling in with the demonization of the Other in post-9/11 war films, *Brødre* does not attempt to humanize a single member of the Taliban force in the camp through any diegetic content that suggests his captors had different lives prior to becoming Taliban fighters, have any sympathy for Michael or Niels Peter's incarceration, or disagree with the forced killing of Niels Peter. Whether this ideological bias is consciously motivated or not, the result is that with an identity-absent mob as the enemy, Michael's responsibility as the individual who wields the weapon is instead emphasized. In other words, the political binary which favours Western characters actually backfires in this instance, illuminating the Western victim as the primary perpetrator of the atrocious 'act'.[3] In addition to this, *Brødre* reinforces the fact that soldiers are trained to kill a faceless, identity-absent enemy, and being a 'cog in the machine' enables this. It is the very anonymity of the enemy which enables career soldiers like Michael to be successful on their missions and to readjust to life back home between postings. However, because Michael knows Niels Peter and has formed an attachment to him, he is unable to process this warzone killing as he does with the others, as this 'act' breaches the 'existing symbolic space' he formally occupied (Žižek *Enjoy Your Symptom* 52).

According to Grigg the act of killing breaks with the big Other moral code of *thou shalt not kill* (Grigg *Lacan, Language and Philosophy* 121) and this rupture with big Other signifies an act of 'absolute freedom' (ibid 131). Acts which don't rupture with the big Other will eventually be repeated (ibid). For example, had Michael killed one of his Afghani captors or even ten of his Afghani captors in order to survive, this would not have broken the moral code of the big Other because (a) the film has constructed those characters as an anonymous group, and (b) killing the identity-absent enemy in order to save one's own life in combat is part of warfare normality. In addition to this, Michael is given further justification for killing the enemy because they were also his captors who imprisoned and tortured him,[4] so these killings sit within the confines of wartime ethics. But killing a junior comrade transgresses these ethics, and in the moment where Michael is expected to feel totally engulfed by reluctance and despair, he instead encounters a 'freedom in being forced', an excuse to kill without responsibility, an 'absolute freedom' which renders the event 'truly subversive' (ibid 121) and subsequently unspeakable. By sharing a cell with Niels Peter and looking after him, Michael breaks the regular 'soldier boundaries' and emotionally attaches to him, which makes killing him even more traumatic and

---

[3] One key difference John Markert notes between the Danish and American version of *Brødre* is the motivation for the act in Afghanistan. He argues that Michael kills Niels Peter to save his own life (self-preservation), while his American counterpart (renamed Sam) killed because he had been physically tortured, which resulted in a PTSD-fuelled assault. Resultantly Michael's 'anguish is the anguish of self-knowledge; Sam's is the result of post-traumatic stress disorder' (Markert 251). Sam's suffering in the American version avoids the additional guilt of being self-aware in the moment of the act. This also reinforces various previously discussed observations from scholars who argue that post-9/11 war films depict the American soldier as an undisputable and primary victim of the War on Terror.

[4] The United Nations [UN] defines torture as any 'act by which severe pain or suffering, whether physical or mental, is intentionally inflicted on a person for such purposes as obtaining from him or a third person information or a confession, punishing him for an act he or a third person has committed or is suspected of having committed, or intimidating or coercing him or a third person'.

psychically troubling. The emotional connection obliterated in this moment (when killing Niels Peter and crossing into the domain of the Real through an encounter with jouissance) remains detached upon his return to Denmark, so that only silence exists in the location where emotion used to be.

Silence and witnessing

The silence surrounding trauma is sometimes linked with sociological stigmas surrounding certain acts (rape and incest for example) (Rutherford 82). However, alternatively, silence can be linked to a fear that no help is actually available for the sufferer – that the fractured subject can't be healed in any way, by any professional, and that confirmation of this will arise when the victim begins to confide in a therapist (ibid). Upon returning to Denmark Michael keeps the event from Afghanistan to himself, out of fear that those he could share it with would recoil in horror or helplessness (further enabling his emotional detachment) or that sharing his suffering would not abate it in anyway.

Silence can also be held in an attempt to protect either the listener or the self. The survivor may not wish to harm the other person with their own terrible experience, or as Rutherford (82) puts it, 'smear the listener with faeces' of memory. As a result, they remain quiet out of a desire to protect another, although this silence is often perceived as a restrictive barrier rather than a protective one, which adds to the emotional disconnection between trauma sufferer and potential listener. Silence can also be maintained in an attempt to 'not-identify' as part of the traumatic event, with the survivor fearing that talking about the experience will encourage other people to only see them in relation to the trauma they have gone through. This attempt to protect the perceived *external* image of the self through silence is somewhat ironic, given that research suggests people who have survived long periods of captivity have an *internal* sense of being fundamentally altered as a result (Lewis Herman 73–89). Arguably the external image is desperately preserved because it is the last relic of a life before the trauma, and (for Michael) his perception of the subject he was prior to moral transgression in Afghanistan.

Anne Rutherford, writing from the position of affect and trauma studies, explains that 'trauma ruptures something that is so fundamental to our existence as human subjects' that by encountering trauma the subject faces an 'existential abyss', their own annihilation (81). The undercutting of one's sense of being human or being alive is something insufficiently conveyed through the mere representational system of language, providing further motivation for silence. For example, Niederland's study of concentration camp survivors found that many experienced major changes in identity since being imprisoned (Coleman 199). Some even transcend the change-in-identity symptom expressed as 'I am a different person now', and move into a true dissociation from the self, expressed as 'I am not a person' anymore (Lewis Herman 95), the subject's annihilation that Rutherford refers to.

Dori Laub, psychiatrist, psychoanalyst and trauma and testimony specialist, argues that the Holocaust was a uniquely atrocious event in history partly because 'the event produced no witnesses' (65) as those who survived it or witnessed evidence of it afterwards (through images, documentation and personal testimony) still have trouble conceiving that it happened. He states, the 'incomprehensible *and* deceptive psychological structure of the event precluded its own witnessing, even by its very victims' (ibid). Laub's discussion connects to a crucial point in *Brødre* – that there are no witnesses to what happened to Michael in the Afghan desert. Technically this is true because Niels Peter is dead and the Afghani captors were either killed or fled, so there is no one to testify to the pressure Michael was under to kill his comrade. In less literal terms the event also defies Michael as a witness because the incomprehensible absurdity of the scenario (being told 'Kill him right now or you both die') is so far beyond humane behaviour that Michael may also doubt the authenticity of his own memory of the event. Therefore, it becomes theoretically and cognitively difficult for Michael to bear witness to something he both suffered through and 'did', further contributing to his sense of detachment from himself (or at least from the ego-ideal he aspired to prior to the event) and his emotional detachment from those around him.

Laub argues that the event which has no witness becomes reduced to silence and this means the event has 'signified its own death' through the failure to retell it or to trust in the recall of it (68). Therefore, in the period of time between Michael returning to his cell immediately after killing Niels Peter and confiding in Sarah during the final scene of the film, the event in Afghanistan 'essentially did not exist' (ibid) as it remains undisclosed by its sole witness, revealing a link between the subject's altered sense of temporality and psychological state. I will refer to this phenomenon (where an event is temporarily nullified until it is brought into the Symbolic through retelling) as the 'absent-event'. In *Brødre* what remains in place of the absent-event is a series of psychological symptoms, predominantly emotional detachment, which communicate that Michael has experienced *something* traumatic. The emotional detachment indicates an encounter with the Real, but the symptom exists in the Symbolic in place of the absent-event. This symptom can be thought of as a placeholder, a signifier of the absent-event, a notion which is confirmed in the final moments of the film when Michael finally begins to tell Sarah what happened in Afghanistan. In this scene, in an equilibrium of symptom and language, Michael begins the process of psychological recovery by essentially exchanging his symptoms for a verbalized description of the event. As his language use increases through the retelling of the event (starting with the words, 'He had a little boy', in reference to Niels Peter), his psychological illness moves towards recovery, his emotional connection with Sarah reattaches and the absent-event re-emerges in the Symbolic as the event, confirming that the subject's experience of temporality changes depending on the psychological state.

Michael's inability to be a witness to his own trauma and his own act in Afghanistan is what Laub describes as 'the true meaning of annihilation … one's identity ceases to exist' (67), because when the witness is silenced and the event becomes the absent-event, it takes the identity of the subject with it, pulling both into the domain of the unspeakable Real. Michael's subjectivity as a deeply ethical and protective senior officer of his men is destroyed through the act of killing one of them. The act tears apart the fabric of his universe so that in killing Niels Peter, Michael symbolically kills himself because after the 'act' the subject is 'not the same as before' (Žižek *Enjoy Your Symptom* 37). This moment that fundamentally changes him is the genesis of his self-annihilation, the initiator of his emotional detachment. But by not disclosing the event to anyone, Michael continues to deny himself (and the absent-event) access to the Symbolic, theoretically living in the no-mans-land of the Real, suffering in *and* from the silence and *remaining* detached from those around him in an atemporal non-place.

Ragland reasserts that the symptom is indicative that something is wrong, 'that something is not symbolized' (*Lacan, the Death Drive* 83). These non-symbolized objects 'are never directly sayable or graspable as totalities' (ibid 84) for 'consciousness itself cannot be directly seen, only through its representations (speech, and behavior)' (Tambling 34). Ragland's quote aligns with the notion that trauma is not only un-representable but is reduced through systems of representation. Therefore, the various physical markers of Michael's emotional detachment are a set of symptoms, something which functions as protection from the trauma he has experienced. The only way to 'escape' the trauma in the Real is through the symptom or what Ragland refers to as an 'unconscious fiction' (*Lacan, the Death Drive* 83).

Michael's silence post-Afghanistan is therefore more telling than words, as Rutherford (88) argues that a lack of articulation illustrates the gap between everyday, communicative language and severe trauma. Language can't adequately bridge that gap so words fail, dropping away into the abyss which is witnessed in the slowing (or halting) of speech. What is most affecting is the silence between the sparse words, for it signifies what can't be said, what can't be conveyed, what can't be unburdened through sharing. In Michael's case, the silence between his limited words is the inexpressible, the trauma of transgressing a moral code and subsequent encounter with jouissance: the Real. *Brødre* therefore conveys the silence of Michael's emotional detachment as particularly meaningful, with the viewer witness to everything that is *not* being said through his restrained manner.

Emotional detachment both facilitates Michael's silence whilst also indicating the presence of his trauma in the Real, beyond the language and temporality of the Symbolic. But what is the mechanism that feeds this emotional detachment? What drives Michael's angst over a trauma in which he was a victim? It is guilt, and of more than one variety.

Guilt: Origin

Guilt is the driving force behind Michael's decline into psychological disorder and is a device of the superego, the subject's internal 'agency' which mediates antisocial behaviours (Freud *Civilisation* 61). The origin of guilt is very divisive; religiously devout people may argue that guilt is actually a sense of having 'sinned', but this explanation still relies on a basic presumption of 'good' and 'bad' actions (ibid). Furthermore, an act does not have to be committed in order for guilt to surface and the subject often feels guilty about the mere intention or thought of the act (ibid). Moreover, a simple allocating of guilt based on whether an act has been committed doesn't take into account more complex situations such as the scenario in *Brødre* where one person is *forced* into committing an act. Michael had no desire (or designs) to kill Niels Peter, so there was no *intention* there, yet it was his hands that wielded the instrument which beat Niels Peter to death. Thus, regardless of being forced, he did commit the act.

Freud locates an aspect of the death drive in the genesis of guilt. The death drive refers both to a 'desire for the inanimate state before life and to that force that produces division, that fragments, castrates, and separates unities' (Bronfen and Webster Goodwin 11). Bronfen and Webster Goodwin argue that death is always involved in 'the subject's narcissistically informed desire for pleasure … to be found in union with the beloved' (11). Although this quote refers to the pre-Oedipal mother-child dyad, that 'inanimate state before life', *Brødre* has a more literal interpretation of death drive dynamics – Michael kills Niels Peter in order to return to the union with his beloved (Sarah), to a time and place that is safe from trauma and where he is deeply emotionally attached to another person. Ironically, the act of killing Niels Peter triggers the emotional detachment of his adjustment disorder, actually severing the emotional connection Michael has with those he loves, which is perhaps not surprising given the close links between a subject's experience(s) with death and disordered psychological states.

Furthermore, Freud deduces that what can be considered generally 'bad' is that which threatens loss of love (*Civilization* 61). The motivation for keeping quiet about the act also reaffirms the idea that the act is equal to the intention – for even if Michael explains the circumstances to his family about Niels Peter's death, he would still have killed a man. Michael believes that Sarah won't understand the desperate duress he was under and fears that she will retract her love for him, thereby remaining permanently emotionally detached from him.

In addition, the death drive, which strives for this 'inanimate state', also 'separates unities'. This is evident in that, by wanting to return to Sarah so desperately, Michael kills Niels Peter, thus preventing Niels Peter from returning to his own 'union with a beloved' in Denmark, where he also has a wife (Ditte) and child (Gustav). Therefore, Michael's act also severs the emotional attachment between Niels Peter and his family. Upon Michael's return to Denmark, he visits Ditte and Gustav. Arriving at the house in his officer's uniform (another visual indication of his ethical perfectionism), Michael's guilt is so insurmountable that he is unable to confide in Ditte that Niels Peter is dead, instead bolstering her hope that he may still be alive somewhere in Afghanistan. The interchange of dialogue between Michael and Ditte is covered with a series of shot-reverse-shots which depict Michael's growing discomfort in response to Ditte's hope. In fact, the first step of Michael's recovery (in the final scene of *Brødre*) reflects his understanding that his desire for reattachment with his own family resulted in the severing of Niels Peter's attachment to his family. Michael's words, 'He had a little boy', is reference to Niels Peter's familial attachment (to Ditte and Gustav) before his death.

Guilt: Mechanism

When Michael is first instructed to kill Niels Peter, he resists; only when a handgun is pressed against his head does he beat Niels Peter with the pole. However, despite his initial resistance, once this threshold is crossed he attacks Niels Peter ruthlessly, landing eleven fast, ferocious blows. I suggest that Michael's sudden aggression is spurred on by the 'freedom in being forced' – he reaches a feverish crescendo in that moment of simultaneous despair and pleasure. This energy is only interrupted by one of the captors, who takes him back to his cell. But psychologically what happens to that energy after the event? Freud argues that 'his aggressiveness is introjected, internalized, it is, in point of fact, sent back to where it came from – that is, it is directed towards his own ego' (*Civilisation* 60). It is this redirecting of aggression which formulates Michael's guilt.

The aggression is channelled back towards the subject's ego by way of the superego (ibid) which, as the subject's conscience, works against the ego, implementing the same 'harsh aggressiveness' that the ego would like to have used (or did use) against another (ibid). In other words, the ferociousness of Michael's attack on Niels Peter undergoes introversion onto himself. This frictional relationship between superego and ego constitutes guilt – the sense that there is a need for the one to punish the other (Freud *Ego and the Id* 166–7). The violence that Michael committed under duress is internalized and introjected (this is made easier by Michael initially not sharing his trauma with anyone else so there is no verbal or emotional outlet). The portion of the superego taunts the ego with a sadistic level of aggression which manifests as the guilt Michael feels (Freud *Civilisation* 60). However, Michael's guilt in *Brødre* functions on two levels – conscious guilt and unconscious guilt. This section of the chapter unpacks how one subject can feel two different 'guilts' over the same incident, how the subject can be aware of one guilt but not the other, and how both types of guilt manifest differently as psychological symptoms.

In referring to the film *Europa '51* Žižek suggests, 'We don't only escape *from* guilt but also escape *into* guilt, take refuge in it' (*Enjoy Your Symptom* 44). In *Brødre* Michael employs and engages with guilt on a conscious level precisely because it is deeply consuming and distracts him from the trauma of his experience of pleasurable freedom while killing Niels Peter under duress. Adopting guilt about the act of killing, temporarily sidesteps the greater guilt of finding pleasure in that act.

In a 1907 paper called 'Obsessive Actions and Religious Practices' Freud refers to 'a guilt that remains unknown' (cited in Johnston *Misfelt Feelings* 88) and several years later his essay 'The Economic Problem of Masochism' refers to 'a sense of guilt which is mostly unconscious' (ibid 161). To elaborate, someone who feels guilty may not know they feel guilty at a conscious level, resulting in a (paradoxical) unconscious sense of guilt. The key factor in understanding how the paradox of unconscious guilt is possible is through acknowledgement that 'not all conscience is conscious' (Johnston *Misfelt Feelings* 92). This occurs because the whole of the superego doesn't operate in a state of conscious awareness; there are sections which remain unconscious (ibid). Michael feels guilt over two aspects of Niels Peter's death, but he doesn't know he feels two levels of guilt because one variety of guilt is located in a part of his superego that isn't operating in the conscious mind. The guilt about killing Niels Peter and transgressing personal and professional ethical boundaries (henceforth referred to as 'transgression-guilt') exists in the conscious part of his superego. The guilt about enjoying the freedom of being forced to kill another person (henceforth referred to as 'jouissance-guilt') exists in the unconscious part of his superego; hence he is aware of the first variety of guilt but not the second. The reason that Michael's transgression-guilt is relegated to the conscious and his jouissance-guilt to the unconscious is explainable in the following way:

> If one is (i.e., one's ego) partly is shaped by who one wants to become (i.e., one's 'ego ideal' or 'superego') and if some of these ideals and facets of conscience are unconscious, then certain aspects of who one is (i.e., one's ego-level identity) are going to be unconscious as well.
>
> (Johnston *Misfelt Feelings* 92)

In other words, as Michael's sense of self (his ego) is shaped by who he wants to be (a self-sacrificing, morally and ethically pristine captain), this ego-ideal is present in the unconscious alongside who he actually is (someone who encountered pleasure upon transgressing boundaries). His guilt about enjoying the killing exists 'down there' in the unconscious. When the unconscious part of the superego relates to the unconscious pat of the ego, Freud calls this 'moral masochism' (what I've been referring to as 'unconscious guilt' and what Freud informally renames 'a need for punishment') (Freud *Ego and the Id* 166). As guilt is generated by the superego harassing the ego, then the unconscious section of superego will harass the unconscious portion of ego as well (in other words the 'bullying' is happening above the surface of the water and below it).

Herman Westerink, who researches in the area of Freudian psychoanalysis, psychiatry and the philosophy of religion, suggests that although unconscious guilt is 'quite common' (204) it is also 'the strongest hindrance to getting well'. This is because unconscious guilt is somewhat sated by the experience of suffering – the moral masochist *wants* to be punished and is hence opposed to a recovery which may alleviate suffering (Freud *Ego and the Id* 166). As a moral masochist, Michael wants to suffer for the jouissance he experienced when killing Niels Peter; his superego is interested in punishing him on the conscious level for killing a junior soldier, but the unconscious portion of his superego is also interested in punishing him because he's masochistic.

Guilt: Displacement and projection

What effect do two levels of guilt have on the subject? Tambling states that the memory-trace (what is left behind when an idea is repressed) 'is transformed – converted – into something bodily' (27). Michael, who in repressing the memory of his encounter with pleasure upon killing, is left with a 'guilt-residue'. This guilt-residue manifests as physical markers of the emotional detachment symptom of Michael's adjustment disorder, etched in his rigid posture, expressionless face and limited language. Each of these physical elements visually displays his emotional detachment from those around him.

Westerink argues that internal states of being are outwardly visible 'in our body movements and facial expressions' (112) and Wagner suggests the subject may perform their trauma in a bodily sense (57). Therefore, Michael's physical and emotional rigidity may also be read as his corporeal performance of guilt, where Michael consumes the dead man after the act and then carries the corpse through symptoms of emotional detachment. This interpretation is particularly relevant to the scene which shows the day Michael arrives back at his home. He silently ascends the stairs to his bedroom and then asks that Sarah and the two girls lay down on the bed with him for a while. Yet, despite the intention of emotional connection in this request, the girls and Sarah make eye contact with one another and curl up against Michael's body but Michael lies still and stiff on his back. A combination of close-ups and wide shots reveal Michael as the still, unmoving form surrounded by wriggling, warming and gentle bodies. Michael is not actually dead in this moment, but his morbid physical presence and emotional detachment suggest the notion of a 'living corpse' (not dissimilar to Reznik in *The Machinist*).

Freud suggests that the subject pushes away the incompatible idea (in *Brødre* this is Michael's jouissance when killing Niels Peter) in 'defense' (*abwehr*) (Tambling 27). But despite pushing away that incompatible idea, something is left behind – what Tambling refers to as a 'memory-trace' (ibid) or what I refer to as 'guilt-residue'. This lingering residue continues to exist on the conscious plane (although the incompatible idea has been pushed into the unconscious) and this residue – in my estimation – manifests as symptoms, clues that something else *was* there (because the symptom after all is a signifier). In Michael's case the residue-symptom is his projection of guilt onto Sarah and Jannik because, at an unconscious level, Michael conceives of himself as guilty so defensively projects this guilt onto other egos. The unconscious guilt Michael feels from the incompatible idea (the transgression of boundaries leading to jouissance) manifests through a projection, which truncates emotional links between Michael and Sarah, and between Michael and Jannik, reinforcing the notion that transgression of boundaries results in broken bonds.

Michael's insistence that there is something else going on 'beneath' Sarah and Jannik's platonic relationship, is another form of projection – because there is something else going on beneath for him in the unconscious. Johnston emphasizes that a sadistic superego which operates (in part) unconsciously still generates 'consciously registered suffering' (*Misfelt Feelings* 97). Johnston also posits that unconscious guilt is [mis]felt 'as anxiety rather than culpability strictly speaking' (ibid 99–100), which supports Michael's unconscious guilt manifesting as suspicion about Sarah and Jannik (anxiety over his wife's relationship with his brother). Westerink also claims that guilt is related to anxiety, stating, 'that for which someone reproaches themselves is also something they fear' (115). This echoes the notion that Michael's unconscious guilt over his encounter with jouissance (that for which he reproaches himself) is redirected as a projection of suspicion about Jannik and Sarah having an affair (something he fears).[5] Projection displaces the internal to the external, although as Westerink explains, this process 'is in reality not a displacement: projection takes place completely within the person's own mind' (113–14),

---

[5] Additionally, *Brødre* doesn't use any dream sequences to depict Michael's guilt about his encounter with jouissance because dreams are in the unconscious and his symptoms manifest 'above surface'. Nightmares (similarly to flashbacks and other re-experiencing symptoms) are not part of the adjustment disorder criterion, as they are to a PTSD diagnosis.

so what Michael believes he is witnessing between Sarah and Jannik is a misinterpretation of reality, distorted by his own guilt-ridden thought process. That being said, projection should still be viewed as anti-attachment in nature; it is fundamentally the displacing and relocating of something initially attached. Essentially, Michael's experience of killing Niels Peter leads him to an encounter with jouissance and subsequent horror at his own response. This discrepancy between his ego and his ego-ideal is repressed, but the sense of reproach he is left with is felt as the presumption that he is considered a bad person by others, which is then projected onto Jannik and Sarah that they are bad people because they are supposedly having an affair. When Michael eventually understands that he is projecting guilt onto other people at the end of the film, it also signifies a re-attaching of projected anger to his own sense of guilt, in other words a movement towards recovery.

Survival anger and the link with jouissance

One major restriction to the recovery of the former-captive subject is the inability to express anger at the captor during the period of captivity because doing so may jeopardize their survival (Lewis Herman 91). Additionally, the captive also feels a deep, unexpressed anger at those who 'failed to help' the captive in a timely manner (ibid), with many people in captivity feeling 'forsaken by man and God' (ibid). Not being able to express anger means it remains within the subject, even after release from captivity, causing further harm to the subject. Resultantly, survivors of captivity with internalized anger often suffer from chronic depression or suicidality and have an increased mortality rate through homicide, suicide and suspicious accidents (ibid 91–2).

The anger residing within the survivor manifests only through occasional outbursts, and these isolate the survivor even more. Such is the case with Michael, who confides the details of Afghanistan in no one and therefore keeps his anger hidden. Resultantly, the anger simmers away beneath the surface, occasionally piercing through his stoic emotional detachment suddenly and seemingly illogical to those around him. For example, when his wife and daughters join in an innocent dinner table joke, Michael is unable to appreciate the humour and instead shouts at his daughters in anger. This outburst puts further emotional distance between Michael and his children and bewilders Sarah – he is not the father or the husband he was before, illustrating Žižek's notion of the changed subject following an 'event'.

Jouissance and anger are experiences bound up in the commonality of emotional intensity. When Michael kills Niels Peter in Afghanistan, he does so with gusto – eleven furious blows to his comrade's head and neck region. His furore in this moment is emphasized through the editing, which only depicts Michael (not Niels Peter or the captors) from a low-angle shot. The cut between each strike relays that each impact of the pipe is a precise and deadly movement, while the visual occlusion of other characters ensures Michael's emotional status is the focus of the scene. Michael's anger at this particular moment is generated by powerlessness and the absurdity of the situation, although because this powerlessness informs the 'freedom in being forced' and pleasure upon transgression, the experience of anger and jouissance are necessarily linked for him from this point. Because anger is bound up in his experience of jouissance in Afghanistan, he also encounters anger in the guilt he feels from that jouissance. The anger is a through-line between event and affect, and Michael's projection of blame onto Sarah and Jannik (which is misplaced unconscious guilt) therefore brings with it anger.

Michael's anger erupts through his cool emotional detachment during the lead-up to the film's revelational scene. After failing to find a cork screw for a bottle of wine one night, Michael suddenly pulls the recently renovated kitchen apart with his bare hands – a signal of the disproportionate response to minor stressors that is key to adjustment disorder. This particular choice of destructive action is symbolic; the kitchen that Michael rips apart was renovated by Jannik in Michael's absence, a domestic symbol of Jannik's new emotional attachment to Sarah and the girls. Indeed, the day after Michael's return he rises early and sets about rearranging the entire contents of the kitchen shelves – an attempt to take control of the domestic setting once more. So, by later pulling out drawers of utensils in a rage and tearing entire cabinets from walls, Michael is destroying what he perceives are signifiers of a challenge to his place as the family patriarch. The kitchen is the trigger for his rage as Jannik's renovations occurred while Michael was held captive; the anger he couldn't express at the captors is instead projected at the activity (the renovation) occurring in Denmark during his absence.

When Sarah comes downstairs to investigate the noise, Michael directs his anger towards her, shouting, 'Do you realize what I did!? Do you realize what I did to get back to you!!?' The correlation between Michael's destructive physical actions and these words is his undisclosed anger. He believes that while he endured torture and killed a man to 'get back to her' she was having an affair with his brother, as signified by the new kitchen. Not only does this infuriate and humiliate him (just as the captors did), but it reinforces his sense of isolation because even his wife does not know what he has been through. By shouting, 'Do you realize what I did!?', Michael finally attaches his residual and internal anger to a specific external object (Sarah). The episode in the kitchen may also be considered an encounter with jouissance, where Michael finds both pain (in the sense of betrayal that the new kitchen symbolizes) and pleasure (in the destruction of that kitchen). Both of these elements, pleasure and pain, are also present in Michael's previous destructive episode – namely the encounter with death which triggered his psychological disorder, the killing of Niels Peter.

The time travelling captive and traumatized speech

The traumatized subject is unique for his or her ability to transcend time; further support for the notion that the psychologically suffering subject and a skewed sense of temporality are linked. As discussed in the previous chapter (in regard to Lisbeth in *The Girl with the Dragon Tattoo*), the trauma victim who survives moves between the temporality of the current day and the temporality of the trauma through a tangle of post-traumatic memories and bodily affects. *Brødre*, however, is a film which not only presents the possibility of temporal transcendence *after* the trauma but also during it. The subject who is captive for sustained periods of time may choose to manipulate their experience of reality by voluntarily entering a state of psychological dissociation (Lewis Herman 90), another form of detachment. Doing this allows the subject to live momentarily in a more pleasant temporality, usually using memories of loved ones and safe spaces to endure 'hunger, cold and pain' (Partnoy 1986 and Sharanksy 1988 cited in Lewis Herman 90). The captive subject can become very skilled at the 'art of altered consciousness', entering a trance-like state, where 'time has no sway' (Razinsky 16), to withstand the reality of the actual environment (Lewis Herman 90).

Michael demonstrates this tactic during his imprisonment in Afghanistan.[6] He is depicted sitting with his back against the earthen wall of his cell for many

---

[6] It should be noted that no explicit time is given for the duration of Michael's captivity in Afghanistan. However, given that the Danish army officially declared him dead, his family had a funeral and the relationship between Jannik, Sarah and her two children is given time to flourish, one can safely assume that Michael was held captive for a period of several weeks or months. The period is unlikely to be more than a year as the children show no clear signs of growth.

hours, where the only light enters through a small, high-up, barred window. The cinematography often moves in from a mid-shot of Michael sitting on the floor to a close-up of his face. As he closes his eyes the image cross-fades into blurred pictures of Sarah and his home in Denmark, suggesting that as his eyes close in the Afghan cell, his consciousness opens in Denmark, allowing him to endure one more day under torture. His temporal dissociation tactic is also confirmed when he returns to Denmark and specifically tells Sarah, 'I sat in a dark room thinking. I thought about you all.'

While this is a veritable skill to have during torture and/or captivity, such practices may later create disturbances to the subject's sense of memory and time, because dissociating from the environment while captured breaches the innate sense of continuity between past and present and this disrupted continuity can linger after the captive has returned to safety (Lewis Herman 90–1; Noll Zimmerman 68). This signifies that transgression of normative temporalities can render the subject detached from contemporary surrounds and contribute to psychological disorder later on. Subsequently, while the formally captive subject returns physically to a safe space, psychologically they can remain 'bound in the timelessness of the prison' (Lewis Herman 90–1). The mind of the captured subject can be thought of as a portal to another time and place, but while this portal is advantageous when imprisoned, its lingering presence deters the subject from recovering from the experience, by remaining open to a temporality in which the traumatic moment is reencountered. Several scenes convey the portal remains open upon Michael's return to Denmark through the visual depiction of him laying or sitting awake at night. Facing the ceiling or the wall with unblinking eyes, silvery white light from a single source outlines his face in the darkness. While the equivalent cinematography in the Afghani cell portrays Michael dissociating from his surrounds to think of favourable conditions in Denmark, the Danish version of this scene reveals the portal to Michael's traumatic past temporality remains open. In more direct terms, although Michael is physically in Denmark, his mind remains imprisoned.

The effect on Michael remaining 'bound in the timelessness of the prison' is evident most strongly in the moments immediately following his (previously discussed) attack on the kitchen. Still caught up in the furore of his suspicions about Sarah and Jannik (symbolized through the renovated kitchen), Michael begins to chase Sarah through the house, yelling 'I'm going to kill you!' repeatedly. Analysis of this dialogue, and awareness of how the traumatized subject transcends time, reveals that Michael is not really saying

'I'm going to kill you' to Sarah, but to the man he killed months previously, Niels Peter.

The key to understanding how this occurs is in those words, 'I'm going to kill you', for Žižek asks, 'indeed is not the very kernel of psychoanalysis embedded in the dimension of language as speech *act*?' (*Enjoy Your Symptom* 36). Language is given agency via speech so utterances become interpellations, 'whereby the subject ... becomes what they purport to be' (ibid 37). Therefore, in saying, 'I'm going to kill you' in the present, Michael actually means 'I can kill you – because I have killed ... I am a killer'. Žižek reiterates that psychoanalysis was considered, after all, a 'talking cure' (ibid 36). Therefore, in unleashing the words 'I'm going to kill you!' on Sarah, Michael is actually engaging in his first moment of therapy. After much time spent maintaining silence and suppressing anger, Michael finally speaks (and admits), 'I'm going to kill you!' to Niels Peter, knowing of course, that he did kill him.

Yet, the utterance of these words ('I'm going to kill you') does not have Michael 'arrive at the factual truth of some long-forgotten event' (Žižek *Enjoy Your Symptom* 37), but has him *recollect* his past *within* the present (so the enunciation is spoken in a future-oriented present rather than past tense). Hence, 'I've killed you' from the past becomes 'I'm going to kill you' in the present because 'remembrance of the past bears on the subject's *present* position of enunciation ... it transforms the very place from which the subject speaks' (ibid). LaCapra endorses this analysis, claiming that when the traumatized subject acts out the past, 'distinctions tend to collapse, including the crucial distinction between then and now' (46). In other words, this present moment statement is really 'meant for' what he did in the past to Niels Peter, but Michael's time-blending faculty, collapses temporal boundaries and this, in turn, disintegrates linguistic boundaries between past and present.

Žižek explains that 'there is no meta-language' (*Event* 100), meaning there is no 'removed' space from which the subject can or may speak with pure objectivity, free of temporalities. Because the adult subject exists within the Symbolic order, time flows behind them into the past and ahead of them into the future. The subject therefore speaks in 'precipitation as well as retroactivity' (ibid). Therefore, Michael's statement, 'I'm going to kill you' is spoken in the present (to Sarah) about the past (Niels Peter), but even in the past (*with* Niels Peter) the statement 'I'm going to kill you' refers to what he is *about* to do in the (immediate) future. This suggests that the traumatized subject never speaks in the present; rather, this subject is psychologically negatively affected by their detachment from 'normal' temporality and the Symbolic, instead eternally caught in a cycle of using language which points towards the past, and perceiving all past language as leading up to the 'event'.

This moment of linguistic retroactivity enables the manifestation of Michael's guilt, bringing silently suffered emotions into a tangible intersubjective space and preventing him from continuing on as he has been – silently and with emotional detachment. In this regard, the moment of 'I'm going to kill you!' is not only a speech act but itself a symbolic event which 'restructures the entire field: although there is not new content, everything is somehow thoroughly different' (Žižek *Event* 124), because this is the moment of Michael's re-attachment to his emotions. Yet, despite this moment signifying a turning point for Michael, his reconnection with emotion offers him no solace. Instead, he feels the full weight of his conscious and previously unconscious (now conscious) guilt, which provokes him into increasingly erratic behaviour.

Suicide as the only successful act

Žižek refers to the film *Sophie's Choice* (Pakula, 1982) wherein the title character's choice results in her acquiring 'a burden of guilt which drives her into madness' (*Enjoy Your Symptom* 80). Similarly to Sophie, Michael makes a so-called 'choice' in *Brødre* but the burden of this forced choice drives him into severe psychological distress, which only feels redeemable through an equalizing act – his own suicide. Several police units arrive at Michael's house in response to his violent outburst against Sarah. Fearing that he has finally acknowledged something he can't take back or amend, Michael responds to the police presence outside his house by becoming even more aggressive. He takes a gun from one of the officer's holsters, points it in their direction and shouts 'Come on! Shoot me!' several times. This is an attempt to provoke suicide-by-cop wherein an individual behaves in a deliberately reckless way which police are trained to respond to by shooting them. The attempt at suicide-by-cop is Michael trying to redeem himself, through one final act which will result in punishment (death). His suicide would thereby appease the conscious and unconscious segments of his superego, which wishes to see him punished for transgressions of moral and ethical boundaries, and for encountering jouissance upon those transgressions. Despite his desperation, Michael eventually lowers the gun in response to Jannik's calm counsel (a sign that Michael is re-attaching emotionally to his brother). Because emotional detachment is both a trait of the soldier and of Michael's adjustment disorder, the moment he re-connects emotionally also marks the end of his military career; he is arrested and spends time in prison – ironically, the very thing he once used to judge Jannik for. This incarceration is one final literal detachment from his family before he begins to tell Sarah about Afghanistan and emotionally reconnect with her.

Because the guilt that Michael feels about killing Niels Peter exists on the conscious plane but the guilt about encountering pleasure while doing it exists on the unconscious plane (until it is 'triggered' by his preoccupation with Jannik and Sarah), he doesn't feel remorse for the encounter with jouissance for most of the film. Only when he gets to the prison at the end of the film does he exhibit signs of remorse, because at this point the unconscious guilt has found its way into his consciousness (by way of the 'I'm going to kill you!' moment at the house and the attempt at redemption through suicide-by-cop). Up until this breakthrough he may be said to feel remorse for killing Niels Peter but not for finding jouissance in the moment.

Conclusion: Return of the repressed, return of the connection and reparation

When traumatic knowledge (Michael's sense of guilt in this case) enters (or re-enters if it has been repressed) the subject's conscious, it generates fundamental change in the subject's understanding of the self. Žižek states, 'after accomplishing it [awareness of the trauma], I am not the same subject as before' (*Enjoy Your Symptom* 37). This statement pertains to Michael's state when he finally confides in Sarah in the grounds of the prison. Only at this point, right at the end of the film, does Michael become fully aware of the trauma he has endured and the degree to which it has impacted him. Yet, the realization of the impact of trauma is also a step towards recovering from it, for if the subject can recognize they have been changed by the 'event', they move towards a new understanding of the post-event self, rather than over-compensation to embody the pre-event self.

This moment for Michael is preceded by a montage comprised of three scenarios: close-up shots of Michael in his cell in the Danish prison, intercut with matching close-ups of Michael in his cell in Afghanistan, intercut with images of Sarah at home. This interweaving of imagery again depicts the portal of temporal transcendence opened in Michael's mind, whilst also contributing to the connection between psychological state and sense of temporality. This time, though, while Michael sits in a Danish prison cell (under significantly better conditions than his previous incarceration), he can return psychically to either Afghanistan or to Sarah. His continual thoughts of Sarah (frequently shown in physically intimate imagery) suggest his desire to emotionally reconnect with her, as well as recognizing that he continues to love her and that she has always been loyal to him.

Michael's emotional re-attachment with Sarah is emphasized in the scene following the montage when Sarah visits Michael at the prison. He goes to meet her at the gate in the outside grounds and the two smile at each other with a warmth and familiarity previously displaced. Sensing that Michael is still reluctant to share his story, Sarah gives him an ultimatum – to tell her what happened in Afghanistan or to get divorced. Sitting by her side on a park bench Michael begins to cry. Eventually, he utters the words, 'He had a little boy. He had a little boy', before the frame fades to black, the sound decreases and the film ends.

As Michael acknowledges the attachment he destroyed between Niels Peter and Niels Peter's family ('He had a little boy'), he exchanges symptoms for words. To elaborate, with each word uttered, he pushes back against the painful silence he has been maintaining since his return, resists the stoic and unaffected demeanour which he's been using to physically display moral and ethical purity, and finally recognizes his ideal ego as an ego-ideal, a bullying superego. Each of his emotional detachment symptoms recedes in the wake of a painful memory recounted aloud. It is here that recovery begins for Michael and, reattaching emotionally, his humanity returns.

5

Copycat (1995)

Introduction to agoraphobia and *Copycat*

Agoraphobia is defined as a 'fear of open spaces' or 'fear of public spaces' (de Beurs 2), but a more nuanced definition regards agoraphobia as a fear of places where the subject feels vulnerable (Capps and Ochs 3). Agoraphobics are afflicted by the sense that they are only safe in their home environment, their 'safe zone', and they experience overwhelming panic when they try to leave (ibid). Paul Carter, published widely in the area of cultural theory and cross-cultural communication, labels agoraphobia a 'chronically debilitating' illness (Carter 209), the suffering associated with agoraphobia is particularly painful because the 'phobic object' (which is space) is frequently a source of pleasure before the onset of the illness (Grose 29). Such is the case in *Copycat* (Amiel 1995), whose lead character Helen celebrated independence and agency prior to becoming agoraphobic. A psychoanalytic reading of *Copycat* suggests that the adult subject (Helen) can be pushed backwards, out of the Symbolic, into a pre-mirror phase dependent state, which is narrativized through the confinement of the agoraphobic safe zone (Helen's apartment). As with Nina (*Black Swan*), Reznik (*The Machinist*), Lisbeth (*Dragon Tattoo*) and Michael (*Brødre*), Helen experiences the symptoms of her psychological distress through her corporeal reality and a changed sense of temporality, following on from a close encounter with death.

Copycat is a 1995 thriller starring Sigourney Weaver as well-known and respected criminal psychologist Dr Helen Hudson. The film opens with Helen delivering a lecture about serial killers to a full lecture theatre at a San Francisco university. Once the lecture has finished, one of Helen's previous patients, Daryll Lee Cullum (Harry Connick Jr), attacks Helen while she is alone in the university bathroom. Cullum attempts to garrote Helen by slipping a metal cord around her neck and suspending her from a pipe running parallel to the bathroom ceiling.

She survives the assault, although a campus security officer who tries to come to her aid is fatally shot, and Helen develops agoraphobia soon after. Given Helen's previous profession as an outgoing and respected public figure, her descent into an isolated and secluded life is particularly embittered. She is deathly scared of, and unable to move beyond, spatial boundaries, which reduces her subjectivity to a pre-Symbolic infantile level of freedom and autonomy.

Thirteen months later, when a series of murders baffle local detectives MJ Monahan (Holly Hunter) and Reuben Goetz (Dermot Mulroney), they approach Helen for advice. Helen deduces that the killer, Peter Foley (William McNamara), is copying some of the most notorious murderers (Berkowitz, Dahmer and Bundy, for example), and she recognizes that she too has become a target as the only living victim of Daryll Lee Cullum. Foley breaks into Helen's apartment and, because she is unable to leave this space due to her agoraphobia, Foley abducts her and takes her back to the university bathroom where Cullum attacked her thirteen months previously. Foley attempts to garrote Helen in identical circumstances, thus committing another copycat crime. However, this time MJ intervenes in the assault and Helen is able to escape the bathroom with Foley in pursuit. MJ follows them both to the building's rooftop and fatally shoots Foley, putting an end to his murderous spree. The extreme outdoors location on the top of a tall building suggests a turning point at which Helen begins to move beyond the spatial constraints of agoraphobia, and return to an existence lived in the autonomy of the Symbolic.

There has been considerably less written about *Copycat* than the more recent films in this book (such as *Black Swan* and *Dragon Tattoo*). In the limited literature which has been published it is agreed that Helen suffers from agoraphobia (Gabbard 82; Robinson 248; Simpson 152), and many authors note how *Copycat* is part of a 1990s trend where serial killers are central to the plot (Bartels; Gabbard; Simpson; Tietchen; Walton). Other films in this canon include *The Silence of the Lambs* (1991), *Se7en* (1995), *Scream* (1996) and *Scream 2* (1997). Interestingly several authors also concur that America's 1990s 'obsession' (Gabbard 82) with 'real and imagined murder' (Simpson 146) contributes to the portrayal of the serial killer Foley as intelligent, artistically informed and aesthetically motivated (Bartels 497; Tietchen 99), part of the proliferation of serial killer narratives which typically approach murder as a fine art (Bartels 497). Rather than analysing *Copycat* through a psychoanalytic lens, several scholars prefer to use a feminist perspective to read the film: Tietchen argues that *Copycat* contributes to the trend of the medicalization and dissection of women's bodies on screen (100); Landstrom examines the link between gender and technology through an anti-humanist framework; Walton argues that it is Helen and MJ's 'shared female gaze of the detective and psychiatrist that counters the voyeurism of the murderer' (Foley) (271) and ultimately defeats him.

Many facets of psychology and psychiatry have explored agoraphobia in the last one hundred years (Carter 29) with modern psychology placing agoraphobia within the broader category of anxiety disorders (APA). In this context, it is understood as an adapted behaviour in response to a sense of fear, threat or vulnerability (ibid). Agoraphobia is diagnosed in individuals who experience a combination of panic (which is disproportionate distress in response to fear, threat or vulnerability) *and* avoidance behaviours which work to prevent such levels of distress reoccurring (APA; Capps and Ochs 46). The clinical symptoms of an agoraphobic panic attack – hyperventilation, fainting, vertigo, raised pulse, emotional verbal outbursts, hand tremors, extraneous movement of limbs, sweating and dry mouth (Craske 16; de Beurs 2) – function as temporary but episodic indicators of overwhelming anxiety (Weber 215) and manifest physically. Capps and Ochs, a psychologist and a sociologist, respectively, suggest the avoidance behaviours of agoraphobia are the outcome of a 'communicative dilemma', where the anxious subject cannot express concerns about the prospect of perceived negative circumstances, and hence avoids the negative circumstances by simply not leaving the house (16–17).

Agoraphobia is most common in urban areas and is higher amongst people who also have relatives with the condition (ibid 4). Anxiety disorders in general are equally present across ethnicities and adult age groups (ibid 1), but females are more likely than males to suffer from anxiety (Craske 1; Bourdon et al. cited in Craske 12; Capps and Ochs 2). Michelle Craske, who researches in the area of psychology, psychiatry and biobehavioural science, points out that women and men are equally susceptible to fear, but that the gender discrepancy in the statistics for anxiety disorders is due to the gendered differences in *reacting* to fear (17). This corresponds with the Kristevan theory discussed in relation to *The Girl with the Dragon Tattoo* that women have a greater tendency to engage in 'internalizing disorders', such as anxiety and depression, while men are more likely to 'develop externalizing disorders such as conduct disorder and attention deficit/hyperactivity disorder' (ibid 15). *Copycat*'s female agoraphobic character conforms to the gender patterns highlighted by Kristeva and Craske, although both disorders (*Dragon Tattoo*'s PTSD and *Copycat*'s agoraphobia) are responses to traumatic experiences where death is a possibility, and hence cannot be said to be a purely internalized disorder.

Psychotherapist Josephine Klein, who specializes in social structures, youth work and sexual abuse, argues for two possible psychological mechanisms in response to a traumatic event (188); dissociation and repression (which involves psychical splitting in an attempt to protect the subject), and anxiety (which also emerges as a protective mechanism against the expectation that even greater anxiety will occur). This is where Helen and Lisbeth (from *The Girl with the Dragon Tattoo*) differ in terms of their respective traumas. Lisbeth, for example, disassociates during her rape, which is depicted in the film through the use of static noise and unstable visual framing during the assault. Because Lisbeth disassociates from the trauma as it happens, and thus psychically splits, some of this traumatic experience is repressed and reappears belatedly (as per Caruth) as post-trauma flashbacks (which are symptomatic of PTSD). Helen, who also experiences a traumatic assault, does not disassociate; instead, she remains psychically present. Therefore, she does not repress the memory of the attack, and her psychological response after the trauma echoes her feelings during the attack – a constant fear, manifesting as an anxiety disorder (agoraphobia) about what *could* happen, rather than re-experiencing symptoms of PTSD that reveal repressed aspects of what *has* happened.

The implication here is that anxiety occurs when dissociation/repression have not. Importantly, a degree of anxiety emerges with the goal of preventing even more anxiety. Yet dissociation/repression also occur to prevent anxiety, albeit within the traumatic moment, by shielding the subject from the trauma unfolding (in Helen's case, the very real threat to her life) (ibid 198). Essentially, both the mechanism of dissociation/repression and the mechanism of anxiety are attempts by the subject to protect themselves. Although these two mechanisms are not necessarily mutually exclusive and can occur simultaneously, Helen appears only to suffer the mechanism of anxiety, rather than repression/dissociation, in *Copycat*. Both Helen's panic attack symptoms and avoidance behaviours intercede as self-preservation to prevent the experience of something even worse. Interestingly, Klein refers to this process as a 'split' which 'has to be maintained between what is being experienced and what might be experienced' (ibid 188). Classic disassociation allows the subject to experience reprieve (splitting) during the actual moment of trauma. However, for Helen, a splitting takes place not psychically but rather temporally, in the interplay between an imagined future (which is made real in the present through her anxiety) and a non-repressed past (the traumatic event which facilitated her agoraphobia); one of the links between the emergence of her psychological disorder and her changed experience of temporality.

The mirror stage reversed

Following the attack by Cullum, Helen loses her identity as an independent and autonomous adult, yet she is constrained by herself: she cannot escape her body, her memories of the attack or her new identity as an agoraphobic because she is trapped inside the safe zone of her apartment. These changes to Helen's subjectivity confirm Shaviro's notion that the post-traumatic subject is 'dispossessed of self, radically decentred, and ... all the more vulnerable and constrained ... It cannot free itself from forces that it is unable to control and that continually threaten to destroy it' (ibid 129). Indeed, although the agoraphobia has turned Helen into a dependent and restricted person, she is unable to break free of the disorder, which renders her helpless and needy. While there is ample discussion of the link between the helplessness of agoraphobia and stereotypical female roles (Capps and Ochs 2; Carter 15; Pile 92), a psychoanalytic reading of *Copycat* reveals that the helplessness of Helen's agoraphobia is linked with the helplessness of infancy.

Lacan argues that 'the default ontogenetic point of departure for subject formation must be an initial state involving anxiety, longing, and unrest' (Johnston *Žižek's Ontology* 212). Although Lacan is referring to the infant subject, who comes into being through an anxiety-inducing separation from the (m)other, this notion is also applicable to Helen; for her subjectivity is changed through encounters with trauma. This first happens when the initial attack by Cullum renders her agoraphobic, but it happens again when she overcomes her anxiety about open and unfamiliar spaces in the second attack by Foley. Helen's sense of herself prior to the initial attack is markedly different to her sense of self afterwards because, as Žižek argues, trauma fundamentally changes the subject (Žižek *Enjoy Your Symptom* 37). Helen Hudson is an extremely unusual subject in that she undergoes three mirror stages. The first (presumably) occurred as an infant for subject formation and entry into the Symbolic, while the second and third mirror stages occur because she is attacked in front of a mirror both times and is changed as a subject each time. *Copycat* therefore suggests that the subject's movement through Lacan's infant phases of human development are not necessarily singular, linear events, in that they may be repeated, they can be reversed and they can (like Nina in *Black Swan*) take place in adulthood. By extension, *Copycat* also suggests that trauma can be so impacting that it results in the dissolution of subjectivity; pulling the subject back into the atemporality of the pre-Symbolic.

The significant relationship between subjectivity and space is evident immediately in *Copycat*; opening shots pan across university students lying in the sun on the campus grounds and stretching out upon the grass of a large outdoor area. The film cuts to the inside of a large building – the lecture theatre – where Helen is the focus. Indoors, space and subjectivity are set up through a combination of cinematography and editing; Helen presents her lecture about serial killers from behind the lectern, captured by long shots which depict her sole, central placement in the middle of a large stage. These long shots are intercut with low-angled close ups of her (which portray Helen's authority in that moment) and point-of-view reverse shots of the audience, demonstrating how Helen scans the faces of her listeners as she lectures. These point-of-view shots succeed at revealing the attentiveness and admiration of her audience members, whilst also cementing *Copycat* as Helen's story, portrayed through her eyes. Dressed in a bright red suit and matching red high-heeled shoes, Helen is immediately recognizable here as ambitious, educated, courageous and successful, her celebrity and importance reinforced by the presence of two security guards who are charged with her safety while delivering public lectures. Her position of power within this environment is also evident through a live video feed which is projecting an enlarged picture of her on the wall behind her, through the spotlights which illuminate her on the stage, and through the prominence of her voice, amplified with a microphone. Her authority and autonomy are further enforced in the following scene when she is shown signing autographs and dispensing advice to female students in the corridor after the lecture. These opening scenes clearly depict Helen operating successfully within the Symbolic order – lecturing fluently and confidently and heralded as an authority within her chosen field. However, her secure place in the Symbolic is upended in the following scene when Cullum attacks.

After checking that the bathroom is safe, Helen's security guard leaves the room and waits for her outside. The bathroom décor is almost completely white (the tiles, doors, sinks, windows and fluorescent lights are all white), so Helen, clad in bright red and shown through a wide shot, is a distinct target moving across the empty space. As Helen enters a stall, Cullum ascends the stall wall between them and slips a metal noose around her neck. Caught off-guard, Helen doesn't have a moment to shout or scream before the noose tightens around her neck and prevents her from speaking – a foreshadowing of her removal from the Symbolic. On the opposite bathroom wall is a large, multi-person mirror above the basins. Resultantly, the entire attack takes place in the floor space in front of Helen but also in the mirror across the room. Silently, she is lifted above the toilet in her stall, hanging from the overhead ceiling pipe. With fingers unsuccessfully grabbing at the chord around her neck, Helen tries to regain her balance by placing the tip of her shoes on the toilet seat. In the process she loses her right shoe but manages to prevent herself from being completely strangled by placing the very tip of her left shoe on the toilet seat. Cullum places a large knife to the guard's throat and a gun to his head, tossing up whether he should 'stick him, or shoot him' before deciding that he'll 'do both' by slashing his throat and shooting him twice. Resultantly, Helen's psychological disorder is not only born out of a fear for her own life but also out of witnessing the death of another. The placement of the mirror ensures that Helen has an unobscured view of herself – clad in red and usually powerful – being disabled, immobilized and assaulted.

In the classic mirror stage, the infantile subject, whose perception of its own body is fragmented and incomplete, sees in the mirror image a unified body that will serve as the basis of its ideal ego in the Imaginary order. This motion is reversed when Helen, perceiving herself as successful, complete and autonomous, sees her mirror image as helpless, paralysed and dependent upon an Other. Resultantly her concept of herself reverts to the pre-mirror phase sense of un-coordination, fragmentation, fragility and incompleteness. As Helen's subjectivity prior to the first attack is based on conceiving of herself as successful, independent and capable, then the attack, by inducing a reverse-mirror stage, reduces her to a pre-mirror phase, infantile self, present in the strange atemporality of the pre-Symbolic. As part of this reverse mirror stage she conceives herself (or re-conceives, because she's been in this position once before as an infant) as unformed or incomplete, fragmentary, uncoordinated and intrinsically connected with the (m)other. Accordingly, as a result of the attack, Helen reverts to being someone who lives inside, or closely connected to, a uterine space, with her agoraphobic safe zone (her apartment) substituting for the safe space of the womb. Helen's apartment is large and modern, with MJ even commenting on it, 'Hell of an apartment you got here. Hell of an apartment.' However, its multitude of corridors and mezzanine levels combined with its predominantly brown colour palette give the space an enveloping aesthetic which corresponds with the uterine function it fulfils for Helen.

When Helen returns to this pre-mirror-stage state, before the pre-Oedipal dyad is divided, whatever was not seen in the mirror as part of her adult Imago (such as fragmentation and incoordination) manifests in her agoraphobic behaviour, connecting her psychological disorder with her sense of corporeal reality. Therefore, her anxiety and panic symptoms are fragmentary and uncoordinated within her apartment *because* she conceives of herself as fragmented and uncoordinated *because* she has returned to the pre-mirror stage. Therefore, everything that wasn't seen in her pre-attack Imago (incompletion, fragmentation and incoordination) becomes manifest when she retreats to the safe-zone of the symbolic uterus (the confines of her apartment). Lacan talks about 'bodily coherence, locomotion, and motor coordination' being the 'necessary condition of ego formation', which relies on an 'imaginary unity of the body' (Shepherdson li-lii). Therefore, in returning to the Imaginary as an anxious adult subject, Helen's panic attack symptoms physically reveal and reflect the dissolution of her subjectivity, explicitly aligning her psychological state with her corporeal reality.

Charles Shepherdson, who specializes in Lacanian psychoanalysis and continental philosophy, claims that anxiety is broadly acknowledged as a 'genuinely psychoanalytic concept' (xxiii) and Lacan is emphatic in pointing out that anxiety 'is not a response to the loss of an object, but rather arises when lack fails to appear' (ibid xxxi). Another way of putting it is that anxiety emerges in response to lack lacking. As Helen engages in a reverse-mirror stage during the attack by Cullum, this goes some way to explaining the formation of her anxiety; the adult subject is consolidated as a person based on their understanding of themselves through the mirror stage, basing their identity on an image separate from the m(other). Therefore, when Helen is sent backwards out of the Symbolic in the attack by Cullum, which returns her to a pre-mirror-stage sense of being unformed and fragmentary, she loses the lack intrinsic to being an autonomous adult (the lack of the (m)other); she experiences the dissolution of her ego. In her uterine-like apartment she is dependent on other people to keep her alive and the normal lack around which adult subjectivity is structured is itself lacking – and according to Lacan this causes anxiety (ibid xxxi). Indeed, Lacan perceives phobia, which is the expressive conduit of anxiety (ibid xxiii), as a 'means for the subject to try to formulate something around a lack' (Grose 29).

Helen's daily experiences as a subject suffering from anxiety are intrinsically linked with the experiences of her past because events are experienced in relation to 'an ongoing story about who we are' and memories exist within a 'web of associations' that link with the subject's narrative (Capps and Ochs 15). The most obvious example of this is that Helen's agoraphobia is induced by the traumatic event of her past (the attack by Cullum). However, while Helen's life within the allegorical womb of her apartment is separated from the outside world, her existence is still part of a continuum in which she used to be active within the Symbolic. Reference is made to this more subtle 'web of associations' in a scene following one of Helen's panic attacks: her friend Andy (John Rothman) encourages Helen to 'Make up your mind … Live or die', implying she can't function as a successful adult (operate within the Symbolic) while remaining strictly in the confines of her atemporal safety zone (cowering in the Imaginary). He alludes to her previous successful existence in the Symbolic when he goes on to say, 'They'll find you years from now amongst the unopened mail, the unread newspapers. The old hermit lady … She used to be a really good shrink once'. Andy's attempt to provoke Helen into becoming a fully functioning adult again is, for the most part, unsuccessful, but his words reconfirm that Helen's identity was not always limited to the restriction and fragmentation of her agoraphobic, uterine-esque confines, and that part of her, while reassured by the safe zone of her apartment, is paradoxically deeply frustrated by the regression of her subjectivity. The bitterness and frustration of Helen's life within the safe zone are only mitigated by the zone's ability to dispel even greater levels of anxiety. That being said, panic attack symptoms still arise within the apartment, presenting suddenly and violently through her corporeal reality, revealing with cinematic visual clarity that her psychological state (agoraphobic) and her physicality are linked.

Anxiety speaks through bodily symptoms

Gold (cited in Pile 30) claims that there are two basic human needs: the need to reduce tension and the need to increase it. Helen's panic attack symptoms (hyperventilation, paralysis, extraneous limb movements and vertigo) may therefore be viewed simply as an attempt to reduce the tension caused by overwhelming anxiety, and viewed through a broader lens, the agoraphobia itself is employed to reduce Helen's tension caused by a consistent sense of threat. Each of these 'levels' is an attempt to prevent Helen encountering the circumstance where her life is threatened, which corresponds with Klein's suggestion that 'anxiety intervenes at the point where' pain is being avoided (188), what Freud referred to as 'signal anxiety' which arises when the subject senses that further danger (and greater anxiety) is about to occur. This manifests in Helen, whose agoraphobia works *for* her in the sense that the restriction from leaving her apartment assists with (a) keeping her alive and (b) keeping panic symptoms (for the most part) at bay. Therefore, the agoraphobia anxiety assists with containing the (greater) threat-anxiety. This deterrence tactic confirms Grose' claim that 'there's something in the logic of the symptom that attempts to quell a difficulty for the subject' (23).

Helen's anxiety formed in response to an assault that, being traumatic, 'escape[s] symbolic and imaginary presentation' (Shepherdson xxvii). As there is no language outside the Symbolic, Helen cannot speak about the traumatic experience and therefore cannot articulate her fear of reoccurrence either. Unable to be formulated as verbalized expression of fear, it lingers, unclarified and uncommunicated as anxiety, endorsing Weber's observation that 'what anxiety seems to discover behind appearances … [is] what Freud calls "trauma"' (217). Additionally, Helen is not capable of stating 'I am terrified' because living in the domain of the Imaginary (in the confines of her apartment), means she no longer has access to the self-confirming language (*I* am terrified) of the Symbolic. Here is where 'symptoms of anxiety form indirect communications' and transmit information that is not transferable through regular verbal communication (Capps and Ochs 103). While Helen's existence in the Imaginary prohibits her from verbalizing her fears, the panic symptoms of her anxiety work as a substitute attempt to communicate what she cannot verbalize. This confirms the notion that the symptom has a language of its own, and more specifically that *anxiety speaks*. Each of Helen's anxiety symptoms during her panic attacks physically manifest what she wants to say but cannot verbalize; they are the physiological expression of the lacking lack of autonomous adult identity, or in other words, they are the physiological expression of the dissolution of subjectivity, and the confirmation that psychological state is intimately linked with the subject's corporeal reality.

Helen's hyperventilation symptom is the physical manifestation of the sense that 'I am being pulled away into another place – help me'. That 'other place' she feels she is pulled into is the Real of her attack. Gasping for breath, grabbing at air, is an attempt at survival (like grabbing at holes in the face of a wall one is falling down). Her eventual loss of consciousness following sustained hyperventilation suggests she has escaped, bodily and emotionally, for a few moments before she reawakens, although not before suffering through the other panic attack symptoms including paralysis, vertigo and extraneous limb movements.

When the panic symptoms arise, Helen is so frightened she can barely move, as if caught by invisible bonds, correlating with Carter's claim that 'the universal symptom of agoraphobia is *movement inhibition*' (16). Yet this is another example of agoraphobia's paradoxical nature, for while paralysis arises in a panic attack, this symptom is born out of the subject's fear of petrification, 'the dread of being immobilized' (ibid 33). Such is the case with Helen, whose attack by Cullum involved physical garroting and suspension. Resultantly, she lost bodily agency in that situation and was unable to run, to escape the noose, to stabilize herself, or eventually to move at all. The relationship between paralysis and agoraphobia can also be found at another level in *Copycat*; hung from the neck, the initial attack inhibits Helen's movement and this sense of helpless immobilization returns in the form of a disorder which keeps her in one place (her apartment), thereby further immobilizing her and re-defining her as a stationary subject who is not moving beyond the confines of the Imaginary into the autonomy of the Symbolic.

Yet Carter clarifies that agoraphobia 'is not the inhibition of *any* movement, but the arrest of a double impulse, a movement outside of oneself towards the other, and a movement away from the other towards the self' (180). Thus, Helen's reluctant and perilous steps down the corridor during her third panic attack suggest not only that she is afflicted by vertigo, but that she is caught in the agoraphobic paradox of wanting freedom from her current life while being afraid to return to her previous freedom. It also suggests fear about moving towards the other ('outside of oneself'), and reluctance about moving away from the substitute womb that Helen's apartment represents (movement away from the [m]other towards an autonomous, adult subjectivity – 'towards the self'). This psychological reluctance and hesitation manifest through Helen's jerky movements, what Carter refers to as a 'voluntary tottering' (92) and the moment when she purposely bangs her head against the wall three times in frustration. Each step that Helen takes down the corridor is a 'willed and perilous plunge over the edge of one's self' (ibid), simultaneously moving towards the feared Other of the abject space beyond the safe zone and the autonomous self who exists beyond the atemporal, uterine apartment, in the Symbolic of the open world.

In a similar vein to the push/pull of Helen's jerky movements, the symptom of vertigo makes the sufferer 'incapable of dropping, even though he is also not in the condition to remain upright' (Weber 214). However, what is particularly interesting about vertigo is 'the absence of that consequence which retrospectively determines vertigo as itself: falling' (ibid). Put another way, though the agoraphobic subject having a panic attack fears falling, the fall never eventuates. If the panic attack also includes sustained hyperventilation the subject may eventually lose consciousness (as Helen does when Reuben and MJ first come to visit), but it is the conscious *sensation* of falling, which makes the subject so afraid. When Helen sees an intruder in her apartment and goes out into the corridor to escape, vertigo is the dominant symptom. Accordingly, she does not fall, despite the heavy tilt of the camera which suggests teetering on the edge of imbalance, and a mid-shot, long-take which moves continually to the left and to the right of Helen. This constant shifting of frame creates a swinging sensation, which also indicates a toppling is imminent, although she does not fall. Helen's vertigo symptom therefore physically plays out the sensation of part-falling and part-restriction of being hung by her neck in the initial attack, and reaffirms the connection between her psychological disorder and her sense of corporeal reality. This semi-suspended state Cullum subjected Helen to is exactly what Carter refers to when discussing the 'always-falling, never-landing' sufferer of vertigo.

Unlike other phobias (arachnophobia[1] or hemophobia[2] for example) there is no option where Helen can remove herself from the trigger of her phobia (space), because, as Pile states, 'there are no mediating terms between the body and the space' (184); Helen cannot get away from or 'out of' space – she's always in space, so long as she's conscious. Her reprieve, then, comes only in the unconsciousness following sustained hyperventilation or through sleep (which is also in short supply for Helen), and the escape from anxiety that this unconsciousness allows is only temporary. However, the positive aspect of retreating from anxiety by losing consciousness comes to an end when Foley re-enters her apartment and injects her with a fast-acting sedative. This invasion reveals her vulnerability is heightened when unconscious, and proves the fallibility of her resurrected boundaries; the paradox of the agoraphobic safe zone.

---

[1] Extreme of irrational fear of spiders.
[2] Extreme or irrational fear of blood.

The agoraphobic paradox and zones

Agoraphobia is perceived as both a response to a problem and a problem in itself (Capps and Ochs 50). The agoraphobic believes their symptoms (both avoidant behaviour and panic attacks) to be problematic since they are debilitating and restrictive, which generates additional feelings of shame, frustration, helplessness and hopelessness. Carter states that 'agoraphobes feel anxiously torn between exposure and suffocation, solitude and the crowd' (9), longing for and fearing open spaces, while both loving and resenting their safety zone. A resultant spiral of agoraphobic behaviour and emotional responses develops in what Capps and Ochs describe as 'an entangled web of feelings of panic' (50). Mixed amongst this spiral, and often ignored, is the initial trauma that facilitated the agoraphobia to begin with. For *Copycat*'s Helen, who was highly independent before the attack, the shame and frustration of her agoraphobic confinement are particularly taxing, complicated by the fact that she both loves and hates the symbolic uterine space she is confined to; she experiences both nostalgia for and deathly fear of the world beyond the space which represents her successful function in the Symbolic order.

Yet, agoraphobia can have positive payoffs, in what Capps and Ochs refer to as something that 'cripples [and] simultaneously supports the sufferer's well-being' (106), which lessens the sufferer's motivation to recover (ibid 100). On the one hand, the sufferer is debilitated by the restrictions of the avoidance affliction and, on the other hand, the affliction deters the onset of unbearable panic. The paradoxical nature of this state can also manifest as contradictory behaviours, painting the sufferer as manipulative (ibid 107). Helen's avoidance behaviour, for example, renders her dependent, as she can't leave the apartment and needs people, such as her friend Andy to help her. Yet, she is also able to get people to travel to her (such as the two detectives MJ and Reuben), which is somewhat empowering and confirms her importance. Additionally, she resents the severe restriction on her life and yet also enjoys the newfound closeness she has with her friend Andy. This resentment/enjoyment paradox is the conscious manifestation of her desire to live as an autonomous subject in the Symbolic, while also enjoying the safe confinement of the Imaginary.

Similarly paradoxical are Helen's panic attacks, which noted Lacanian psychoanalyst Roberti Harari argues may be performed for the understanding and sympathy of the Other, but in a way that is 'inducing, aggressive, and challenging' (70–81). He refers to this as 'acting out' which 'appeals to the gaze and calls for attention – doubtless in a provocative way ... a message for the Other' (ibid 79–81). Indeed, Helen's largest panic attack occurs in her apartment and emerges suddenly and confrontationally in the presence of the two police detectives (MJ and Reuben) when they show her photographs of the recent homicide scenes. Sensing that her safe zone has been contaminated by the two strangers and the photographs they carry ('I don't want these here. I don't want to see these here!'), Helen responds with hostility towards the pair by swearing at them and snapping, 'You can spare me the bullshit inspector ... The beautiful part is I don't give a fuck!' The onset of this panic attack is portrayed visually through an increased use of close ups (both on Helen and on the brief case containing the photos) but more poignantly through aural cues including a sudden increase in volume, an echo effect, the sound of an ominous hiss as the case is clicked open, a rhythmic ticking (which sounds like a time-bomb) and the use of synths in a minor key. Helen then begins to shout repeatedly for Andy and to hyperventilate. Her body movements become jerky and uncoordinated (a visual confirmation that the more distressed her psychological state, the more she experiences corporeal symptoms) and she drops a drinking glass which shatters. Andy arrives with a paper bag for Helen to breathe into but she faints and collapses on the floor.

Each of these symptoms is an external sign of Helen's internal state, which Harari claims are calling out for attention from the Other in lieu of having the language to express herself (given she exists within the pre-Symbolic at this point). Those who witness the attack are shocked, with MJ asking 'Should we call the paramedics?' Andy responds calmly, 'Oh no. Just a good old-fashioned panic attack. She hyperventilates 'till she passes out then her breathing returns to normal and she's fine,' which implies he has seen this multiple times before. But rather than Helen's panic attack symptoms (which are a substitute for language) garnering understanding from MJ and Reuben about her anxious state, they find the whole episode bewildering, with Reuben referring to her as a 'strange ranger' and MJ as a 'pill-popping, juice-head, hyperventilating, agoraphobic asshole' on their way back to the car.

Part of the paradox of agoraphobia is that the terrified subject reinforces their own fear by resurrecting boundaries, which intrinsically suggest someone needs to be 'kept out'. For example, the agoraphobic fears the city, more than any other space, with the idea of being caught up in its 'uncontrollable and instinctual flow' filling the individual with dread (Carter 31). Yet de Beurs suggests that, at the crux, it is not the location, or a repeat of the situation, that the agoraphobic subject fears, but the threat 'about one's well-being in these situations' (3). Therefore, Helen does not so much fear large or open spaces beyond her 'safe zone'; rather, she fears being alone in those spaces with an attacker who wishes her harm, and such a person may exist unnoticed in the 'uncontrolled, uncoordinated movement' of a public space in the city. It is the 'slipperiness' and unpredictability of a malicious Other (Carter 20), as opposed to the location itself which frightens the agoraphobic. Yet, in the case of *Copycat*, the malicious Other is tempted by the resurrection of boundaries and walls. Foley, for instance, appears as an innocent bystander within walled zones, his face just one of several in a crowd in the opening scene's lecture theatre and in the police station later on. He also perceives Helen's protective apartment and her reclusive behaviour as confirmation that she is a worthy target – he frequently studies her from a building across the street and collects newspaper clippings and photographs, believing she will make him famous if he attacks her and she writes a book about him.

Although Helen is not inside an institution at any point, her apartment denotes her as both separate from others and 'not normal'. In this regard, agoraphobia institutionalizes Helen, albeit not in the literal sense of a psychiatric care facility; rather, her regression to the pre-mirror stage and pre-Symbolic reintroduces psychic boundaries as spatial boundaries. *Copycat* is therefore a film which delineates identity through physical borders and boundaries, such as walls, doorways, corridors and windows. Pile suggests that 'aspects of identity or self develop in relationship to places ... but places set a brute limit on what individuals can make of themselves' (55). Helen's apartment, for example, although very modern and large (representing her pre-attack professional success) is also utterly limiting of her subjectivity. Because she cannot physically move beyond those walls, she is limited in her ability to form new aspects of her identity, to build on her career, to meet new people or to develop new relationships; she is, in other words, existing within an atemporal, pre-Symbolic uterine space which negates development, or even maintenance, of an autonomous subjectivity.

Indeed, Francis Pheasant-Kelly (who typically publishes on the topic of cinema and identity) suggests that 'abjection emerges in films in which space, institutions and subjectivity intersect' (*Abject Spaces* 11), confirming that literal and psychological iterations of the border are crucial to Kristeva's abjection theory (ibid 154). The areas beyond Helen's apartment walls are perceived by her to be abject spaces, because they are contaminated by the trauma of her first attack by Cullum. This supports Pheasant-Kelly's argument that abject spaces are usually locations occupied by the 'Other' (ibid) and that the abject is excluded 'through maintaining homogenous boundaries' (ibid 6). To cross the border of an agoraphobic's safe zone is to enter into an encounter with the abject: 'Any transgression that "disturbs identity, system, order" and that "does not respect borders, positions, rules" is liable to abjection' (ibid).

For Helen, everything beyond the safety of her apartment is part of a dark and troubling space, beginning with the hallway leading to her front door. The sinister nature of this space is revealed, for example, when she attempts to move down this hallway during either of her panic attacks, where point-of-view shots depict the lengthy space as distorted and undulating. When Helen attempts to escape the intruder in her apartment, the danger of the hallway is also shown through a sideways tilting of the visual frame, which mimics the instability of her vertigo. Again, the paradox of Helen's apartment is that, while Capps and Ochs refer it to as 'a safe haven within a chaotic, often unwelcoming universe' (3), Pheasant-Kelly also argues that such a space can be abject if 'it involves either a return to a symbolically uterine state, or loss of subjectivity' (*Abject Spaces* 18). Therefore, in *Copycat*, the safe zone of Helen's apartment is also an abject zone, given that it functions as *both* a substitute for the enveloping womb of the pre-Symbolic and a substitute for the lacking lack (or dissolution of subjectivity).

Furthermore, the abject also finds its way into this safe space either literally (when Foley enters her apartment) or mentally (through Helen's memories of Cullum's traumatic attack), thereby crossing the sacred boundary of her domestic sanctuary. To elaborate, Helen's attack by Cullum initially takes place in the Symbolic (before she regresses to the pre-Symbolic through her reverse-mirror-stage). Yet, given the trauma of the assault, Helen's memory of it is based in the Real, 'an unreachable place where what is missing from the Symbolic, or for Freud what is unacceptable or traumatic, is deposited' (Pile 138). Therefore, every time something (like photos of crime scenes) or someone enters her apartment from the outside and triggers her overly stimulated senses, it brings forth the memory of her trauma so that the Real punctures through into her present, pre-Symbolic sanctuary.

Helen's pre-Symbolic uterine apartment has the illusion of safety but *Copycat* reveals the fallacy of this agoraphobic paradox by identifying the resurrection of a zone as an invitation to transgression, by revealing the limitations of the sufferer's adult subjectivity, and by highlighting that the trauma of the Real can be carried into the 'safe zone' through visitors and objects which enter from the outside and from the agoraphobic's memories. The authority of the safe-zone border is therefore rendered impotent.

Fear as the 'felt reality' of future threat

While the symptoms of panic attacks temporarily detract from Helen's constant state of anxiety, the anxiety is not reduced when the panic attack symptoms subside and she regains consciousness. What then, drives the panic symptoms of anxiety? What can generate such rapid psychological and physiological decline? Razinsky states, 'the seemingly basic answer is: a threat to our existence' (107). It is existential threat that makes the subject anxious.

Living with an anxiety disorder, Helen experiences the emotion of fear in response to 'a signal at the level of the ego of a danger' (Lacan *Seminar X* 20). Pile argues that it is natural for humans to respond to the stimulus of their environment but notes that interpretations of these environments 'are subject to other "functions and factors"' (such as previous trauma) (42). Responses will also vary depending on how close the subject perceives the danger to be; an imminent danger at close proximity will elicit escape actions, while a more distant danger will encourage avoidance techniques instead (Craske 22). The avoidance behaviour of Helen's anxiety disorder is her agoraphobia (avoiding leaving the safety zone), while her panic attack symptoms occur when she perceives that something dangerous is within close enough quarters that she needs to escape it instead (albeit, as previously mentioned, the escape to unconsciousness is only temporary, as panic attack symptoms don't reduce the underlying anxiety).

Brian Massumi, whose academic work often pulls together the strands of political theory, sociology and philosophy to discuss power and affect, claims that something can be feared so strongly that it comes into existence from the future, as threat's representative in the present is fear (*Future Birth* 54). He continues, threat 'is the felt reality of the non-existent, loomingly present' and that 'if we feel a threat, there was a threat' because threat is 'affectively self-causing' (ibid). In relation to *Copycat*, threat can be linked to a particular environment or space because when threat 'self-causes, its abstract quality' materializes as affect in the form of anxiety and 'its quality suffuses the atmosphere' (ibid 62). The notion that threat 'suffuses the atmosphere' is especially relevant to the agoraphobic subject, such as Helen, whose constant anxiety is bolstered by hyperawareness of her environment. In fact, her supposed safe zone is not immune to the ambience of threat, revealed through the fact that she suffers panic attacks within the apartment walls.

Although anxiety is the affect through which threat can 'come into being' (Weber 216), the physical body and the traumatized mind, which are closely linked, don't differentiate between anxiety about threat (which is possible future danger), anxiety about present danger, and anxiety about previous danger (which is trauma) (Massumi *Future Birth* 64–5). For example, if a sleeper is woken by a fire alarm, the heart rate rises regardless of whether there is a real fire or whether it is a false alarm. Similarly in *Copycat*, Helen's panic attack symptoms (her disproportionate reaction to the stimulus of her environment) occur regardless of whether the threat eventuates as a present danger, or remains as 'just a threat' (possible future danger). The body finds both possibilities equally distressing in what Massumi refers to as 'activated flesh' (*Future Birth* 64–5). In addition to the physical symptoms (hyperventilation and extraneous limb movement) of her panic attack in front of MJ and Reuben, such activated flesh is witnessed in a scene where Helen's newspaper is delivered several steps from her front door. The prospect of having to reach out into the corridor activates laboured breathing, sweating and a bodily agitation which has Helen run a shaky hand through her hair, slide down to the floor and throw her reading glasses across the room. Additionally, she closes her eyes, in an attempt to block out her altered vision, which is depicted through a point-of-view shot of the distorted and undulating corridor. The difference between the sleeper woken by a fire alarm and the subject with anxiety disorder is that the signal for danger (whether it remains as threat or transforms into actual danger) is constantly present for the anxious subject. Therefore, although Helen's physical symptoms subside once she has retrieved the newspaper and firmly closed the apartment door, and although no harm came to her when retrieving the newspaper, her sense of threat remains, activated within her mind, as a 'virtual state before being actualized' (Ewald 222).

Part of threat's omnipotent quality stems from its ability to regenerate, multiply, intensify and persist, for as Massumi states, 'threat is not real in spite of its non-existence. It is superlatively real, because of it' (*Future Birth* 53). No matter how the event occurs (either the threat emerges as danger or the threat remains as threat) there is always the possibility it could have been different – and this is what continues to generate threat going forward; threat is always an emerging danger rather than a 'clear and present danger' (ibid). Put another way, if the threat doesn't actually come to fruition, it still always had the *possibility* of coming to fruition, while if the threat does come to fruition, this confirms that the future possibility of the occurrence of danger had 'rightly' been there in the past. Resultantly, if the threat does unfold into the clear and present reality of danger, this means 'the preemptive action is retroactively legitimated by future actual facts' (ibid 56). In addition to this, the anxious subject's uncertainty about what could come next is never 'consumed' by whatever emerges in the present, as there is always a 'surplus of indeterminate potential' (ibid 53) because threat is never 'over'. There is also the possibility that the 'next time' will be worse and the time after that will be worse and so on, providing threat with an exponential, as well as omnipotent, quality. Therefore, Helen's experience retrieving the newspaper from the corridor but coming to no harm, does nothing to allay her anxiety about the space beyond her front door. In fact, if anything, her physical reaction, the 'flesh activated' by her anxious mind, contributes to and re-informs her inherent fear about something ominous lurking beyond her safe zone.

The link between agoraphobia and temporality is further tied to anxiety because the negative incident that threatens to occur in the future is rooted in fear derived from an incident in the past, meaning the origin of threat comes from within – from the subject's memories (Razinsky 107). For example, Helen's anxiety disorder exists because of a traumatic past incident (the attack by Cullum). This situation, which threatened her life and made her a witness to the security guard's death, continues to haunt her, by placing a lens of fear over her current and future experiences. As a result, the source of the threat is internalized, carried as memory – it exists within Helen as part of an 'ongoing story' (Capps and Ochs 15) which includes her pre-agoraphobic life in the autonomy of the Symbolic.

We should note, however, that this is part of the 'double play' of *Copycat*, which as a film in the thriller genre plays tricks with central characters and the viewer. To elaborate, even though Helen's anxiety disorder is a psychological response to the attack by Cullum, which generates a sense of threat from within, the film eventually reveals that there actually is someone (Peter Foley, the copycat killer) out to harm Helen *again* and the threat is therefore also from without. Ironically the knock-on effect of Foley's external threat reinforces and adds validity to Helen's internal sense of threat so that (as previously mentioned) 'the preemptive action is retroactively legitimated by future actual facts' (Massumi *Future Birth* 56). Admittedly, at the end of the film, despite Foley's death and her escape to a rooftop, Helen is extremely vulnerable to developing an even more severe anxiety disorder based on the verification of her initial anxiety symptoms.

The phobia conduit: Linking fear, anxiety and threat

As an agoraphobic Helen is overly sensitive to environmental stimuli and reacts to it disproportionately, and this sensitivity is informed by Cullum's initial attack on her. Helen's heightened state of awareness, rooted in fear, results in the affect of anxiety. Anxiety, as the affect through which threat comes into being, has the 'quality of indefiniteness ... the fear of something that is nothing' (LaCapra 57). It is a fear that doesn't have an object to focus on (a 'thing'); it is something indefinable, lurking 'out there' in time and space, as a shapeless possibility. Likewise, Razinsky (268) summarizes that anxiety is characterized by 'absence rather than a presence'. For instance, Helen is frightened by the prospect of what *might* be in her apartment or beyond her apartment walls – it is what she can't see, but does imagine, which provokes such anxiety. Yet, as previously discussed, Helen's anxiety is a response to trauma (Tambling 58) and 'anguish is not without an object' (Voruz 170).

Helen's anxiety disorder is initiated by an attack by (an)Other, which does not mean that Helen's anxiety is focused *on* the attacker, but that her anxiety emerged in response to something – it has traumatic cause, specifically an attempt to kill her. Anxiety has an inherent 'generic-ness' which Weber refers to as 'free-floating' (215) and Lacan refers to as 'unfastened' (*Seminar X* 14). They refer to the notion that anxiety is a generalized affect resulting from trauma, but it requires a conduit in order to be expressed, and the generic anxiety Helen experiences following the attack by Cullum is expressed as agoraphobia. This upholds Lacan's emphatic point that affect is not repressed (Lacan cited in Johnston *Misfelt Feelings* 133); in fact, the expression of the affect – in this case the agoraphobia hosting the anxiety – openly plays out in Helen's life, in her atemporal environment and through her body and behaviour.

Helen is not unique in feeling threatened by the trauma of her past. In fact, individuals who suffer from agoraphobia spend a lot of time and energy preoccupied by previous encounters with trauma whilst also contemplating similar scenarios occurring again (Capps and Ochs 21). The anxiety resulting from past traumas is nebulous and non-specific, while fear is focused and targeted, what Harari refers to as a 'localizable empirical object' (32). Yet anxiety is a 'means for the subject to try to formulate something around a lack' (Grose 29). Helen's anxiety therefore finds its focus *through* her phobia because it is more bearable for the subject to be afraid of something specific rather than something undefined (Grose 27–9; Shepherdson xx). As Shepherdson explains, the anxiety over an undefined danger is empowered by 'its excessive character in relation to representation, its capacity to escape symbolic and imaginary presentation, and the ego's faculties of codification' (xxvii). In other words, the danger to the subject's ego, which generates the anxiety, may be a *literal* thing but is in effect a *lingering* thing, an unrepresentable threat which exists in the domain of the Real, having escaped representation in the Symbolic.

Helen's anxiety is a response to her sense that something unspeakably awful will happen to her again. But in order to avoid that situation reoccurring (and therefore encountering even more anxiety), Helen substitutes the non-specific anxiety-inducing threat for a phobia, specifically a phobia of spaces which consequently prevents her from leaving her apartment while it protects her from another encounter with the unspeakable trauma, existent in the horrific Real. Her phobia, in this sense, is very logical – not only as a substitution for more anxiety but also as a barrier (literally this time) to encountering another attack. If a phobia is, as Freud believed, the 'externalized manifestation of an unconscious thought that the subject cannot bear to confront directly', it is also an object through which unbearable anxiety 'can be expelled and partially contained' (Shepherdson xx). Agoraphobia therefore 'isn't a psychic structure in itself', but *part* of the affect of anxiety (Lacan cited in Grose 29).

In fact, Carter claims that claustrophobia and agoraphobia are two sides of the same coin, merely opposing symptoms manifesting from the same anxiety (Carter 32). This anxiety oscillates between the two pillars of a desire for contact with the Other and panic/fear at the thought of contact with the Other, who exists in the space beyond Helen's apartment walls. The fear that Helen feels at coming into contact with the Other is appeased somewhat by a set of rules about staying within the safe zone of the home, but the fear comes back full throttle (as panic attack symptoms) when those rules or conditions are breached (Carter 91).

For example, her third panic attack takes places within the corridor directly outside of her apartment (again), because she sees the silhouetted figure of an intruder (Foley) on the mezzanine level of her apartment. The fact that a frightening Other has infiltrated her apartment already breaks the rules which appease her anxiety (obviously her apartment is not a safe zone given it has been broken into), but when she ventures out into the hallway to escape the Other, her panic symptoms activate so strongly that she struggles to stay upright and conscious as hyperventilation and vertigo alter her vision and balance. Ironically, her specific spatial phobia, born out of generic anxiety of the Other, is so powerful that she goes back into her apartment, knowing that a specific Other (the intruder) is in there. Fortunately for Helen, the intruder leaves when he realizes Reuben is on his way to the apartment to check on Helen.

For Helen, because threat is carried 'within', and because her apartment can be broken into, her safe zone, resurrected in response to threat, is only a façade of safety. In *Copycat* constructing a safe zone only invites a crossing of the zone's boundaries by the perceived threat. By its very nature the 'zone' makes itself, and those who exist within it, vulnerable to anxiety and panic. In fact, it is Foley's crossing of this zone which prompts the final act of the film – Helen's second assault and third mirror stage.

The third mirror stage

After breaking into Helen's house and physically assaulting her, Foley injects her with a fast acting sedative. When she next wakes she finds herself in the horror of her previous attack – the same bathroom, the same rope strangling her, the same red suit, the same mirror reflecting the scene and the body of another security guard dead on the floor; it seems to her that she has woken up within the exact nightmare of the trauma which informed her anxiety disorder to begin with, a movement to the temporality (time and location) which generated her agoraphobia. This moment also highlights the interplay between Helen's anxiety disorder (which feared a return to the previous scene of trauma above all other spaces) and the thriller genre (which being a copycat homicide film takes her back to the scene of the original attack). Yet, aside from her assailant being Foley rather than Cullum, there are some crucial differences to this copycat scenario and it is these differences which facilitate Helen's escape from the situation and her return to the Symbolic.

The first difference occurs when Foley approaches Helen and attempts to further frighten and control her by referring to his presence in the film's opening lecture, saying, 'I remember watching you on a big screen in that red dress. God, you looked huge. Look at you now. So sad'. As per the first attack Helen has an unobscured view of herself in the mirror, garroted and helpless, confirming her status as a subject who is dependent on, and controlled by, an Other. But as Foley's obsession with his own fame becomes evident, his self-centred monologue enables Helen to perceive of him as the insecure and developmentally stunted young person he is. From her position in the toilet cubicle several metres back, Helen watches Foley's reliance on his own mirror image; he combs his hair and studies his reflection while saying excitedly, 'I am gonna make you the world's most famous victim. Guess what that makes me!?', before comparing himself to the serial killer idol, Jack-the-Ripper. Comprehending that Foley is trapped by the illusion of the mirror-stage (where his identity is based upon a fraudulent external image which disguises true incompleteness, fragmentation and incoordination), Helen realizes that her own position as vulnerable and dependent on an Other is fundamentally no different to his; adult subjectivity is, at its essence, formed on the basis of this external image and rooted in lack. As he approaches her and boasts, 'I've been practicing ... I can make it last for hours', the low-angled, close-up of Helen's face zooms in further. Finally, sick of his rambling, she articulates her perception of him, saying, 'Fuck you! ... You heard me, you little twerp. You think I'm afraid of you? ... I know all about you. You're just a sad, second-rate, boring, impotent little copycat ... Daryll Lee couldn't get it up either.' Foley is enraged and stops her from talking further by gagging her, but having recognized that Foley is insecure and voiced this observation, Helen has already done the damage (so to speak). The gag only succeeds in preventing her from forewarning MJ, but her transition back into the autonomy of the Symbolic has already begun through her re-acquaintance with language and recognition that adult subjectivity is based in lack, rather than lack of the lack.

The second major difference between Cullum's attack and Foley's copycat attack is that it is the female detective MJ, rather than an anonymous male security guard, who comes looking for Helen. When MJ enters the bathroom, Foley reiterates the copycat nature of his crimes by pretending to be the dead security guard lying on the floor of the bathroom (putting the real dead guard in a toilet cubicle). Not realizing that Foley is 'playing dead' he surprises MJ from behind, the two struggle and Foley shoots MJ twice in the torso. The force of the bullets at close range push MJ backwards into the bathroom mirror, which shatters into multiple pieces and falls to the floor. MJ slides to the ground, supposedly unconscious, and Foley presumes she is dead. However, as MJ is wearing a bullet proof vest beneath her clothes this is not the case and she beats Foley at his own copycat game by also 'playing dead' on the floor for a few minutes. When Foley attempts to cut MJ's throat with a huge knife, Helen initiates the third discrepancy between Cullum's and Foley's attacks.

Helen attempts to prevent MJ being killed by making the choice to hang herself. True to the original attack by Cullum, the tiny bit of control she has over her body is the tip of one foot on the toilet seat, but when Helen sees MJ is about to have her throat slit she foregoes the slight stabilization of the toilet seat and tries to strangle herself. The *choice* to take her death into her own hands by completely destabilizing herself marks another step in her transition back into the Symbolic, with her decision signalling agency (whilst also confirming the subject's corporeal reality is linked with both their subjectivity and their psychological state). This is not part of Foley's copycat plan and he has to shoot the noose mechanism to release her and stop her from strangling herself. She falls to the floor amongst the broken glass of the mirror and removes the noose from around her neck. When Foley tries to pull her up she stabs his thigh with a large shard of glass from the ground, which allows her a few seconds to escape him.

The significance of Helen stabbing Foley with a shard of her fragmented self is not lost here – particularly in relation to Nina's similar action in *Black Swan*. In *Black Swan* Nina stabs her own reflection with a piece of glass (a shard from the broken mirror containing the Black Swan reflection) to avoid acknowledging the truth (that she is fragmented). Yet she uses a shard of her Black Swan reflection (from the mirror) to break the shell of the White Swan imago, in an attempt to 'free' the truth. Therefore, although for the majority of the film, the Black Swan had appeared to be a malevolent force, this scene reinforces that the White Swan imago is as much a symbol of Nina's psychological disorder as the Black Swan. In a similar vein, Helen stabs her attacker with a literal fragment of her pre-Symbolic, suffering self (a shard of glass from the mirror which reflected her as helpless and dependent), which facilitates a transgression beyond her agoraphobic suffering by allowing her to flee to the roof. Like Nina, Helen therefore uses a segment of the visualization of her own psychological order to help herself and harm her attacker. Furthermore, her fluent and effective action (raising the glass shard and thrusting it deeply into Foley's thigh) conveys a command of her physical body and recovery from the ill-defined, extraneous movements of her recent panic attacks which grounded her presence in the incomplete and fragmented pre-Symbolic, her return to a more autonomous physicality, aligning with a shift in her psychological state.

Suddenly, successfully beyond the boundary

The final scenes of *Copycat* take place on the rooftop of a tall building, not purely for dramatic effect, but because, as Carter states, the rooftop of a tall building is the ultimate visual extension of the agoraphobic's abyss (44). Having been drugged, physically assaulted and choked, Helen is not in the best physical condition when she reaches the top of a stairwell while fleeing Foley. Exhausted, she leans against a door to open it and suddenly finds herself confronted with a monstrous abyss; in this location there is no limit to her vision – no roof, no walls and no barrier to a fall of several stories on all sides. The crescendo of the dramatic orchestral 'escape' music comes to an immediate halt and is replaced by near-silence; only the faint sound of air is heard, aurally conveying the infinity of her vision. The camera completes a wandering 360° pan of the rooftop and the night sky and returns to settle on Helen's shocked face.

Used to the uterine space of her pre-mirror phase apartment, and unable to tolerate a location without borders, she takes a step back inside the stair well, pulling the door closed. Only the approach of Foley's footsteps up the stair case (made uneven because of his now-injured thigh) provokes Helen into reopening the door and stepping outside. Clutching rooftop air conditioning units for support, Helen begins to move forward away from the door. Several metres from her starting point, Foley arrives on the roof and begins to follow her. Despite his limping, he closes the gap between them quickly, with Helen still moving unsteadily and slowly from one air conditioning unit to another. Carrying his large knife in hand he begins to taunt Helen saying, 'Hey Helen, looks like I cured your agoraphobia!' The irony of this comment, designed to further disable her emotionally and physically, is that Foley is actually right; the second attack pushed her into entering a limitless location, open to sky and air. Realizing that she is no longer trapped by the suffocating safety of the pre-mirror-phase or the misconception that she is helpless, she recognizes the remaining symptoms of her agoraphobia are absurd – they lose meaning without the confines of the pre-uterine apartment. She straightens up, turns to face him and starts laughing spontaneously and heartily, the camera now encircling her in a visual suggestion of liberation and autonomy. This inversion of the previous 360° pan of the rooftop and night sky suggests she has psychologically overturned her fear of open spaces and her need for uterine-esque safety.

Helen's behaviour enrages Foley and he lifts his knife menacingly but a bullet pierces the knife-wielding arm and he turns to see MJ at the rooftop doorway with her gun raised – a scenario he did not consider, given he presumed she was dead in the bathroom. When he reaches for his own gun, she shoots him four more times in the torso and once cleanly through the head and he falls to the ground dead. Helen takes several deep and calming breaths, before kicking the gun away from Foley's still hand and walking smoothly and steadily back towards MJ. This rehashing of Helen's original trauma with a new twist corresponds with Grose's argument that when phobics recover they are 'left with a new story that follows the shape of the old story, but without such unnerving affect' (30). This means that Helen survives near-identical traumatic conditions but with very different outcomes – indeed, the first 'story' sees Helen descend into psychological disorder (and the associated physical symptoms and atemporal existence of the pre-Symbolic uterine space), while the second 'story' sees her transcend out of it (to reassert control of her corporeal reality and live within the temporality of the Symbolic). And yet, both the descent into agoraphobia and the ascent out of it are initiated by her encounter with death.

Conclusion: The *Copycat* method in returning to the symbolic

From a clinical standpoint Lacan suggests that 'anxiety should be administered in small doses' (Shepherdson xxiii), meaning that exposing the anxious subject *gradually* to the focus of the anxiety facilitates a steady and potentially successful recovery. This is markedly different to what happens to Helen, who following abduction, assault, reconnection with the scene of trauma and an eventual escape to a rooftop, hardly receives the gradual exposure to space that Lacan suggests works for the anxious subject's recovery. Yet *Copycat* suggests that this sudden exposure to the spaces beyond Helen's apartment work as a painful but effective remedy in transitioning her from a pre-mirror phase state back into an autonomous subjectivity, where she moves beyond the restrictions of her atemporal, agoraphobia and returns to the Symbolic. Arguably this is because the gradual, 'bit by bit' approach that Lacan recommends is an incarnation of the agoraphobic condition; a 'gently gently' approach which actually reinforces the legitimacy of the condition (fear of space beyond borders) through the careful, cautious and hesitant pushing of boundaries. Instead *Copycat* blows this approach apart by literally having Helen bursting through a boundary into the open night air, thereby launching her into instant and total immersion of the feared object (space beyond the boundaries). In this (albeit unusual) instance, the approach works, with the anxious subject exposed to the phobic object (space) and the root cause of anxiety (a malicious Other) all in one go. Helen's conscious realization that phobia and anxiety are intimately connected (through a cause and effect relationship) frees her from compliance to the agoraphobic 'rules', which are finally revealed as deceptive.

Copycat (1995)

Copycat is a film which delineates identity through the construction of physical boundaries. By focusing on a subject afflicted with agoraphobia following trauma, this text reinforces clinical psychology's placement of agoraphobia within the wider DSM-V category of anxiety disorders. *Copycat* also demonstrates what happens when the subject doesn't psychologically disassociate during trauma; remaining psychically present in the first attack means Helen does not repress the memory of the assault, and her psychological response after the trauma (which is anxiety) echoes her feeling during the attack (anxiety). Using the clinical psychology approach, the safe zone of Helen's apartment denotes her as separate from others and abnormal, whilst using a psychoanalytic approach the safe zone of Helen's apartment reveals that the adult subject can be pushed backwards, out of the Symbolic, into a pre-mirror phase state.

Intrinsic to the anxiety disorder that Helen suffers is a looming sense of threat which can never be expelled, decreased or ignored. It is this generic and ever-present threat, derived from the trauma of Cullum's assault, which becomes channelled into agoraphobia; in order to avoid a reoccurrence of massive anxiety (another assault), Helen embraces the lesser anxiety of agoraphobia. But, as with all agoraphobics, Helen's psychological suffering is complicated by the way she both cherishes and resents her safe zone. She fears the world beyond her apartment where danger lurks, but misses her 'old' life in the autonomy of the Symbolic order. Additionally, part of the paradox of agoraphobia is that the resurrection of boundaries (which impose restriction and suffering) are ineffective at banishing anxiety; the safe zone of Helen's apartment can be entered by the Other, by objects brought in from the outside and through Helen's own memory of trauma. Furthermore, the erection of a 'zone' only encourages the malicious Other (Foley) to transgress the boundary. While Helen is afflicted by the feeling that she is only safe within the boundaries of her apartment, she still has panic attacks within this safe zone. Symptoms of panic manifest physically, functioning as a language which (ineffectively) expresses fear in lieu of access to *actual* language in the Symbolic.

When Helen is sent backwards out of the Symbolic in the attack by Cullum, she returns to a pre-mirror-stage sense of being unformed and fragmentary, and loses the lack intrinsic to being an autonomous adult (the lack of the (m)other). In other words, she experiences the dissolution of her ego. This dissolution confirms the argument that trauma fundamentally changes the subject, even to the extent of the nullification of subjectivity. Yet, in homage to the title of the film and thriller genre, *Copycat* reverses this situation by creating a replica scenario – essentially, the *reverse* reverse-mirror stage. By recognizing her assailants' reliance on his mirror image (in other words, his own lack at the centre of his subjectivity), Helen is able to linguistically undermine him and recognize the agency which remains to her. Her return to the normal temporality of the Symbolic is marked by her re-acquaintance with language and the autonomy of her corporeal reality in the bathroom. Additionally, her agoraphobic symptoms are revealed as meaningless and futile once she psychologically and physically survives being thrust into the unrestricted infinity of a starlit night.

6

The Shipping News (2001)

Introduction to melancholia, depression and *The Shipping News*

The terms 'melancholia' and 'depression' refer to the same composite condition, which holds an established place in both clinical psychology and psychoanalytic theory. The DSM-V specifies 'major depressive disorder' as a period of at least two weeks, where the individual experiences either a 'depressed mood' or a 'loss of interest or pleasure' which causes 'distress or impairment in social, occupational or other important areas of functioning'. Individuals must also suffer three of the following symptoms for a diagnosis of major depressive disorder: significant weight loss; insomnia or hypersomnia; psychomotor retardation or agitation; fatigue or loss of energy; feelings of worthlessness and/or guilt; diminished concentration and decision-making skills; or recurrent thoughts of death. Whereas the DSM-V refers to this combination of symptoms as major depressive disorder (or clinical depression), psychoanalysis refers to it as 'melancholia', manifesting either episodically or chronically in the affected subject (Kristeva *Black Sun* 9).

Kristeva famously uses the black sun as a metaphor to describe the melancholy status of the depressed individual (Kalsched 206). The black sun is a light that doesn't illuminate, a presence that is characterized by absence, which Kristeva refers to as 'the Thing' (*das Ding*) (ibid). Yet, ironically, the familiar emptiness which the melancholic clings to offers the suffering subject neither nurturance nor comfort. In a life characterized by apathy, grief and sorrow (Lechte and Margaroni 82), Kristeva perceives melancholia as 'an abyssal suffering' (*Black Sun* 189). Similarly, psychoanalytic and hermeneutics scholar Liran Razinsky claims that melancholia is death's encroachment on life (216), while literary psychoanalyst Anne Juranville refers to it as 'a disease of mourning' (88). Juranville's notion of disease draws on Freud, for whom the difference between mourning and melancholia is that mourning is part of normal human behaviour, whereas melancholia is pathological (Razinsky 184). Similar differentiation is drawn between sadness and depression in the DSM-V, with the diagnosis of depression being reliant on a *sustained* period of low mood, which is not attributable to other causes (such as medication or comorbidities), and has significant impact on the individual's capacity to function in daily life.

The Shipping News (Hallstrom 2001) is the film adaptation of E. Annie Proulx's Pulitzer Prize-winning novel of the same name. Kevin Spacey stars as Quoyle, a depressed and despondent ink-setter for the *Poughkeepsie News* near the east coast of the United States. The film opens with Quoyle remembering an abusive childhood and it is immediately apparent, through Quoyle's dour voiceover and negative reflections on the meaninglessness of his life, that he is a chronically depressed individual. When the adventurous and promiscuous Petal (Cate Blanchett) enters his life, Quoyle quickly falls in love with her, although she is abusive towards him. Several years later Quoyle is attempting to process the sudden deaths of his parents and Petal when his estranged Aunt Agnis (Judy Dench) convinces him to move to the ancestral homeland of the Quoyle clan in Canada. Agnis, Quoyle and his daughter Bunny, move to the fishing village of Killick-Claw, Newfoundland, where Quoyle reluctantly begins working as the shipping news reporter for the local newspaper.

Quoyle's transition to this new life is marked by a series of learning curves and changes; he learns about the abuse Agnis suffered under her brother Guy (Quoyle's father), he learns to form relationships with his colleagues and he learns to love a woman who loves him in return. Most importantly, through his new job as a writer, Quoyle is forced to engage with the currency of the Symbolic (language), on a frequent and skilled basis. Resultantly he begins to move away from the asymbolia of melancholia to cultivate words, which previously signalled only emptiness, into published stories with meaning. Each of these changes contributes to a subtle but steady shifting away from the isolation, emptiness and passivity of melancholia, which, for all of his previous years, had defined him. *The Shipping News* conveys a subtle shift into the Symbolic during adulthood, where a life previously rooted in nothingness gently transitions into meaning.

Prince describes *The Shipping News* as having 'very limited box-office appeal' (25), when it was pitted up against massive blockbusters *The Fellowship of the Ring, Harry Potter and the Philosopher's Stone* and *Spider-Man* in 2001. Perhaps it is not surprising then that scholarly work regarding *The Shipping News* is primarily about Proulx's Pulitzer-winning novel, rather than the film adaptation. Although only a small amount is written about *The Shipping News* film, most pieces share a common recognition of rural space as a major theme (Cooke; Hernaez Lerena; Requena-Pelegri). Admittedly not all analyses are favourable; Hernaez Lerena claims the novel was 'violently attacked and ridiculed' (25) for reducing the Newfoundland language and people to 'quirky characters full of folksy charm' (25), an insult that was only added to with the release of the film, which strayed even further from the authentic Newfoundland spirit (25). Cooke also acknowledges the film depicts contemporary realities for Canadian rural communities including the exhaustion of natural resources, globalization, isolation, and the negative effects of the oil industry and other 'big business' (109), but concurs with Hernaez Lerena that the Newfoundland people are portrayed as quirky caricatures (109). Mingled in with the literature which acknowledges the environment in *The Shipping News* is a quiet discussion of class, with particular reference to food. Everett considers the ways food is intricately connected to socio-economic status, class and identity when discussing the inclusion of seal flipper pie in *The Shipping News* (72). The seal flipper pie is contentious, not only because of its links with working classes and rural customs, but because of the anti-seal hunting rhetoric and discussion surrounding 'responsible ecological stewardship' in the Newfoundland and Labrador regions of Canada (74).

There is some discussion of identity in *The Shipping News* literature. Krainitzki looks briefly at the depiction of sexuality, arguing that Agnis is not Othered in the same way most older Lesbian characters are; she possesses a 'temporal dimension' of past (the history with her abusive brother), present (her forging of new relationships with Bunny and Quoyle) and future (her new female partner Mavis) (19). Wang, Jaten and Requena-Pelegri all discuss Quoyle's identity in *The Shipping News*; Wang argues that memory and a return to homeland are central themes; Jaten argues that Quoyle's self-identity is a continuing quest through multiple life stages; Requena-Pelegri argues that Quoyle becomes a 'caring and emotionally involved' father by opposing his own 'hegemonic father' (120). Polack writes about the novel, rather than the film, but her approach to the text from a psychoanalytic perspective aligns her work with my own. She argues that Quoyle must pass a series of psychological challenges as part of his 'return' to his 'homeland', where '[i]n the process, both self and place are reconceived' (95).

Symptoms and affect of melancholia: Suffering, sadness, self-hate and speech

The melancholic's lived experience is dominated by affect, where the suffering of overwhelming sadness manifests and lingers. Despite its negative impact on daily functioning, melancholia is actually a means by which the subject is able to continue living; the melancholic subject abides by an unwritten contract with depression where the possibility of death is deferred in exchange for a 'living-death' rooted in despondency, rather than a meaningful and purposeful life (Ragland *Lacan, the Death Drive* 81). Accordingly, Quoyle's melancholia manifests through symptoms such as low mood (what the DSM-V describes as depressed mood or loss of interest or pleasure), limited verbal communication with others (psychomotor retardation), depleted self-esteem (feelings of worthlessness and guilt) and indetermination (limited decision-making skills).

In voiceover and dialogue Quoyle speaks minimally, slowly and in a monotone – classic signs of severely low mood. These linguistic symptoms correspond with Kristeva's description of melancholia as 'a non-communicable grief' that is 'heavy with daily sorrows' (*Black Sun* 4). Indeed, Quoyle's depression has a heaviness which is similar to the bleak grey colour palette of the film. This aesthetic is the visual depiction of what Christian Kläui, a psychoanalytic practitioner who specializes in melancholy and depression, refers to as the 'heavy spirit' (*schwermut*), 'despondency' (*bedrucktheit*) and 'dejection' (*niedergeschlagenheit*) of melancholia (136). Quoyle's depleted self-esteem is evident from his voiceover section, when he states, 'My failure to dog paddle was only the first of many failures.' His lack of self-esteem is perpetuated by an abusive father who makes his disappointment in Quoyle clear, with Quoyle also saying in his opening voiceover, 'When I got admitted to the junior college my father figured it was a clerical error. When I dropped out a year later he wasn't surprised.' As an adult Quoyle seems no more able to stand up to his father than when he was child. This is not to say that the abuse necessarily continued into adulthood, but that at the time when the autonomous adult subject is usually able to recognize the vulnerability and innocence of being a child, Quoyle continues to reprimand his 'child-self' and, by extension, excuse his father's actions. Quoyle is not able to recognize that he was a victim as a child because, as an adult, he does not conceive of himself beyond that stage; as a melancholic who has failed to live successfully in the Symbolic, Quoyle can't contextualize his childhood abuse because he has not moved into the domain of self-recognition beyond it. He remains trapped in the non-space of the pre-Symbolic, signalling the close link between his psychological disorder and his skewed sense of temporality. Additionally, Quoyle's unwillingness to address his father's abusive nature or his own potential to cultivate a better life for himself conveys the depressive's limited decision-making abilities referred to in the DSM-V, or what psychoanalysis refers to as the passivity of the melancholic.

Before discussing more sophisticated notions of symptomatic grief and language, it is important to note that as a melancholic Quoyle is characterized by a deep sadness. As the cornerstone of depression, sadness 'stamps the entire behavior and all the sign systems' (Kristeva *Black Sun* 21) as 'affect swamps the subject' (ibid 64). Therefore, beneath each of Quoyle's symptoms – the communication difficulties, the indecision and self-hate – is an unshiftable sadness. This sadness is best described as a wound manifesting as 'rank pain' (Kläui 137), a gaping hole that invariably exists inside Quoyle regardless of the circumstances of his life. While the sadness of the melancholic subject is witnessed at a surface level, through symptoms such as low self-esteem and lethargy, it is not fixable at that level. This is because the sadness exists on a conscious and unconscious level for the subject, generating a subjectivity and lived experience which *consists* only *of* that emptiness, with the subject reduced to 'a thriving wound, pain in its pure state' (ibid).

At the start of *The Shipping News* Quoyle is the embodiment of this 'thriving wound'; his sadness is visible in the way he talks (slowly and infrequently), the way he walks and moves (listlessly and heavily), the bland clothes he wears and his expressionless face. At this point in the film Quoyle is the personification of melancholia; he is a wound on screen and a visualization of the link between psychological state and corporeal reality. Kristeva posits that such sadness indicates a primal self who is 'wounded, incomplete, empty' and that melancholics affected in this way believe *themselves* to be fundamentally flawed, as opposed to 'wronged' by another (*Black Sun* 12). As previously stated, Quoyle believes himself to be responsible for his depressed state, claiming to have had 'many failures' and to have merely 'stumbled into adulthood', rather than recognizing that he was raised by an abusive parent. Kristeva claims that melancholic sadness is a 'perverse display' which simultaneously 'fills a void and evicts death'; that is, it protects the melancholy subject from suicide, but only to an extent (*Black Sun* 48). The overwhelming sadness of melancholia, the affect to which melancholics so steadfastly cling, is therefore also a shield, 'sometimes the last one – against madness' and against a final act such as suicide (ibid 42). Not unlike anxiety (see Chapter 5), melancholia is a life-line which saves but also harms the subject. So while it seems, in the opening scenes of *The Shipping News*, that Quoyle is so terribly depressed that he has nothing to live for and no barrier to attempting suicide, it is actually the identity-forming effect of that state (the crippling sadness) which keeps him clinging to life, again highlighting the link between psychological suffering and the subject's relationship with death.

The most pronounced symptom of Quoyle's melancholia is the effect on his language and communication with others. Classically the speech of the melancholic is repetitive with a flat quality (Lechte and Margaroni 82), featuring sentences 'that are interrupted, exhausted, come to a standstill' (Kristeva *Black Sun* 33). Capps and Ochs argue that when the speaking subject pauses or has false starts, this signals that the information being shared is particularly important, as these elements can indicate 'tentativeness, distress, or self-doubt' (28). The melancholic subject then, whose speech is chronically heavy with pauses, false starts and silences, is signalling something important with every word – that they are suffering because they find no meaning and no comfort in language, as the language the melancholic utters seems 'built up with absurd signs' (Kristeva *Black Sun* 53). Kristeva argues that the melancholics' delivery of words is elongated and punctuated by silences because melancholics, so connected with their anguish, 'no longer concatenate, and consequently, neither act not speak' (ibid 34). In other words, the melancholic descends into the meaninglessness of asymbolia where it seems that words come 'frozen' as if 'somewhat removed from the head and body of the person who is speaking' (ibid 43). Quoyle, for example, even during dramatic moments (such as pleading with Petal to come home), fails to either break his monotone or increase the speed of his slow expression.

Symptoms and affect of melancholia: An alternative temporal reality

Temporal transcendence is seen in various psychological disorders – for example, Lisbeth (*Dragon* Tattoo), Michael (*Brødre*) and Helen (*Copycat*) all experience movement between temporalities in response to traumatic circumstances – but melancholics experience a 'skewed' temporal reality, feeling that time does not 'pass by' and that the concept of 'before' and 'after' does not exist as it does for non-depressed subjects (Kristeva *Black Sun* 60). As a melancholic Quoyle lacks a sense of being alive in the present, but also has no sense of his future. Though he exists in the present he is consumed by the past, believing that 'everything' has already 'gone by' (ibid). This feeling that life has already 'been and gone' is part of the melancholic sense that time is meaningless, or even non-existent, thereby rendering the melancholic insignificant or even absent. This melancholic affect is demonstrated by Quoyle's belief that he is not really present in the physical world of the diegesis when he states, 'I got used to being invisible.'

The Shipping News features several instances of temporal transcendence, where Quoyle has a different experience of time and space to other people. The first example of this melancholic affect occurs in the construction of the opening scenes of the film, when as a child Quoyle is pushed off a wharf into water by his father, which informs a life-long fear of deep water. Not being able to swim, Quoyle fights on the surface for several moments before sinking down into the water. His frantic movements slow as his body comes to a rest on the lake bed. His child's face, placid in drowning, slowly morphs into his equally placid adult face, to depict that, despite the passing of many years, Quoyle still feels as if he were that young boy: powerless, passive and drowning. This episode remains a traumatic memory for Quoyle, (he does not speak about the event or conceptualize it as part of his narrative memory), but rather re-experiences it like a flashback, triggered in later life by other bodies of water. The time between this childhood trauma and Quoyle's adult age is as much as two or three decades, yet the reoccurring nature of traumatic memory (as discussed in Chapter 3) eliminates temporal distances in the normative sense. This means that Quoyle's traumatic childhood lake experience feels as recent to him as events which happened in the past day or even hour, depicted through the seamless visual merging of his child and adult faces.

The transition to the following scene is enacted by maintaining this same adult image of Quoyle (in the water) but changing the background around him. The cloudy lake water dissolves into an environment where Quoyle is first depicted waving through an endless line of anonymous faces passing by a ticket booth. The background dissolves again to show him rinsing an endless mountain of crockery in a restaurant kitchen, and then dissolves again as Quoyle watches thousands of issues of *The Poughkeepsie News* going through the printing press. The monotony of these tasks, and the maintenance of his image against a changing background, generates a sense of timelessness, as if Quoyle's life is not measurable in years and is experienced only as an endless repetition of meaningless movements, without beginning or end.

The other pertinent example of Quoyle's skewed sense of temporal reality is echoed in the aesthetic of the film's settings, first in the relentless rain of the Poughkeepsie township and then in the Newfoundland landscape. The repetition of Quoyle's car's windscreen wipers, constantly and fruitlessly shifting off Poughkeepsie raindrops, generates the same monotonous despair as the people at the ticket booth, dishes in the restaurant and newspapers at the factory. Likewise, through a grey and white palette, and a small township with only basic facilities, the geography of Killick-Claw also gives the impression of timelessness and alienation, as if Quoyle were not separated from his ancestors by centuries or from his former life in Poughkeepsie by kilometres. Rather, there is a gaping void which separates Quoyle from others: the abyss of melancholic mourning.

Cause of melancholia

The mourning of the melancholic subject is akin to a nostalgia for something from a prior time. Etymologically 'nostalgia' means 'suffering from return', so melancholia is a yearning for a return to a primary state of things (Juranville 82). However, the nostalgia of the melancholic is specifically connected to 'the loss of a reprehensible love object' (Westerink 205), what Juranville describes as the 'absolute, mythic object' (82) and Kristeva refers to as 'an archaic other' (*Black Sun* 14). It is this ongoing loss which afflicts Quoyle – it is a 'calling out to' the subject from another place and time, although the melancholic subject, frequently unaware of the origins of their affliction, fails to recognize they are being called out to, and experiences only the affect.

Kristeva questions how and why melancholia comes to afflict the subject when she asks, 'Where does this black sun come from? Out of what eerie galaxy do its invisible, lethargic rays reach me?' (ibid 3). Each infant goes through the process of separating from the (m)other, followed by entrance into the Symbolic, as part of becoming an autonomous subject (Jonte-Pace 20). The subject's entrance into the Symbolic order, the realm of signs and language, is dependent on their ability to identify with something other than the lost object (the mother), whether it be 'father, form, schema' (Kristeva *Black Sun* 23). However, melancholia is generated when the subject has a constitutive inability to move into the Symbolic (Juranville 83), reconfirming that for Kristeva 'how one is in the symbolic is more important than *that* one is the symbolic' (Lechte and Margaroni 72).

Yet each human subject must separate from the m(other) in order to enter the Symbolic; this separation is crucial to the development of autonomous subjectivity. Therefore, the sense of lack, which is felt in response to separation from the m(other), is encountered by each person. This means that the catalyst for melancholia (the lost object) is present in everyone, for without this proclivity to melancholia 'there is no psyche' (Kristeva *Black Sun* 4). The yearning for the lost object is therefore a normal part of human development, although most subjects (who are not melancholic) accept language as a replacement for the lack. Therefore, in Kristeva's eyes, 'melancholia is the failure to have *faith* in language' (Lechte and Margaroni 84), to trust it as a replacement; it is the absence of the transcendence into the Symbolic. The melancholic rejects language as an adequate substitute for the loss of the Thing and instead adopts sadness as 'a sole object', to signify the lack (Kristeva *Black Sun* 12). Therefore, Quoyle, intrinsically and fundamentally sad, has adopted this affect in homage to the 'archaic other', the mother who is always lost to him, and this is how, as an adult, he remains outside of the Symbolic in the atemporality of the pre-Symbolic, depressive psychological state.

Sociologist John Lechte and Maria Margaroni, who researches in the area of continental philosophy, psychoanalysis and aesthetics (68), explain that, as language is the way in which 'contact is made with the other (with the mother, in the first place)', it always signifies distance. It is also the only way the subject 'finds solace' after separation from the mother. The word is therefore not only a linguistic sign but a carrier of affect, for every time the subject uses language the subject receives confirmation that they exist in the Symbolic, which is simultaneously a confirmation that they are no longer in the Imaginary, connected with the m(other). As Lacan insisted language is based in lack, but the melancholic subject rejects language as an acceptable substitute for the loss of the mother and therefore lives in a *constant* state of lack; loss is felt when the melancholic subject uses language yet also when they don't, and they therefore live permanently in lack. Quoyle's melancholy is based on the loss of his primal object (his [m]other), but he continues to feel the lack in his adulthood, despite continued attempts to negate the loss of the (m)other through his choice of love interests. The mourning for the lost object can't be represented or symbolized and manifests instead as an unshiftable sadness (which the melancholic latches onto). With loss the basis of Quoyle's reality, sadness and pain become central to his lived experience.

However, crucial to understanding the mechanism of melancholia is the addition of another powerful affect, the aforementioned self-hate which dominates the melancholy subject's perception of self, and frequently inhibits recovery and even reflexivity and awareness. To understand the presence of this self-hate, the melancholic's anger must first be acknowledged – frequently forgotten or ignored as the sadness of melancholy actually hides the anger the subject feels towards the lost object. Kristeva describes the emotional and psychological mechanism in the following way:

> 'I love that object,' is what that person seems to say about the lost object, 'but even more so I hate it; because I love it, and in order not to lose it, I embed it in myself; but because I hate it, that other within myself is a bad self, I am bad, I am non existent, I shall kill myself'. The complaint against oneself would therefore be a complaint against another, and putting oneself to death but a tragic disguise for massacring an other. (*Black Sun* 11)

In *The Shipping News*, Quoyle loves the (m)other but also hates her for 'abandoning' him during the process of the development of his subjectivity. To counter the feeling of being abandoned, Quoyle places the essence of the (m)other within himself, but this also means anger at the (m)other has now become internalized, and inverted hate for another becomes self-hate. However, if Quoyle were to be so overcome by sadness and self-hate that he chose suicide, he would be hurting the (m)other (who he has internalized). Therefore, the option of suicide is particularly complicated for the melancholic and has a significant drawback; it is a 'way out' but it hurts the melancholic's most significant 'Other' in the process.

The other outcome of inverting and internalizing primal anger for the mother is that it sets up a pattern whereby the melancholic subject (Quoyle) consistently absorbs and inverts the anger and violence of all Others directed towards him. Where the non-melancholic's response to abuse may be to get angry or violent in return, the melancholic internalizes the others' anger as further fuel for his constitutive sadness. Resultantly, the sadness of melancholy has a dual function: it both resists suicide, and informs the melancholic's well-known passivity (Lechte and Margaroni 80). Quoyle has a passive response (or no response at all) to the various maltreatments inflicted on him through his life, including physical and verbal abuse at the hands of his father, and emotional abuse from Petal. In these circumstances, when he is hit, hurt, ignored or ridiculed, the immense sadness inside Quoyle inverts the violence with which he might otherwise defend or protect himself. For example, as previously discussed, in the opening scenes of *The Shipping News*, Quoyle's voiceover immediately reveals that he takes on the burden and responsibility of his father's abuse, stating, 'My failure to dog paddle was only the first of many failures,' thereby interpreting an incident of child abuse, in which he was the victim, as his own fault. Because he perceives that it was *his* failure to dog paddle in the water, rather than his *father's* abusive actions, there is no hate for his father here, only for himself.

Mechanism of asymbolia

But how is it that language comes to be meaningless for the melancholic? For the non-depressed subject, language begins with the negation of loss (Kristeva *Black Sun* 43), since the non-depressed subject goes through the following mechanism: 'I had lost my mother but now I have re-found her through language' or even 'I consented to losing my mother so have actually not lost her and I am with her again through using language.' The denial of losing the mother, because it was consented to, is what Kristeva refers to as 'negation' (ibid). Therefore, entrance into language is based on the denial of any loss, retrieving the mother through language instead (ibid 63). Negation is therefore a paradoxical process in which the repressed knowledge (of losing the mother) is represented through language only because it is denied (ibid 44).

However, as a depressed subject Quoyle disavows the negation (*verleugnung*), which means the Thing of his loss (his lost love object) remains keenly felt, having no replacement salve (language) to soothe the wound (ibid 43). The disavowal of negation lays the foundation for the melancholic's sense of a nonsensical language which lacks meaningful signifiers to express their constitutional sadness. For the speaking subject life is meaningful, but 'when meaning shatters [in melancholia and asymbolia], life no longer matters' (ibid 6), which corresponds with Kristeva's observation that the melancholic subject speaks as if removed from their own corporeal reality. Kristeva goes on to clarify that the disavowal of negation 'deprives the language signifiers of their role of making sense for the subject' by being pulled out of their 'signifying neutrality' and made 'repetitive, or simply alliterative, musical or sometimes nonsensical' (ibid 42). Words are then perceived as being hollow and absurdly meaningless by the depressed subject (ibid 52). Hence the melancholic is reluctant to use language due to its perceived ridiculousness, although this ridiculousness is itself an effect of the disavowal of the negation that would have made language meaningful.

The denial of negation devitalizes signification, meaning that everything for the melancholic is 'reduced to senselessness and emptiness' (Kläui 138). For example, when Quoyle's father leaves a voice message for him announcing his and his mother's suicides, the words he uses are absurd, even obscene, to Quoyle:

> Quoyle? This is your father. Lost your home number. It's time for your mother and I to put an end to it. I left instructions with the undertaker, Datton and Sons. Told 'em to notify my sister, Agnis Ham. Not much of a life. Nobody gave me nothing.

These words, heard through the filter of the melancholic's ear, are separated from the weight of their own meaning. When one of Quoyle's shocked workmates asks, 'Were they sick or something?', Quoyle's response is typically despondent; he does not reply to his workmate (verbally or otherwise) and the vacant expression eerily remains on his face. This is because, for the melancholy subject, his own speech also becomes 'like an alien skin' (Kristeva *Black Sun* 53), depleted of meaning or value, so responding verbally to his workmate seems futile and nonsensical to Quoyle. The discomfort he feels about using this 'foreign skin' is evident from his early voiceover statement, 'I stumbled into adulthood.' This statement not only expresses his shame at having not transitioned into a successful adult, but also reflects, at a deeper level, his rejection of the Symbolic as a replacement for the lost object, claiming he 'stumbled into' the Symbolic rather than embracing it, and is therefore not comfortable using that system of signs in the way other people do.

For example, before Quoyle begins to move away from his melancholic symptoms, especially asymbolia, he fails to process words from those surrounding him, even in traumatic or emotional circumstances, such as from Petal ('Find yourself a girlfriend'), Bunny ('Why are you so scared Daddy?'), his parents ('It's time for your mother and I to put an end to it'), his boss ('Work not stimulating enough for you Quoyle?') and even the police ('She was mercifully killed on impact'). These words fall upon Quoyle as meaningless sounds, drowned out by the roar of an ever-present loss which can't be substituted by a system of menial signs.

However, when his Aunt Agnis shows up at his house, she is the first person to understand that he has no faith in himself; she thus *forces* him to make a change, rather than assuming he has the capacity to do so himself. Arriving on his doorstep, she immediately introduces herself ('Agnis Hamm. I'm your Aunt') before stepping inside the house and scolding Quoyle ('Potato chips won't do you any good'), then firmly instructing him, 'Drink your tea'. Agnis functions in a small but vital supporting role as a catalyst for Quoyle's transition, and it is Agnis' acerbic tones saying, 'The move will help. You'll see', which resonate with Quoyle on the ferry ride north to Canada. Agnis is the catalyst for Quoyle's move to Newfoundland, for she is the character who mobilizes Quoyle's psychological as well as geographical movement, and whose sharp and domineering words finally pierce through the fuzz of his previously impenetrable asymbolia. As a chronically depressed person Quoyle feels helpless; a reluctance to invest in a life believed meaningless is a logical behavioural solution to a problem believed unsolvable. He can't commit suicide because this would kill the internalized part of the self which is the Thing, and yet he can't change what he perceives is unchangeable – his own failure to thrive. It is only the entrance of new people (Petal and Agnis) who destabilize the stalemate of his melancholic bind.

The melancholic 'in love' but suicidal

Petal's sudden entrance into Quoyle's life in Poughkeepsie changes the monotony and isolation of his existence. For example, the first time Quoyle meets Petal he says (in voiceover), 'I got used to being invisible. Until someone noticed me.' In this moment Petal looks at Quoyle and sees the benefactor of her next meal, but for Quoyle the interaction is special and he believes Petal's interest in him is authentic. This is because, for the melancholic, falling in love can provide the sense that the part that was missing (the lost object) has been found once again. This desire to re-find the lost object provides the melancholic with a degree of desperation, which in turn, enables easy delusion of the true circumstances.

Klaui claims that love and depression are linked by this misconception that the love partners 'complete each other' (143), whereby falling in love is like re-finding the lost object. Yet ironically, the only way for the melancholic subject to possess the lost object (an object which they never had and therefore was always lost) is to treat the object that they have as if it were already lost (Žižek *Event* 23). For example, Quoyle appears to be in love with Petal but he never really 'had' Petal because she never had genuine feelings of love for him in return and was therefore always lost to him. Quoyle is besotted with Petal from the very start of their relationship and for him there is nothing beyond the two of them. Several hours after they first meet, post coitus, he declares, 'I love you … I love you' confirming Lechte and Margaroni's (63) claim that 'love, for the lovers, is a web that has no position exterior to it'. As Petal appears to be filling in the void felt by Quoyle for so long, he is desperate to keep this miscalculated closeness, beseeching her to come home several years later, 'Petal, Petal, you're the only woman I've ever loved.'

In *The Shipping News* love and depression are also linked by Quoyle's propensity to suicide while in the 'relationship' with Petal. Teresa De Lauretis, distinguished author in the areas of semiotics, psychoanalysis and film theory, claims that the melancholic seriously contemplates suicide when resentment about abandonment and betrayal emerges, arguing it is the inverted and internalized hatred for the Other 'that overwhelms the melancholic subject and produces the tendency to suicide' (36). Therefore, the most likely time for Quoyle to commit suicide is during the six-year period that Petal is still alive and having multiple affairs, because Petal (who fulfils the role of the lost object), both abandons and explicitly betrays Quoyle on a regular basis. Indeed, the scene in which Quoyle hears Petal's sexual noises with another man through the wall depicts Quoyle's despair by using the image of fast water rushing into the room to visualize being overwhelmed by painful feelings. Quoyle's inclination to suicide is evident in the fact that he does nothing to avoid drowning, and instead lays back on the bed and lets himself sink passively beneath the surface, conveying one of the ways in which Quoyle's psychological suffering links with his complex relationship with death.

Each time Petal hurts Quoyle, she re-wounds the original pain of being abandoned by the mother. Only her death alleviates this pattern of abuse, and to some extent reduces the acute circumstances which facilitate Quoyle's suicidal ideation. That being said, Petal's death does nothing to ease Quoyle's melancholia, and in Newfoundland he continues to struggle with a sense of powerlessness, ineffectiveness and, of course, deep sadness. For the melancholic, suicide appears to be a veritable option in terms of removing oneself from the sense of constant lack. However, Kristeva claims that the melancholic's denial of negation, which 'destroys the meaning of the symbolic also destroys the act's meaning and leads the subject to commit suicide without anguish of disintegration' (*Black Sun* 19). Therefore, the melancholy subject commits suicide, not so much out of despair, but out of misunderstanding the full significance and finality of the act because of their perception of the meaninglessness of the Symbolic order. In other words, the melancholic seeks an end without realizing what this end actually entails – another example of the way in which death and psychological state are complexly linked.

Ejected from the Imaginary but barred from entering the Symbolic, Quoyle is theoretically left no place to exist; it is hardly surprising he contemplates suicide in the face of being forever caught in the 'in between' atemporality of melancholia. This 'in between' status is felt most acutely every time Petal leaves him – her abandonment generating a sharp sense of isolation which echoes the primal separation from the mother. While suffering Petal's abuse, Quoyle clings to the memory of the initial emotional and physical connection between them. But what Quoyle interpreted as love, Petal perceived differently, for as a female narcissist she receives a pathological satisfaction from relationships which are fast-burning and disposable.

The female narcissist: Petal

Elizabeth Grosz, working from the area of feminist and gender studies, argues Petal is a classic narcissistic woman; she is conceited, superficial, duplicitous and most importantly, Petal is motivated by a burning need to be loved (Grosz 128). The female narcissist is particularly dependent on any man who might either withhold or withdraw love from her and she measures her own worth by attempting to entice and maintain relationships with at least one lover (ibid). Petal beguiles a variety of men (including Quoyle) with little thought for how they feel about being only one of many, in an attempt to gain confirmation of her value from multiple partners. Yet regardless of how many men Petal has 'on the go', she never achieves the sense of worth she yearns for.

Quoyle meets Petal when she is in the midst of a screaming row with a boyfriend at the petrol station. Catching sight of Quoyle watching her through his rain-streaked windscreen, Petal simply walks to his car, gets in and demands, 'Let's go. Wake up, go!', confirming that Petal attracts and 'catches' men very quickly. In the car she declares she's 'starving' and Quoyle takes her to a diner to eat. Halfway through their meal, Petal reaches across the table, takes Quoyle's hand and says, 'So what'd'ya think? You wanna marry me, don't ya? It's 8.05. Think I'm gonna fuck you by 10.' By the end of the evening she has managed to have sex with him, and as previously stated, he is so besotted by her that he proclaims his love for her immediately afterwards. Petal has multiple partners over the next six years, and the car crash which finally ends her life is caused by the last of her lovers, who loses control and drives their car over a bridge and into a river.

Break-ups are particularly hard for the female narcissist as they become aware that the male partner is withdrawing his love (ibid). This much is evident in Petal's first scene, where she is introduced to the viewer and to Quoyle while having a row with her boyfriend in a public space. Arguably, this is why Petal never 'officially' leaves Quoyle – despite having multiple other partners, disappearing for long periods of time and encouraging Quoyle to 'Find yourself a girlfriend', she still returns to their house occasionally and keeps her belongings there, perhaps because this is an easier option than formally ending it with Quoyle. Had she not been killed in the car crash, it is likely Petal would have maintained this semblance of a relationship with Quoyle for many more years.

That being said, part of the female narcissist's pathology is that she will never be 'sated', so Petal never has enough lovers despite picking them up and amassing them quickly. Therefore, while she doesn't value or love Quoyle, as part of her repertoire of lovers he still adds something to her attempt to build self-worth. Quoyle appears to please Petal least of all, though – she walks out on him multiple times, refuses to let him touch her physically and even brings other men she has sex with back to their home.

Petal is the least pleased with Quoyle because she can't get the confirmation of value she needs from him due to his melancholia. Arguably this is because melancholics can't truly love and instead can only long for the lost object (for which Petal is merely a substitute). Kristeva suggests that the melancholic cannot love because they have a 'reduced emotional investment' in language (due to the disavowal of negation), which is central to the daily interaction of love (Lechte and Margaroni 63). Resultantly, unconsciously, Petal senses that Quoyle 'needs' her, rather than 'loves' her. Essentially, both Petal and Quoyle are using each other for their own gains. Although it seems that Quoyle's intentions are less conceited and hurtful than Petal's (and he claims to truly love her), Petal, underneath her harmful actions, is also suffering, since the narcissistic woman, 'in spite of her aura of power, aloofness, and confidence … feels worthless, a mere fragment of a person' (Grosz 128).

As a narcissistic woman Petal has the capacity to genuinely love her own child (ibid). This is because the child emerges from her own body, and in loving that child she both loves herself and an Other who is very similar to her and comes *from* her. In this instance the female narcissist's classic self-love is extended out to a maternal love (ibid). Yet, Petal shows very little evidence of caring for Bunny.

Following Quoyle and Petal's first sex scene the film cuts to several months later when Petal, who is heavily pregnant, leaves a doctor's appointment and angrily states, 'If I end up with stretch marks I'll sue his arse', and her final act before dying in a car accident is to sell Bunny to a black market adoption agency for US$6000. Despite multiple lovers Petal fails to gain a sense of autonomous and intrinsic self-worth prior to her death; therefore, it is my estimation that, although Grosz believes female narcissistic love can be extended to a child, this is not the case with Petal and Bunny.

It is difficult to know exactly why this is (because the film does not elaborate upon it), but the two scenes mentioned above illuminate Petal's disgruntlement about perceived changes to her agency following the conception of her child. For instance, despite the numerous people in Petal's life, none of them have any influence over her behaviour; she simply uses each man for her own benefit and then discards him. However, the child growing inside Petal is the first person to have some control over her; even before being born, the child makes changes to the way Petal looks and feels about her body. Selling Bunny on the black market also suggests that Petal was eager to get some 'use' out of her (monetary profit in this case), in the same way that she only engages with men who she can benefit from. Therefore, rather than Petal perceiving Bunny as an Other who is very similar to herself (and resultantly someone she can love as an extension of narcissistic self-love), she identifies her as the unwanted anomaly who impacted negatively on her agency and as an unfortunate link to one of her discarded lovers, Quoyle. Perhaps the black market sale is her last attempt to establish that she is in control of Bunny, not the other way around.

Yet, while it may initially appear that Petal is the film's antagonist, causing havoc and heartbreak for the gentle protagonist Quoyle, she is also broken, sad and self-destructive. And, even if there were a way to redeem her abhorrent actions, she has never given the opportunity, dying in a car crash several hours after selling Bunny. Quoyle's move to Newfoundland following Petal's death confirms that *The Shipping News*' antagonistic force exists internally, not externally, for Quoyle; his melancholia is much more of barrier to his happiness than Petal ever was.

Love and loss: Wavey

Quoyle's two love interests in *The Shipping News* are an example of his 'constructive repetition', a phrase used by Shlomith Rimmon-Kenan, who researches representation, psychoanalysis and subjectivity, to describe the way a subject emphasizes difference to 'achieve mastery over a disturbing, wounding event' (Bronfen *Risky Resemblances* 104). For the melancholic Quoyle the source of primal wounding is the separation from the mother and unsuccessful entrance into the Symbolic. When Quoyle seeks to fill the void inside him through a relationship with Petal and she invariably fails to provide him with the nurturing he desires, she re-wounds him. Each time she walks out on him, he re-experiences the original wound of separation from the (m)other. However, as his new love Wavey (Julianne Moore) is not a replica of the first woman, Quoyle is able to take the step of loving again whilst acknowledging that she cannot fill the void in him the way he expected Petal to, and thereby gains mastery over the disturbing wounding event of the past that Rimmon-Kenan refers to.

Despite the head-first infatuation Quoyle demonstrates for Petal, Kristeva claims that the subject is always aware they will lose their lovers eventually, simply because every subject enters into a loving relationship knowing for certain that it will end, possibly with death (*Black Sun* 5); as Razinsky (186) states, 'future loss is the fly in the ointment of love'. When a loved one dies the subject feels the need to 'decathect every single path of cathexis to the object' (ibid), yet the 'forging of every such path was done under the intimidating possibility that the attachment might end one day' (ibid). Quoyle encounters this loss when Petal leaves and again when she dies, but he dares to repeat that same loss when he takes the risk of falling for a woman called Wavey in Killick-Claw.

Yet, while Petal's death solidifies that she is 'properly' lost to Quoyle (as opposed to seeing other men and being absent for long periods), Bronfen claims that once a female partner has died, the male denies that she is gone and her absence 'brings about a second kind of liminality' (*Risky Resemblances* 111). Therefore, following her death in the car crash Petal exists on the edge of Quoyle's reality, in the liminal space where he first idealized her as his 'perfect' woman. As an 'inanimate' presence, Petal 'hovers between the two realms because he will not let her die' (ibid). Quoyle's lingering connection to Petal's not-quite-presence is portrayed in the scene where Quoyle explains to Bunny that Petal has died. With Aunt Agnis looking on disapprovingly from the kitchen window, Quoyle reads through a book designed to teach children about the death of a loved one. Tracing the words on the page with his finger, he slowly reads aloud to Bunny, 'Your loved one has not left your heart or your thoughts, but is sleeping peacefully.' When Bunny questions him, 'She's sleeping?', Quoyle nods in consent. It is almost as if Quoyle is engaging in an adult game of fort-da – attempting to gain mastery over absence by remembering her fondly (not as she actually was) and by thinking of her in a way that doesn't fully acknowledge that she is fully gone.

When Quoyle moves to Newfoundland and meets Wavey, he discovers she is a good mother to her son Harry and a gentle person. He begins to recognize how awful Petal was but it takes some time for Quoyle to build a romantic relationship with Wavey, as opposed to seeing her as a maternal substitute, and initial meetings with her are awkward and even confrontational. Quoyle never really 'had' Petal because she never had genuine feelings of love for him in return and was therefore always lost to him. Quoyle's response to this is to initially push away the woman he does actually 'have' (Wavey), treating her as if she also was inaccessible, mourning for her although she is still there. It is the comparison between the two women which illuminates the reality of the first (that Petal was unkind and abusive towards Quoyle and Bunny). Without Wavey's entrance into Quoyle's life he may have gone on mourning for Petal indefinitely, perceiving her in the liminal space occupied by those neither living nor dead.

The mourning subject may attempt to replace the former lover (the dead spouse, for example) with a new one who seemingly fulfils the same purpose (Bronfen *Risky Resemblances* 107). However, the 'new' woman may be similar to or different from the previous woman; as Petal and Wavey are totally different women, Wavey does not merely 'affirm the first woman's death' or serve as an 'identical substitute for her predecessor' (ibid). Instead, Quoyle recognizes Wavey for the person she actually is, rather than what he wants her to be (as was the case with Petal), for Wavey, like Quoyle, is a melancholy subject. Wavey is also struggling to bring up a child alone and suffers from low esteem; she, too, is 'the melancholy woman … [who] wastes away by striking moral and psychic blows against herself' (Kristeva *Black Sun* 30). Her fragile sense of worth takes a further setback when Quoyle, drunk and grieving, mistakenly calls Wavey by Petal's name – a slip of the tongue (parapraxis) – triggered by 'the shadow of a long-lost former loved one' in the current lover (ibid). This incident is a double blow for Wavey, who, other than having been invalidated through the inappropriate naming of another woman, is also reminded of her own ex-husband, who had multiple affairs with numerous women in the village; in both cases she is not the first choice of partner. Yet, where Quoyle's behaviours towards Petal revealed an attempt to plug the 'mother-whole', Quoyle genuinely loves Wavey; as a fellow melancholic Wavey can't be used to merely 'plug' the void left by the mother, because as a melancholic, she has a void of her own.

As Quoyle's move to Newfoundland is the first step in moving away from melancholia, his initial relationship with Wavey is rocky. However, they find more solid ground as his asymbolia recedes, meaning that eventually, he does not 'need' Wavey (or anybody) to 'plug the hole' left by the mother. *The Shipping News* suggests that, indeed, the melancholic cannot truly be in love, but once the 'invisible, lethargic rays' of his own black sun pull back, Quoyle can.

The void, the thing and the lack

There is an inherent emptiness to subjectivity, given that it is intrinsically linked with separation from the Other and subsequent loss. The split required for the subject to move beyond the Imaginary and into the Symbolic is constantly embodied by the subject who engages with language, which (as a system) marks the primal loss. Therefore, Lacan theorizes that, all people, regardless of who they are, have an emptiness at the centre of their being and are driven to attempt to fill this space (Ragland *Lacan, the Death Drive* 81). Addictive behaviours can be viewed as an attempt to fill the hole and detract from the void because they entirely consume the subject on a physical, mental, emotional and spiritual level, and are therefore fairly successful at functioning as a temporary distraction from the hole. Depression has a similar positive effect, which goes some way to explaining the re-occurrence of depression in some individuals and the chronic duration of it in others.

This raises the question of whether Quoyle's melancholia is the void itself, or the thing that he engages with to cover or camouflage the void. It would seem, given its roots in his mourning for the lost object, that Quoyle's melancholia *is* the void, and yet as something which is comforting in its familiarity, melancholia also seems to be a defence mechanism that Quoyle clings to. Yet Ragland (*Lacan, the Death Drive* 82) claims that people attempt to fill the void with behaviours which actually feed into it and resultantly they are never fully successful in their attempt. Quoyle's attempt to 'stop up' the hole left in him by his mother can be seen in his attachment to Petal and his initial interactions with Wavey. Evidence of his maternal yearning is revealed in these interactions with both women; after Quoyle and Petal have sex for the first time she straddles him, feeds him a soft marshmallow treat and encourages him, in a baby-like voice, to 'Nibble, nibble little mouse'. His first moment of intimacy occurs with Wavey when he stumbles on the uneven surface of the shoreline at Killick-Claw and re-steadies himself against her body, before resting his head upon her thigh.

Similar to the 'lurking' quality of the void, Lacan's concept of the Thing (*das Ding*), posits that something unnameable exists behind everything, since 'order and representations [are] built around something that is not there' (Razinsky 218). Kristeva (*Black Sun* 15) describes the Thing as 'a waste', which Quoyle as a melancholic merges with because 'depressive persons cannot endure Eros, they prefer to be with the Thing' (ibid 20). When the melancholy subject forgoes signification (using language meaningfully) and enters into asymbolia, they sink into a torment that signals 'a reunion with the Thing' (ibid 41). This torment is experienced as the subtle agony of melancholia, a pain visually portrayed in *The Shipping News* through setting and environment: firstly through the endless rain in Poughkeepsie (with a monotony that matches Quoyle's dreary and repetitive jobs), and secondly through the barren grey landscape of Newfoundland (which is both bleak and enveloping). And yet '*das Ding* is our absolute other; it is the object we look for' (despite being lost to start with) (Razinsky 218). People attempt to fill the gap left by the lost object with other objects (which can broadly speaking mean people or actual objects), but never succeed at permanently doing this.

The non-depressed subject 'comes into being through speaking', swapping the absence of the Thing for the word, ensuring that 'in every speech uttered there is death' as they have struck a bargain with existence by coming to terms with the Symbolic (ibid 209). The speaking subject is therefore aware of death because language is rooted in lack and signifies 'the possibility of our own demise' (ibid 219). To speak is to therefore acknowledge one's own mortality, while the mute subject, such as the asymbolic melancholic, keeps the sense of death at bay, indicating a further link between the subject's psychological state and interaction with death.

Writing, the move away from asymbolia and melancholia

Prior to meeting Agnis, as a subject living in mourning for the lost object, Quoyle hadn't moved beyond the pre-mirror phase self and had failed to develop an adult subjectivity characterized by successful entrance into the Symbolic. In taking a journalist job at the local newspaper *The Gammy Bird*, however, Quoyle begins to secure an autonomous subjectivity by being forced to employ language to counter the predominant symptom of his melancholia (his asymbolia). At first Quoyle is reluctant to take the job at *The Gammy Bird* because, in addition to reporting the shipping news (which means being around water a lot), he also has to cover local car crashes, which is difficult for him after Petal's traumatic death. Unfortunately for Quoyle, his first day at *The Gammy Bird* takes him to the scene of a car crash, where an errant moose crossing the road caused both occupants of the vehicle to be killed on impact. When Quoyle arrives on the scene the bodies (of the people and the moose) are spread around the wreckage.

Having witnessed the salvaging of Petal's crashed car, Quoyle encounters some traumatic re-experiencing symptoms from the sight, namely a repeated flashback of the moment the waterlogged car, with Petal's dead body still in it, is pulled from the water in Poughkeepsie. This is the last image Quoyle has of Petal, and the suffering he experiences because of it, combined with his inability to articulate it, places this image in traumatic memory (alongside the memories of his father abusing him) – unspeakable, temporally transcendent and utterly distressing. When Quoyle arrives at the car crash scene in Killick-Claw, this traumatic memory is triggered by the similar carnage in front of him. The dead driver's lifeless leg hangs from the car door, but Quoyle sees Petal's fishnet stockings and high-heeled boots instead. He responds viscerally to the image by vomiting into the roadside gutter, a Kristevan revealing of the link between psychological state and corporeal reality.

Yet as Quoyle struggles with the grisly scene, the attending fire officer and his photographer colleague discuss the luck of hitting such a large moose; 'a gift really, when you think about it, out of season like that, a moose that size'. This dislocation between Quoyle's agitated psychological state and the blasé attitude of the people around him reaffirms and echoes the sense of isolation and difference which the depressive suffers from in group situations. Furthermore, the disjuncture between the gruesomeness and trauma of the scene and the flippancy of the words used to discuss the moose, ('I suppose we could split it four ways right? How much could you fit in that station wagon there?'), also reaffirm the senselessness of language for the melancholic suffering from asymbolia; the words being exchanged between the other two men seem utterly absurd to Quoyle in that horrendous moment.

Customarily Quoyle would respond to this situation by retreating further into asymbolia, perhaps not speaking for hours, or even days, finding some vague comfort in the disconnection of an asymbolic universe. However, because Quoyle is now employed to write about this event he is forced to engage with it linguistically. With his livelihood dependent on this engagement, he writes about the car crash, but rather than producing a succinct and provocative story he generates a soulless, lengthy article containing multiple, banal details. Firstly, this approach mirrors what he perceives as the absurd 'gabbling' of the fireman and photographer at the scene. Secondly, it demonstrates his asymbolia, but this time through the written word rather than the spoken word; his excessive use of words, bereft of meaning, simply get churned out and churned out, much like the thousands of copies of the *Poughkeepsie News* that he previously watched rotating through the printing press.

The newspaper owner Jack chastises him later by saying, 'I took a chance on you Quoyle. Don't let me down' (thereby implying that he already has). These words resonate with Quoyle because they echo the negative things his father used to say to him. Characteristic of the melancholic who turns hatred for the m(other) into self-hate, rather than assertively responding to Jack's threat, Quoyle internalizes and inverts Jack's anger, converting it into more self-doubt and sadness. Quoyle's colleague Billy encourages him to 'Find the center of your story, the beating heart of it', a metaphorical reference to Quoyle developing his own subjectivity through his writing. Interestingly, Billy's gentle encouragement, as opposed to derisive disappointment, fosters some motivation in Quoyle to continue. Obvious though it is, where Quoyle has an inherent mechanism which turns the anger of the Other into self-hate, he doesn't have an inherent mechanism which automatically turns the kindness of the Other into self-love. Consequentially, Quoyle writes a controversial article about a locally berthed yacht which formally belonged to Hitler, despite Jack asking him to write about something else entirely. This display of subtle persistence suggests an internal change in Quoyle, a slight hardening of his resolve and challenging of hopelessness. This is depicted visually through several low-angled close-ups of his face, which suggest small gains in power, and aurally by the soft, uplifting plucking of a string instrument, which suggests a quiet but meaningful victory. Quoyle's article is guided by his genuine interest in the yacht's owners – a wealthy, bickering, American couple whose marriage is coming apart. By writing about their lives in a meaningful way, he reclaims his own, exchanging previously senseless signs for meaningful stories, and engaging with the Symbolic in a way he never has before.

The newspaper owner Jack is delighted with the article; he assigns Quoyle a weekly additional column to cover human interest stories and bids Tert (another writer) to order Quoyle a computer. With the journalism increasing his affinity with language (both written and verbal), Quoyle has a sense of subjectivity emerging for the first time in his life. He walks to Tert's desk and states, 'IBM [computer] please'. When Tert looks displeased he repeats, 'I. B. M'. This brief exchange indicates Quoyle's increasing conceptualization of the meaning behind words; by specifying what brand of computer he wants, Quoyle understands that he is an increasingly important employee at *The Gammy Bird*, but more importantly, the *repetition* of the acronym – 'I. B. M' – signifies that Quoyle is able to secure these unstable signifiers (arbitrary because they are an acronym) to meaning. In other words, the process of writing (and therefore engaging heavily with language) facilitates Quoyle's movement away from the meaninglessness of asymbolia, generating new depth and connection where there was previously only hollowness.

In addition to a shift away from asymbolia, Quoyle's writing has other positive effects on his melancholia. Firstly, the success of his article lifts his self-esteem by confirming that he is a capable writer and a valuable employee at *The Gammy Bird*. Secondly, the choice he made to write the unsanctioned piece verifies that positive things can come from his productivity, rather than from his passivity. And thirdly, his increased command of language allows him to communicate freely with his colleagues, who become his friends, thereby reducing the chronic sense of isolation the melancholic suffers. Essentially, Quoyle's interaction with language sees him integrating properly into the Symbolic and moving away from mourning for the lost object. This new acceptance of language as a substitute for the lost object is evident in the scene when he re-introduces himself to Wavey by saying, 'I … I'm a journalist myself'. This reference to himself ('*I … I'm* a journalist myself') signifies his movement into the Symbolic where he distinguishes himself as separate from the m(other) through use of the term 'I'. The ownership of his profession ('I … I'm a *journalist* myself') signifies an embracing of identity which, somewhat ironically, actually revolves around language, rather than the asymbolic shunning of it. In other words, Quoyle's work as a journalist enables his development of a subjectivity outside of melancholia, a subjectivity beyond a life full of death.

Death and surprising survival

Despite the way in which language enables Quoyle to shift away from a subjectivity intrinsically linked to death, death can also be witnessed through language; another connection between the subject's psychological state and relationship with death. This is because death can be seen 'in the dissociation of form itself, when form is distorted, abstracted, disfigured, hollowed out' (Kristeva *Black Sun* 27). Therefore, as death can be seen in the fragmentation of form, this reaffirms that Quoyle's work at the newspaper, which gradually sees him stringing disconnected words into publishable paragraphs, is synonymous with movement away from death, and a 'normatively' increased fear of it. So, Quoyle's shift away from the melancholic state is demonstrated by his new engagement with language, but it is also acutely depicted in a scene where his death seems imminent and frightening. Razinsky claims that people fear death because it is external to them (135). For example, one is hit *by* a car or *contracts* a disease, and yet melancholia is death internalized. Melancholia is the living death which defies Kristeva's horror about the corpse; Kristeva argues that the corpse is the ultimate signifier of abjection, the actualization of crossing the life and death boundary, and yet the melancholic subject breeches this boundary every day. Because Quoyle embodies the living-death of melancholia, he has a ghostly presence on screen (similar to Reznik in *The Machinist*), as if he is not really present in the physical world – a further confirmation that a subject's psychological state is intimately connected with their corporeal reality, their sense of temporality and their relationship with death. This spectral quality, combined with his suicidality during his time with Petal, suggests a disinterest in resisting death the way other (non-melancholics) do. However, at a pivotal moment in the later part of *The Shipping News*, when death seems both ingrained in Quoyle and imminent for him, he chooses instead to fight for life – another indication that he is moving further away from melancholic despondence and towards a 'normative' fear of death.

After Quoyle's confidence is boosted by the success of his journalism, he faces his fear of water and braves the bay outside Killick-Claw on a small motor boat. He turns the rudder too quickly, floods the vessel and ends up capsized in the middle of the sea. Not being able to swim, just as when he was a child, he begins to sink beneath the water. His panicked psychological state is conveyed through a series of quickly intercut point-of-view shots, with frames that are highly mobile and covered in water and bubbles. A dramatic orchestral track featuring string instruments, the distorted sound from beneath the water surface, and Quoyle's own gasps for breath, aurally accompany the visuals to reinforce his terror. As he struggles, two flashbacks intrude up on his vision – a low-angled image of his father, Guy, standing on the wharf after pushing him in, and the image of Petal, rowing away from Quoyle in a small boat. The appearance of Guy and Petal at this critical moment has three separate meanings.

Firstly, as Quoyle attempted to use Petal to fill the void of the lost object, the image of her receding into the distance represents Quoyle's movement away from an identity rooted in mourning for the (m)other, in exchange for entrance into the Symbolic. Secondly, the images confirm that Quoyle's recollections of his father's and Petal's abuse linger in his traumatic memory, and that they re-emerge at this moment because they are triggered by other traumatic encounters (such as the moose car crash scene, or in this case, the fear of drowning). Thirdly, the appearance of Guy and Petal at the moment when Quoyle is drowning suggests that Guy, Petal and the water are all part of the same abusive force – equally antagonistic and all indifferent to his suffering. This three-way alignment between the ocean, Petal and Guy reveal them each as signifiers of death: the ocean as the force which threatens death by drowning; Petal as the substitute for the (m)other who threatens death by melancholia; and Guy as the abusive force who perpetuates self-hate and worthlessness, and therefore also threatens death by melancholia.

When Quoyle catches sight of a cooler bin floating several meters away, he splashes towards it, shunning the images of his abusers and moving away from death in the process. He clings to the cooler bin for several hours, determined to stay afloat, even into the darkness of the night. Quoyle's rare show of tenacity is depicted through a medium close-up of his frightened face, which pulls out into an extreme long shot, of him bobbing alone in the empty ocean. The fight that Quoyle puts up to survive comes as something of a surprise, as for most of the film he is living the figurative death of the melancholic, and for some of the film he is even suicidal. However, at the opportunity for suicide, so near the death he believed he sought, his movement away from melancholia is explicitly conveyed in his struggle to survive the capsize. By kicking himself back above the surface, moving towards the cooler bin and holding onto it into the freezing hours of the night, Quoyle affirms that, rather than 'letting go' and drowning, he *chooses* to stay alive. This action both undermines any lingering inclination to suicide and rejects the melancholic's typically passive and defeatist response to struggle; Quoyle's changing relationship with death (which moves from an embrace to a shun) reveals a shift in his psychological state from despondent melancholic to a subject who is temporally present in the Symbolic.

Conclusion: The struggle with sadness and subtle shift

Where clinical psychology refers to the experience of persistently suffering from a low mood, causing impairment to functioning, as major depressive disorder (or more colloquially 'depression'),[1] psychoanalysis recognizes this experience as melancholia. Yet, where the described symptoms of depression and melancholia are essentially identical, clinical psychology's DSM-V focuses only on symptomatology, diagnosis and treatment, whereas the psychoanalytic approach is also interested in psychosocial origins and mechanism. In either case, the subject suffering from depression/melancholia is dominated by affect.

As a melancholic, Quoyle's lived experience is characterized by overwhelming sadness and despondency. Believing himself to be fundamentally flawed, he struggles with suicidal ideation, feelings of worthlessness, self-doubt, hopelessness and a skewed sense of temporal reality which perpetuates isolation. *The Shipping News* reflects Quoyle's melancholia through a dreary colour palette and subdued settings, while also depicting his psychological state through the physicality of the character; he dresses blandly, looks tired and expressionless, and moves slowly and blunderingly. The most significant characterization of Quoyle's melancholia, however, is his decreased and difficult relationship with language. In both dialogue and narration Quoyle's voice has a monotonous, flat quality. His speech, which is limited to begin with, is also riddled with stuttering, unnecessary pauses and silences. These linguistic symptoms come from the affect of asymbolia, which fosters the sense that language is meaningless.

Each infant goes through the process of separating from the (m)other and encountering the void of the lost object. However, where most subjects adopt language as a substitute for the loss of the mother, the melancholic refuses the exchange, and constantly encounters the void instead. Kristeva refers to this melancholic mechanism as the 'denial of negation', and the subject fails to enter successfully into the Symbolic, remaining dedicated to mourning the lost object instead. As a result, the melancholic finds the signs of language (words) to be meaningless, hollow and nonsensical – and this is the symptom of asymbolia. In an attempt to fill the void incurred by separation from the mother *and* the denial of negation, Quoyle enters into two romantic relationships where he

---

[1] The persistently low mood must also be accompanied by three of the following symptoms: significant weight loss; insomnia or hypersomnia; psychomotor retardation or agitation; fatigue or loss of energy; feelings of worthlessness and/or guilt; diminished concentration and decision-making skills; or recurrent thoughts of death or suicidal ideation (APA).

perceives the 'new' woman may be able to fill the void. But in both cases, Quoyle is unsuccessful in this goal – firstly because Petal, the female narcissist, has an agenda of her own, and secondly because Wavey, the female melancholic, has a void of her own. In both cases the woman cannot be used to plug the void left by primal wounding. The only way for Quoyle to be free of his ever-present sense of the void is to go through the process of negation, to accept language as a substitute for the absent (m)other and to belatedly enter the Symbolic as an adult.

Quoyle is able to counteract the asymbolia by taking a journalist job which forces him to engage with language on a regular basis and in a skilled, meaningful way. In essence he exchanges the senseless and hollow signs of asymbolia for stories about local people which hold interest for him. His work therefore generates a currency which enables, for the first time, the development of his subjectivity beyond melancholic mourning for the lost object. At the start of *The Shipping News* Quoyle does not fear death, embracing it instead through his melancholia. However, as the melancholia retreats through increased engagement with language, a fear of death emerges. This fear helps Quoyle to stay alive when he previously would have let the ocean take him to a watery end, and affirms Kristeva's notion that Quoyle, who is no longer melancholic, can endure Eros, the life drive.

Conclusion

This book sought to explore psychological disorder as part of human reality by using cinematic texts as investigative tools. Although this book acknowledges the more common and topical psychological disorders of the present period through its inclusion of six particular film characters, it did not set out to investigate sociological trends or population movements in the area of mental health. Instead, this book has sought to acknowledge disordered psychology as an intrinsic, normative and common aspect of the human lived experience.

My initial approach to this subject area was through the consideration of internal, psychological suffering as part of the lived experience for *some* people; it appeared that certain individuals were consistently plagued by it, while others encountered it occasionally, and others still seemed to avoid that occurrence entirely. It also seemed that psychological disorder was best addressed by using the diagnostic tools and treatments of the modern medical profession, since these are both pragmatic and culturally pervasive. At this point, it had not occurred to me that states of psychological disorder which inflicted suffering upon the individual were actually *part* of the experience of being alive; rather, I perceived them to be extraneous to the normal lived experience.

Upon reading key literature by Freud and Lacan, it became apparent that psychoanalysis is open to an exploration of psychological suffering beyond the confines of diagnosis and treatment. Indeed, Lacan, Kristeva and Žižek – the latter two themselves heavily influenced by Lacan – argue that the lived experience intrinsically involves suffering because of the subject's self-alienation. Through an increasing familiarity with psychoanalysis as a philosophy, I came to understand that psychological suffering has varied manifestations, multiple and complex origins, and no 'hard and fast' answers or solutions. In other words, I recognized that psychoanalysis accepts psychological suffering, not as extraneous to the normal lived experience, but as inherent to it.

At this realization I embarked on this research, wanting to bridge the approach that holds psychological disorder to be part of the human lived experience *and* the approach that holds psychological disorder to be diagnosable using particular criteria. In an area dedicated to assisting with human suffering, it seems vitally important that the two approaches (modern clinical psychology and psychoanalysis) are applied together more often. Rather than devoting the research to a strict divide that uses one of these philosophies while deriding the other, I wanted to acknowledge the merits of both approaches, and have them work together to better understand and assist people who are suffering.

Herein lies the oft-ignored common denominator of modern clinical psychology and psychoanalysis: they both attempt to decrease human suffering and therefore need to engage in a more effective and productive dialogue to allow this to happen. This book acknowledges the merits of both approaches – complementing and enhancing the other, rather than detracting from each other. Psychoanalysis, for example, looks at where the suffering stems from: why is it there? what initiated it? how did it evolve? when did it start? Through the Diagnostic and Statistical Manual [DSM], clinical psychology is more engaged with how that suffering manifests through symptoms: what behaviours have changed? what thought processes are occurring? how do these changes impact daily functioning? A theoretical framework which combines origin and evolution *with* symptomatology and diagnosis is essentially utilizing the 'best of both worlds' for the most rounded and complex understanding of the subject. This philosophy, which argues that origin, development, manifestation and classification are best acknowledged as an interconnected set of factors, also highlights that the lived experience consists of a multitude of psychological states (as opposed to a binary between 'mentally ill' and 'mentally healthy'), and these states may lie dormant, manifest or resolve themselves at any point in the life cycle.

Another positive benefit of recognizing that psychological disorder is part of the normal lived experience is that post-diagnosis there are more options for the individual; without a deviant versus normative dichotomy putting pressure on treatment and cure, notions of 'overcoming', 'healing' or 'fixing' have less imperative. Indeed, part of the draw of applying psychoanalysis here is that it avoids pathologizing the subject and therefore avoids the suggestion of 'returning' to an improved or 'better' state of health. By overlaying the DSM, clinical psychology's diagnostic tool, onto psychoanalysis, this investigation suggests that being alive includes a range of psychological variability, and that, while I am not suggesting that 'anything goes', I do argue that everyone is abnormal to some extent.

With psychological disorder acknowledged as a normative aspect of the lived experience, the suffering individual can instead focus on better self-knowledge and improved comprehension of their state as opposed to a focus on a 'return' to a 'normal' state. This development alone may be enough to alleviate suffering in some individuals. Others may use their new self-knowledge to live more effectively *with* the disorder by negotiating an existence which involves perceiving the disorder as part of their reality or part of their subjectivity (either temporarily or permanently). This book therefore has subtly avoided making definitive summaries of how, when or if, the cinematic characters' disorders ended, focusing instead on cause (the origin of the disorder), mechanism (the psychical process and development of the disorder) and affect (the symptoms which manifest) within the narrative trajectory of each film.

Keeping in mind the intention to use clinical modern psychology and psychoanalysis in *conjunction* with one another, each film features a central character who is, firstly, diagnosed using the DSM-V's categorization of symptomatology and, secondly, is observed from a psychoanalytic standpoint. The psychoanalytic approach predominantly uses either Lacanian, Žižekian or Kristevan philosophy and enables, beyond symptomatology, a discussion of cause, mechanism and affect. The findings elicited by using this dual approach are informative, complex and deeply useful for better understanding the human experience of psychological suffering.

Psychological disorder, and the associated suffering, can be studied from an exclusively clinical perspective. However, I chose to address these issues through film because the use of a mediating element provides insight and perspective which is otherwise unavailable through a purely clinical methodology. Clinical case studies are often emotionless and empirical, limited by the professional discourse between patient and analyst, and heavily dependent on the author's literary skills. Because film uses a combination of still and moving imagery, sound, special effects and editing, it is a particularly adroit means of conveying complex internal psychical states. In other words, the aesthetic versatility of the medium, which transmits to both visual and aural senses, is able to portray psychological disorder and suffering more effectively than often straightforwardly factual methods. Additionally, film is a socially situated medium, meaning it is influenced by the socio-cultural context of its production. Recent film (from within the last 25 years) therefore reflects the prevalence of psychological disorder and suffering in contemporary society. By serving as both a reflexive art form and cultural phenomenon, film offers a rich sociological basis for an investigation into the human lived experience.

Other than the fact that all six films feature a central character with a disorder that is diagnosable using the DSM-V, there were two motivations for including these particular films. Firstly, I included an equal combination of male and female characters who, as a group, reflect that psychological disorder and suffering affects both genders, albeit often in differential ways depending on how gender roles or expectations relate to the depicted disorder. Secondly, none of these films attempt to solve or heal the character in a way that undermines the psychoanalytic philosophy of promoting self-knowledge. Instead, these texts are content to portray the diegetic arc of psychological disorder without an onus on improvement or recovery. This leaves the narrative free to concentrate on the trajectory of suffering, and allowed me, the analyst, to concentrate on origin, mechanism and affect.

The *Black Swan* chapter used the Lacanian mirror stage to investigate the acute psychosis of a prima ballerina (Nina) in the New York City Ballet. The mirror stage theory proposes that, by first identifying with a reflection, the subject forms an identity based on an image so that the understanding of 'the self' is founded on the *image* of the self. The resultant internalization of the external image and subsequent development of subjectivity disguises the pre-mirror phase, non-unified subject. This chapter also utilized Lacan's writing about the cause of psychosis; when primal repression is foreclosed, no Name-of-the-Father paternal metaphor develops and no Oedipus complex occurs. Therefore, because Nina never moved through the Oedipus complex, as an adult she continues to live in the pre-Oedipal dyad with her mother Erica, rather than in the Symbolic of adult autonomy, and her realization of this anomaly, combined with huge professional pressure, generates the onset of an acute psychotic episode.

I used the mirror phase theory to argue that Nina's ego is grounded in her ability to perform herself as bodily image, which means that the mirrors in *Black Swan* function as visual depictions of 'her' as an identity based predominantly on image, thus depriving her of a place in the Symbolic. The primary symptom of her psychosis (hallucinations) reveal that, while fruitlessly striving to be her imago (the White Swan), Nina subconsciously interprets herself as fractured and incomplete, depicted through the emergence of Black Swan body parts within her own flesh. However, the presence of the White Swan is as much a manifestation of Nina's psychosis as the Black Swan; the White Swan cannot provide Nina with stable self-hood and is only an image to aspire to in the same way that the Black Swan is an image to fear. Furthermore, Nina's final statement ('I was perfect') suggests that her psychosis actually assisted her movement into the self-actualization of the Symbolic, where she uses language to distinguish herself as an autonomous subject for the first time. Ultimately, Nina's psychological disorder (brief psychotic disorders) is actually the catalyst which breaks her perfectionist delusions, her dependence on her mother, and her confinement in the Imaginary, pushing her into the autonomy of the Symbolic, where she can identify as something beyond an image.

Lacan's mirror stage theory also has relevance to *The Machinist*, given Reznik's relationship with his own bodily image. Yet, rather than these reflective surfaces portraying conscious and unconscious representations of the ego (as with Nina in *Black Swan*), they demonstrate the compartmentalizing of Reznik's psyche, where his superego is projected outwards onto a separate person (Ivan). The battle in *The Machinist* therefore involves *reunifying* Reznik's divided subjectivity through an admission of guilt, rather than the recognition in *Black Swan* that the two mirror images (White Swan and Black Swan) are both *separate* aspects of Nina's subjectivity.

Reznik is a visually unusual and memorable character because of his emaciated physique, yet his emaciation is just one sign of several clues that he is suffering psychologically. *The Machinist* is a film full of cinematic red herrings which distract both the viewer and Reznik to keep them from recognizing that the strange things occurring originate in an internal space – his own psyche. The trauma of killing a child (and then fleeing the scene to avoid punishment) is located in the Real, which resists representation in the Symbolic. Reznik's knowledge of this incident is therefore repressed in his unconscious, to exist for a year as what Žižek refers to as an 'unknown known'. Having repressed the memory of the fatal car accident, *The Machinist* is a film which confirms how physically, socially and psychologically destructive guilt can be when it is not acknowledged on a conscious level, manifesting instead through insomnia, emaciation and paranoia.

As Nina in *Black Swan* hallucinates the appearance of swan body parts emerging through her own body, Reznik hallucinates a man called Ivan, whose presence is also threatening and sinister. However, as Ivan is the hallucinatory projection of Reznik's own superego, the internalized Name-of-the-Father, his portrayal as someone who can't be trusted is an unconscious projection of how Reznik feels about himself – untrustworthy and guilty. As Reznik's superego,

Ivan's presence transcends normal limits of time, space and significance. Žižek acknowledges that Ivan functions, not as a father-figure, but as the embodiment of law. Encouraging Reznik to hand himself over to the police (which allows him to sleep), Ivan functions in a similar role to the Black Swan in *Black Swan*, where the figure who first appears to be a menacing antagonist is eventually revealed to be the visual projection of unconscious knowledge, and an unlikely facilitator of psychological progress.

Lisbeth Salander from *The Girl with the Dragon Tattoo* also visually projects her traumatized psychological state. Yet, where Nina and Reznik project aspects of their psyche onto separate 'people' (the Black Swan, the White Swan and Ivan), Lisbeth portrays her internal psychological state through the vehicle of her own body. Using Kristeva's theory of abjection in conjunction with psychoanalytic trauma theory, the chapter argues that *Dragon Tattoo* confirms that traumatic experience fundamentally changes the subject. Through the transgression of corporeal and ethical boundaries during rape, Lisbeth's body is rendered a site of abjection. Lisbeth visualizes this trauma through her physical appearance, thereby engaging in a simultaneous movement towards and away from the abject. By displaying her internal anger and hostility on an external surface (her appearance), she engages in a Kristevan attempt to expel the abject. This attempt to rid herself of the abject is unsuccessful because, by trying to externalize it, she instead expresses and embraces it as an aspect of a new, post-trauma identity.

Following an abusive childhood and the sexual assault at age twenty-four, Lisbeth develops post-traumatic stress disorder [PTSD]. Her symptoms extend over several sub-groups including 're-experiencing', 'mood alterations' and 'increased arousal', which manifest predominantly as nightmares, flashbacks, inter-personal hostility, hypervigilance and irritability. These post-trauma symptoms emerge belatedly in response to a mind overwhelmed at the time of the assault, which psychically dissociates in an attempt to protect itself. Lisbeth's trauma, located in the horrific Real, is therefore not reducible to a single event but transcends the confines of normal temporal realities through the repetition of PTSD symptoms that re-enact the trauma *and* through her continual engagement with the abject. Because the Real isn't directly representable, trauma is essentially witnessed through the affect it has on the subject, or what I refer to as 'the carnage it leaves in it its wake'. Yet, while Lisbeth's re-experiencing symptoms and embodiment of abjection seem counter-productive in many ways, they also fuel her survival and strengthen her resilience in a frightening post-trauma landscape; she is fundamentally changed by the trauma, but she is not broken.

Michael is another character who is fundamentally changed by traumatic experience in *Brødre*. As a former prisoner of war he discerns an unequivocal and integral difference between himself and others, which prevents him from emotionally connecting with people. Forced to kill a junior comrade in the captive situation, Michael's ethically and morally unblemished ego is ripped apart, replaced by two levels of substantial guilt which inform his adjustment disorder upon return home. As part of the canon of post-9/11 films, *Brødre* also works in a similar way to Lisbeth's traumatic memory, with the proliferative viewing of this subgenre functioning like replays of the traumatic moment in the traumatized subject's mind; the 'subject' of this scenario being the Western hemisphere and the trauma referred to being 9/11. However, unlike *Dragon Tattoo*, in which Lisbeth's sense of difference spawns from the actions of an(Other) transgressing her boundaries, Michael's traumatized psychological state is based on his own transgression of boundaries.

In the moment where Michael is forced to kill his junior comrade he experiences a totally unexpected moment of pleasure, which emerges in response to a rare release from the restriction of his own superego. I refer to this encounter, where he is forced into killing and therefore escapes the normal inhibitions of responsibility, as the 'freedom in being forced'. Yet this transgression ruptures Michael's perception of himself so fundamentally that it functions as what Žižek refers to as an 'Event', which radically reframes his lived experience and identity. When Michael returns home he adopts rigid emotional detachment as the primary symptom of his adjustment disorder, attempting to assuage his guilt and reinstate his moral cleanliness through behaviour which is strictly militaristic and unemotional. At this point *Brødre* reveals that transgression of boundaries and subsequent guilt cannot be 'undone' through emotional detachment and Michael's psychological suffering only increases when he adopts this approach and further isolates himself. When Michael eventually confides in an(Other), the Event, which had been rendered temporarily nullified (in what I refer to as an 'absent-event'), is pulled into the Symbolic again through Michael's retelling. Each of his emotional detachment symptoms, which had functioned as placeholders for the absent-event, is exchanged for representation in the Symbolic – words. It is at this point of emotional re-attachment that Michael's humanity begins to return and the *possibility* of recovery appears.

Where Michael emotionally detaches from society following trauma, *Copycat*'s Helen Hudson physically detaches by remaining behind the walls of her safe zone. Helen's agoraphobia develops following a traumatic attack and consists of panic symptoms and avoidance behaviours in response to anxiety. Unable to transcend spatial boundaries, agoraphobia reduces Helen to a pre-Symbolic infantile level of freedom and autonomy, with her apartment functioning as a uterine space. Like *Dragon Tattoo*'s Lisbeth and *Brødre*'s Michael, Helen is fundamentally changed by the trauma she encounters. However, unlike Lisbeth, who psychically dissociates during her rape, Helen has an uninterrupted view of her assault as it plays out in a large reflective surface. The result of this unremitting view is that Helen engages in a reverse mirror stage; helpless, immobilized and dependent on an Other in the attack, Helen's ego (which is usually autonomous, successful and independent) is inverted, inducing a dissolution of her subjectivity which removes her from the Symbolic. *Copycat* therefore highlights that the subject's movement through the stages of human development does not necessarily consist of singular, linear events; rather, they may be repeated, reversed and, as with Nina's delayed Oedipal complex in *Black Swan*, these stages can occur in adulthood.

However, where *Black Swan* draws a link between subjectivity and image, *Copycat* delineates identity through physical and spatial boundaries. Helen's agoraphobic restriction to her apartment denotes her as abnormal, expelled from the world of adult autonomy and psychologically suffering. While Helen makes these sacrifices in exchange for a sense of safety, the weakness of her psychological disorder is that the resurrection of such boundaries is an invitation to infringement – either through individuals entering her space, through objects contaminating her space or through her own memories of the trauma. Additionally, confined to the domain of the pre-Symbolic, she lacks the tools to state, 'I am anxious', resorting to bodily panic attack symptoms to express her anxiety. Eventually recognizing that the Other she fears is also insecure and dependent, Helen demonstrates a show of agency and autonomy during a replica attack. She further solidifies her movement back into the Symbolic by verbally degrading her assailant and then physically assaulting him with a literal fragment of her own image (a shard of mirror glass). The notion that Helen re-enters the Symbolic (but this time as an adult) is confirmed in the final scenes, which show her transcending the space of her uterine apartment.

The Shipping News also asserts that movement into the Symbolic is not limited to infancy, featuring a character who spends a significant period of his life suffering from the asymbolia of melancholia. In a lived experience constituted by sadness, the melancholic is dominated by affect. For much of *The Shipping News* Quoyle manifests this severe and sustained depression through low mood, passivity, and most importantly, the limited language of asymbolia. As a melancholic he also experiences a warped sense of temporality, feeling cut off from the present and failing to detect a future. As the walking personification of depressive disorder Quoyle is an onscreen wound, representing the presence of death within life. In a similar way to Reznik in *The Machinist*, Quoyle has a ghostly capacity, as if not quite alive in the physical world, yet anchored there by his own corporeal reality.

Rejecting language as a substitute for the loss of *das Ding*, the disavowal of negation lays the foundation for Quoyle's constant sense of lack. He fails to move successfully into the Symbolic order, finding neither comfort or meaning in words, with language appearing nonsensical and hollow. Similarly to Nina in *Black Swan* and Helen in *Copycat*, Quoyle is a character who, despite his adult years, exists outside the Symbolic order, struggling (and failing) to generate an autonomous subjectivity in the face of this banishment. By taking a new job as a journalist Quoyle is forced to engage with the currency of the Symbolic (language) consistently and adroitly. In an exchange of meaningless signs for meaningful stories, he begins to integrate properly into the Symbolic, finally embracing language as an adequate substitute for the Thing. This transition also signals the development of his subjectivity beyond mourning for the lost object and the personification of 'death in the living world'. Quoyle's presence in the Symbolic is confirmed in a scene where, faced with the proposition of death, he instead chooses to fight for his life, moving against the suicidality, passivity and mournfulness which had characterized his melancholia.

Three other themes emerge when these films are viewed collectively, as opposed to individually or in comparison to one other. Firstly, the relationship between corporeal reality and psychological state is evident in every one of these films; Nina's psychosis develops in response to a stressful career in the 'aesthetic profession' of ballet and a fear of her incomplete subjectivity literally pushes through the boundaries of her corporeal reality; Reznik's body deteriorates in response to his guilt; Lisbeth uses her body to project anger and hostility after her corporeal reality is violated; Michael attempts to abate his guilt by engaging in emotionally detached behaviour which is visualized through bodily posture, gesture and facial expression; Helen is unable to express her anxiety linguistically so conveys it instead through bodily symptoms of panic; and Quoyle embodies severe depression through his listless physicality. As the subject's corporeal reality can express guilt (Reznik and Michael), fear (Nina, Lisbeth and Helen), or despair (Quoyle), the manifestation of these physical symptoms confirms the link between the suffering subject's internal, psychological condition and corporeal state; the experience in, and of, one's own body is therefore integral to the lived experience.

The second common element in all of these films is the subject's altered sense of temporality; Nina's psychosis is, by definition, a break from the reality of the moment, with her hallucinations allowing her to enter into an atemporal conversation with her own unconscious; Reznik's combination of insomnia, emaciation and paranoia gives him a spectral quality, as if he is not really present in time or space. His post-trauma amnesia also succeeds at (temporarily) erasing a specific, traumatic moment in time; the re-experiencing symptoms of PTSD pull Lisbeth back into the time and location of her trauma; as a captive subject, Michael uses voluntary dissociation techniques to transcend the confines of his current place and time (his cell), while the nullification of the 'absent-event' shifts the traumatic incident from Symbolic temporality to the atemporal landscape of the Real, until he recounts it; Helen's physical panic symptoms, which are induced by anxiety, transcend temporalities by pulling her back into the same psychological space as her assault. In addition, her agoraphobia promotes the dissolution of adult subjectivity by allowing her to psychically regress to the apartment-womb of her infantile pre-Symbolic; Quoyle's melancholia promotes a skewed sense of time where it seems life has already 'gone', and he exists neither in the present or future. Each of these characters' sense of temporality is affected by their psychological disorder. Frequently this altered sense of time is part of the affect of the disorder (as with Nina, Lisbeth, Helen and Quoyle) but temporal abnormalities can also be employed, consciously or unconsciously, as defence or coping mechanisms (as with Reznik and Michael). In either case, the alteration to the subject's sense of temporality inflicts further suffering, confirming that a sense of time (altered or not) is inherent to every lived experience.

Finally, death has a strong presence in all of these films. Nina's belated movement into the Symbolic occurs at the moment of her death; Reznik's insomnia develops out of causing the death of a child; Lisbeth's PTSD is the result of surviving a situation where death is a strong possibility; Michael's adjustment disorder is derived from being forced to kill another person, or die himself; Helen's agoraphobia is a response to surviving a situation which nearly killed her; and Quoyle's melancholia is the personification of death in the absence of subjectivity. The presence of death within each of these narratives suggests that, in addition to death being a part of every subject's lived experience, it is also has strong connections with the subject's psychological state. For example, when the subject is *threatened* with death by an Other (as with Lisbeth and Helen), psychical mechanisms kick in that attempt to protect the subject through dissociation in the moment, or through defensive mechanisms afterwards. A subject who *causes* the death of an Other (as with Reznik and Michael) is also traumatically affected but suffers the psychical mechanism of guilt, as opposed to protection. Furthermore, the subject who remains overly *connected* with death through their inability to separate from the m(Other) (as with Nina and Quoyle) suffers the existence of a life without autonomous subjectivity, a life without 'self'. Indeed, *all* subjects must live with death, as none of us is immortal. Yet the subject's proximity to, and engagement with, death can – and often does – lead to their psychical suffering, reinforcing the notion that psychological disorder is part of the spectrum of human experience, rather than a binary of order and disorder.

Using a combined clinical psychology and psychoanalytic approach, the individual readings of these films illuminate how complex the origin, mechanism and affect of psychological disorder can be. They suggest that psychological suffering may occur at any of these stages, and that psychological disorder, as a deeply complex and hugely varied reality, is part of the normative lived experience, rather than extraneous to it. The interpretation of these texts as a collective group confirms the link between psychological suffering and the normal lived experience, with three generic existential elements emerging as commonalities across all six films. Together, embodiment, time and death constitute the human lived experience; the psyche its interface with the physical, the temporal and the transcendent.

Works cited

Allen, Richard. 'Psychoanalytic Film Theory.' *A Companion to Film Theory*, edited by Toby Miller and Robert Stam, Oxford: Blackwell, 1999, pp. 123–45.

American Psychiatric Association [APA], editor. *Diagnostic and Statistical Manual of Mental Disorders: DSM-5*. Online edition, Washington DC: APA, 2013. https://dsm-psychiatryonline-org.ezproxy.auckland.ac.nz/doi/book/10.1176/appi.books.9780890425596.

Amiel, Jon. *Copycat*. Regency, 1995.

Amnesty International. 'Torture and Other Ill-Treatment.' 2017, https://www.amnesty.org/en/what-we-do/torture/. Accessed 7 March 2017.

Anderson, Brad. *The Machinist*. Filmax, 2004.

Andrade, Pilar. 'Cinema's Doubles, Their Meaning, and Literary Intertexts.' *Comparative Literature and Culture*, vol. 10, no. 4, 2008, Article 8.

Anzieu, Didier. 'Formal Signifiers and the Ego-Skin.' *Psychic Envelopes*, edited by Didier Anzieu, translated by Daphne Briggs, London: Karnac, 1990, pp. 1–25.

Anzieu, Didier, and Gilbert Tarrab. *A Skin for Thought: Interviews with Gilbert Tarrab on Psychology and Psychoanalysis*. London: Karnac, 1990.

Archer, Neil. '"The Girl with the Dragon Tattoo" (2009/2011) and the New "European Cinema".' *Film Criticism*, vol. 37, no. 2, 2012, pp. 2–21.

Aronofsky, Darren. *Black Swan*. Fox Searchlight, 2010.

Astrom, Berit, et al. *Rape in Stieg Larsson's Millennium Trilogy and Beyond: Contemporary Scandinavian and Anglophone Crime Fiction*. Kindle, London: Palgrave Macmillan, 2013.

Bartels, Klaus. 'Serial Killers: Sublimity to Be Continued. Aesthetics and Criminal History.' *Amerikastudien* [*American Studies*], vol. 43, no. 3, 1998, pp. 497–516.

Baudry, Jean-Louis. 'Ideological Effects of the Basic Cinematographic Apparatus.' *Film Quarterly*, vol. 28, no. 2, 1974, pp. 39–47, doi:10.2307/1211632.

Baughan, Nikki. 'The Reel World: Interview with Female Film Directors Susanne Bier and Haifaa Al Mansour, from Denmark and Saudi Arabia.' *Index on Censorship*, vol. 44, no. 4, 2015, pp. 11–13.

Beardsworth, Sara. *Julia Kristeva: Psychoanalysis and Modernity*. New York: State University of New York Press, 2004.

Bégin, Richard. 'The Objective: The Configuration of Trauma in the "War on Terror", or the Sublime Object of the Medium.' *Žižek and Media Studies: A Reader*, edited by Matthew Flisfeder and Louis-Paul Willis, London: Palgrave Macmillan, 2014, pp. 53–66.

Belau, Linda. 'Introduction: Remembering, Repeating, and Working-Through: Trauma and the Limit of Knowledge.' *Topologies of Trauma: Essays on the Limit of Knowedge and Memory*, edited by Linda Belau and Petar Ramadanovic, New York: Other Press, 2002, pp. xiii–xxvii.

Belau, Linda. 'Trauma, Repetition, and the Hermenutics of Psychoanalysis.' *Topologies of Trauma: Essays on the Limit of Knowedge and Memory*, edited by Linda Belau and Petar Ramadanovic, New York: Other Press, 2002, pp. 151–75.

Berger, Richard. *Active Adaptations: Killing the Girl with the Dragon Tattoo*. Poole: Bournemouth University, 2012.

Bergman, Kerstin. 'From Literary Girl to Graphic Novel Hero: Trans-Medial Transformation of Steig Larsson's Lisbeth Salander.' *The Journal of Specialised Translation*, no. 22, 2014, pp. 93–109.

Bergman, Kerstin. 'Transforming Tattoos of the Girl with the Dragon Tattoo.' *Tattoos in Crime and Detective Narratives: Marking and Remarking*, edited by Kate Watson and Katherine Cox, Manchester: Manchester University Press, 2019, pp. 95–110.

Bier, Susanne. *Brødre [Brothers]*. Two Brothers, 2004.

Bignall, Simone. 'Black Swan, Cracked Porcelain and Becoming-Animal.' *Culture, Theory and Critique*, vol. 54, no. 1, 2013, pp. 121–38, doi:10.1080/14735784.2012.749110.

Bould, Mark, et al. 'The Thin Men: Anorexic Subjectivity in Fight Club and The Machinist.' *Neo Noir*, New York: Wallflower Press, 2009, pp. 221–39.

Bourke, Joanna. 'Afterword.' *The War Body on Screen*, edited by Karen Randell and Sean Redmond, London: Continuum, 2008, pp. 266–8.

Braunstein, Nestor. 'Desire and Jouissance in the Teachings of Lacan.' *The Cambridge Companion to Lacan*, edited by Jean-Michel Rabaté, Cambridge: Cambridge University Press, 2003, pp. 102–15.

Bray, Isabelle, and David Gunnell. 'Suicide Rates, Life Satisfaction and Happiness as Markers for Population Mental Health.' *Social Psychiatry & Psychiatric Epidemiology*, vol. 41, no. 5, 2006, pp. 333–7, doi:10.1007/s00127-006-0049-z.

Brazil, Horus Vital. 'Psychoanalysis and the "Life Cycle": An Introduction.' *American Journal of Psychoanalysis*, vol. 46, no. 4, 1986, http://search.proquest.com.ezproxy.auckland.ac.nz/docview/1301636053/citation/992B61BB87374352PQ/1?accountid=8424.

Brewin, Chris. *Posttraumatic Stress Disorder: Malady or Myth?* New Haven: Yale University Press, 2003.

Bronfen, Elisabeth. *Night Passages: Philosophy, Literature, and Film*. Translated by David Brenner, New York: Columbia University Press, 2013.

Bronfen, Elisabeth. 'Risky Resemblances: On Repetition, Mourning, and Representation.' *Death and Representation*, edited by Elisabeth Bronfen and Sarah Webster Goodwin, Baltimore: Johns Hopkins University Press, 1993, pp. 103–29.

Bronfen, Elisabeth, and Sarah Webster Goodwin. 'Introduction.' *Death and Representation*, edited by Elisabeth Bronfen and Sarah Webster Goodwin, Baltimore: Johns Hopkins University Press, 1993, pp. 3–25.

Brown, Laura. 'Not Outside the Range: One Feminist Perspective on Psychic Trauma.' *Trauma: Explorations in Memory*, edited by Cathy Caruth, Baltimore: Johns Hopkins University Press, 1995, pp. 100–12.

Brunette, Peter. 'Post-Structuralism and Deconstruction.' *Film Studies: Critical Approaches*, edited by John Hill and Pamela Church Gibson, Oxford: Oxford University Press, 2000, pp. 89–93.

Capps, Lisa, and Elinor Ochs. *Constructing Panic: The Discourse of Agoraphobia.* Cambridge, MA: Harvard University Press, 1995.

Carlsten, Jennie. 'Constructing the Terrorist Subject: Michael Collins and The Terrorist as Models of Agonistic Pluralism.' *The War Body on Screen*, edited by Karen Randell and Sean Redmond, London: Continuum, 2008, pp. 154–64.

Carter, Paul. *Repressed Spaces: The Poetics of Agoraphobia.* London: Reaktion Books, 2002.

Caruth, Cathy. 'An Interview with Jean Laplanche.' *Topologies of Trauma: Essays on the Limit of Knowedge and Memory*, edited by Linda Belau and Petar Ramadanovic, New York: Other Press, 2002, pp. 101–25.

Caruth, Cathy. 'Recapturing the Past: Introduction.' *Trauma: Explorations in Memory*, edited by Cathy Caruth, Baltimore: Johns Hopkins University Press, 1995, pp. 151–7.

Catharina, Landstrom. 'Technosubjects on Film: Taking Feminist Technology Studies to the Movies.' *Kritikos: An International and Interdisciplinary Journal of Postmodern Cultural Sound, Text and Image*, vol. 1, 2004.

Chiesa, Marco. 'Research and Psychoanalysis: Still Time to Bridge the Great Divide?' *Psychoanalytic Psychology*, vol. 27, no. 2, 2010, pp. 99–114, doi: 10.1037/10019413.

Choudbury, Poulomi. *Negotiating Identity from the Margin of Modifications: 'Reading' Larsson's Lisbeth through Transformation of the Body.* Seattle: Amazon Digital Services, 2015.

Chow, Rey. 'Film and Cultural Identity.' *Film Studies: Critical Approaches*, edited by John Hill and Pamela Church Gibson, Oxford: Oxford University Press, 2000, pp. 167–73.

Clover, Joshua. 'The Looking Class.' *Film Quarterly*, vol. 64, no. 3, 2011, pp. 7–9, doi:10.1525/fq.2011.64.3.7.

Coleman, Lindsay. '"Damn You for Making Me Do This": Abu Ghraib, 24, Torture, and Television Sadomasochism.' *The War Body on Screen*, edited by Karen Randell and Sean Redmond, London: Continuum, 2008, pp. 199–214.

Cooke, Dervila. 'Tradition, Modernity, and the Enmeshing of Home and Away: The Shipping News and Prouxl's 1990s Newfoundland.' *Studies in Canadian Literature*, vol. 38, no. 1, 2013, pp. 190–209.

Cooper, Rachel. *Diagnosing the Diagnostic and Statistical Manual of Mental Disorders.* London: Karnac, 2014.

Corpus, Rina Angela. 'Ballet in the Dark: A Critical Review of Black Swan by Darren Aronofsky.' *Humanities Diliman*, vol. 8, no. 2, 2011, pp. 157–60, https://doaj.org/article/8841dbdb32ff4f7a9818c6f5768b0226.

Craske, Michelle G. *Origins of Phobias and Anxiety Disorders: Why More Women than Men.* Amsterdam: Elsevier, 2003.

Creed, Barbara. 'Film and Psychoanalysis.' *Film Studies: Critical Approaches*, edited by John Hill and Pamela Church Gibson, Oxford: Oxford University Press, 2000, pp. 75–88.

de Beaurs, Edwin. *The Assessment and Treatment of Panic Disorder and Agoraphobia.* London: Thesis Publishers, 1993.

de Bruyn, Dirk. *The Performance of Trauma in Moving Image Art.* Cambridge: Cambridge Scholars Publishing, 2014.

de Lauretis, Teresa. *Freud's Drive: Psychoanalysis, Literature and Film.* London: Palgrave Macmillan, 2008.

De Vos, Jan. 'Psychologization or the Discontents of Psychoanalysis.' *Journal for the Psychoanalysis of Culture and Society*, vol. 16, no. 4, 2011, pp. 354–72, doi: 10.1057/pcs.2010.29.

Demyttenaere, Koen, et al. 'Prevalence, Severity, and Unmet Need for Treatment of Mental Disorders in the World Health Organization World Mental Health Surveys.' *Journal of the American Medical Association*, vol. 291, no. 21, 2013, pp. 2581–90, doi: 10.1001/jama.291.21.2581.

Dixon, Wheeler Winston. *Film and Television after 9/11.* Carbondale: Southern Illinois University Press, 2004.

Dolgopolov, Greg. 'High Stakes: The Vampire and the Double in Russian Cinema.' *Transnational Horror Across Visual Media: Fragmented Bodies*, edited by Dana Och and Kirsten Strayer, Abingdon-on-Thames: Routledge, 2014, pp. 44–66.

Dor, Joël. *Introduction to the Reading of Lacan: The Unconscious Structured Like a Language.* New York: Other Press, 1998.

Dor, Joël. *The Clinical Lacan.* Edited by Judith Feher Gurewich and Susan Fairfield, Lanham: Jason Aronson Inc, 1997.

Dryden, Linda. *The Modern Gothic and Literary Doubles: Stevenson, Wilde and Wells.* London: Palgrave Macmillan, 2003.

Easthope, Anthony. 'Classic Film Theory.' *Film Studies: Critical Approaches*, edited by John Hill and Pamela Church Gibson, Oxford: Oxford University Press, 2000, pp. 49–55.

Easthope, Anthony. *The Unconscious.* Abingdon-on-Thames: Routledge, 1999.

Everett, Holly. 'Food, Class and the Self: Seal Flipper Pie and Class Conflict.' *Food for Thought: A Multidisciplinary Discussion*, edited by Robert Stewart and Susan Korol, Sydney (Canada): Breton University Press, 2012, pp. 71–91.

Ewald, Francois. 'Two Infinities of Risk.' *The Politics of Everyday Fear*, edited by Brian Massumi, Minneapolis: University of Minnesota Press, 1993, pp. 221–8.

Failler, Angela. 'Narrative Skin Repair: Bearing Witness to Mediatized Representations of Self-Harm.' *Skin, Culture and Psychoanalysis*, edited by Sheila Cavanagh et al., London: Palgrave Macmillan, 2013, pp. 167–87.

Fielding, Julien. 'The Machinist.' *Journal of Religion and Film*, vol. 10, no. 1, 2006, Article 11.

Fisher, Mark, and Amber Jacobs. 'Debating Black Swan: Gender and Horror.' *Film Quarterly*, vol. 65, no. 1, 2011, pp. 58–62, doi:10.1525/fq.2011.65.1.58.

Fouz-Hernandez, Santiago. 'Performing Fatness: Oversized Male Bodies in Recent Spanish Cinema.' *Performance and Spanish Film*, edited by Dean Allbritton et al., Manchester: Manchester University Press, 2016, pp. 204–19.

Frances, Allen. 'DSM in Philosophyland: Curiouser and Curiouser.' *Making the DSM-5: Concepts and Controversies*, edited by Joel Paris and James Phillips, New York: Springer, 2013, pp. 95–103.

Freeland, Cynthia. 'Explaining the Uncanny in The Double Life of Veronique.' *Horror Film and Psychoanalysis: Freud's Worst Fear*, edited by Steven Jay Schneider, Cambridge: Cambridge University Press, 2004, pp. 87–105.

Freud, Sigmund. *Civilization and Its Discontents*. Edited by James Strachey and Masud Khan, Translated by Joan Riviere, London: Hogarth Press: Institute of Psycho-analysis, 1979.

Freud, Sigmund. *The Standard Edition of the Complete Psychological Works of Sigmund Freud: The Ego and the Id and Other Works*. Edited by James Strachey, New edition, vol. 19, London: Vintage, 2001.

Friman, Patrick C., et al. 'Changes in Modern Psychology: A Citation Analysis of the Kuhnian Displacement Thesis.' *American Psychologist*, vol. 48, no. 6, 1993, pp. 658–64, doi:10.1037/0003-066X.48.6.658.

Fristanty, Sandra. *An Analysis of Trevor Reznik's Guilt in Brad Anderson's Film 'The Machinist'*. Malang: University of Muhammadiyah Malang, 2013, http://eprints.umm.ac.id/27122/.

Fritz, G. K., and R. O. Poe. 'The Role of a Cinema Seminar in Psychiatric Education.' *The American Journal of Psychiatry*, vol. 136, no. 2, Feb. 1979, p. 207–10, doi: 10.1176/ajp.136.2.207

Gabbard, Glen. 'Copycat.' *The Psychoanalytic Review*, vol. 83, no. 2, 1996, pp. 282–4.

Garland, Caroline. 'Thinking about Trauma.' *Understanding Trauma: A Psychoanalytical Approach*, edited by Caroline Garland, Abingdon-on-Thames: Routledge, 1998, pp. 9–31.

Gates, Philippa. '"Hidden in the Snow": Female Violence against the Men Who Hate Women in the Millennium Adaptations.' *Rape in Stieg Larsson's Millennium Trilogy and beyond: Contemporary Scandinavian and Anglophone Crime Fiction*, edited by Berit Astrom et al., London: Palgrave Macmillan, 2013, pp. 193–213.

Gemzoe, Lynge Agger. 'Brødre vs. Brothers: The Transatlantic Remake as Cultural Adaptation.' *Akademisk Kvarter [Academic Quarter]*, vol. 7, 2013, pp. 283–97.

Grant, Michael. 'Cinema, Horror and the Abominations of Hell: Carl-Theodor Dreyer's Vampyr (1931) and Lucio Fulci's The Beyond (1981).' *The Couch and the Silver Screen: Psychoanalytic Reflections on European Cinema*, edited by Andrea Sabbadini, Hove: Brunner-Routledge, 2003, pp. 145–56.

Gregersdotter, Katarina. 'The Body, Hopelessness, and Nostalgia: Representations of Rape and the Welfare State in Swedish Crime Fiction.' *Rape in Stieg Larsson's Millennium Trilogy and beyond: Contemporary Scandinavian and Anglophone Crime Fiction*, edited by Berit Astrom et al., London: Palgrave Macmillan, 2013, pp. 81–96.

Grigg, Russell. 'From the Mechanism of Psychosis to the Universal Condition of the Symptom: On Foreclosure.' *Key Concepts of Lacanian Psychoanalysis*, edited by Dany Nobus, New York: Other Press, 1999, pp. 48–74.

Grigg, Russell. *Lacan, Language, and Philosophy*. New York: State University of New York Press, 2008.

Grose, Anouchka. *From Anxiety to Zoolander: Notes on Psychoanalysis*. London: Karnac, 2018.

Grosz, Elizabeth. *Jacques Lacan: A Feminist Introduction*. Sydney: Allen and Unwin, 1990.

Gusain, Renuka. 'The War Body as Screen of Terror.' *The War Body on Screen*, edited by Karen Randell and Sean Redmond, London: Continuum, 2008, pp. 36–49.

Halberstam, Judith. *Skin Shows: Gothic Horror and the Technology of Monsters*. Durham: Duke University Press, 1995.

Hallström, Lasse. *The Shipping News*. Miramax, 2001.

Hansen, Miriam. 'The Mass Production of the Senses: Classical Cinema as Vernacular Modernism.' *Modernism/Modernity*, vol. 6, no. 2, 1999, pp. 59–77, https://muse-jhu-edu.ezproxy.auckland.ac.nz/article/23266

Harari, Roberto. *Lacan's Seminar on 'Anxiety': An Introduction*. Edited by Rico Franses, Translated by Jane Lamb-Ruiz, New York: Other Press, 2001.

Henry, Claire. 'The Girl with the Dragon Tattoo: Rape, Revenge, and Victimhood in Cinematic Translation.' *Rape in Stieg Larsson's Millennium Trilogy and beyond: Contemporary Scandinavian and Anglophone Crime Fiction*, edited by Berit Astrom et al., London: Palgrave Macmillan, 2013, pp. 175–92.

Hernaez Lerena, Maria Jesus. 'Tourist or Native? Consequences of Tourism on the Literary, Filmic, and Critical Practices of Newfoundland.' *Journal of Tourism and Cultural Change*, vol. 13, no. 1, 2015, pp. 22–38.

Hickam, Becca, and Cara Meixner. 'Transforming Leadership: Film as a Vehicle for Social Change.' *Journal of Leadership Education*, vol. 7, no. 2, 2008, pp. 40–6. http://journalofleadershiped.org/index.php/issues/vol-7-iss-2/234-transforming-leadership-film-as-a-vehicle-for-social-change

Hill, John. 'General Introduction.' *Film Studies: Critical Approaches*, edited by John Hill and Pamela Church Gibson, Oxford: Oxford University Press, 2000, pp. xiii-xv.

Hojbjerg, Lennard. 'The Visual Style of Susanne Bier's Films.' *Journal of Scandinavian Cinema*, vol. 7, no. 3, 2017, pp. 253–66.

Janoff-Bulman, Ronnie. 'Victims of Violence.' *Psychotraumatology: Key Papers and Core Concepts in Post-Traumatic Stress*, edited by George Everly Junior and Jeffrey Lating, New York: Plenum Press, 1995, pp. 73–86.

Jaten, Melissa Anna. *The Eternal Return: The Shipping News and the Consideration of Faith*. Montana State University, 2002, https://scholarworks.montana.edu/xmlui/bitstream/handle/1/8259/31762103697577.pdf?sequence=1.

Johnston, Adrian. 'Part II: Misfelt Feelings: Unconscious Affect between Psychoanalysis, Neuroscience, and Philosophy.' *Self and Emotional Life: Philosophy, Psychoanalysis, and Neuroscience*, edited by Adrian Johnston and Catherine Malabou, New York: Columbia University Press, 2013, pp. 73–276.

Johnston, Adrian. *Žižek's Ontology: A Transcendental Materialist Theory of Subjectivity*. Evanston: Northwestern University Press, 2008.

Johnston, Emily. *Split Wounds: Diverging Formations of Trauma in the Diagnostic and Statistical Manual of Mental Disorders V, Girl with the Dragon Tattoo, and The Rat Laughed, and Once Were Warriors*. Normal: Illinois State University, 2016.

Jonte-Pace, Diane. 'Situating Kristeva Differently: Psychoanalytic Readings of Woman and Religion.' *Body/Text in Julia Kristeva: Religion, Women, and Psychoanalysis*, edited by David Crownfield, New York: State University of New York Press, 1992, pp. 1–22.

Juranville, Anne. 'Hysteria and Melancholia in Woman.' *Lacan in the German-Speaking World*, edited by Elizabeth Stewart et al., translated by Elizabeth Stewart, New York: State University of New York Press, 2004, pp. 79–100.

Kalsched, Donald. *The Inner World of Trauma: Archetypal Defenses of the Personal Spirit*. Abingdon-on-Thames: Routledge, 1996.

Kaplan, Ann. 'Introduction.' *Psychoanalysis and Cinema*, edited by Ann Kaplan, Abingdon-on-Thames: Routledge, 1990, pp. 1–23.

Kay, Sarah. *Žižek: A Critical Introduction*. Cambridge: Polity, 2003.

Kenny, Dianna. *God, Freud and Religion: The Origins of Faith, Fear and Fundamentalism*. Abingdon-on-Thames: Routledge, 2015.

Kinghorn, Warren. 'The Biopolitics of Defining "Mental Disorder."' *Making the DSM-5: Concepts and Controversies*, edited by Joel Paris and James Phillips, New York: Springer, 2013, pp. 47–62.

Kläui, Christian. '"But It, the World … It Shames My Mute Pain": Some Thoughts on Melancholia and Depression.' *Lacan in the German-Speaking World*, edited by Elizabeth Stewart et al., translated by Elizabeth Stewart, New York: State University of New York Press, 2004, pp. 131–46.

Klein, Josephine. *Our Need for Others and Its Roots in Infancy*. Abingdon-on-Thames: Routledge, 1997.

Kolker, Robert P. 'The Film Text and Film Form.' *Film Studies: Critical Approaches*, edited by John Hill and Pamela Church Gibson, Oxford: Oxford University Press, 2000, pp. 9–21.

Krainitzki, Eva. 'Ghosted Images: Old Lesbians on Screen.' *Journal of Lesbian Studies*, vol. 19, no. 1, 2015, pp. 13–26.

Kristeva, Julia. *Black Sun: Depression and Melancholia*. Translated by Leon S. Roudiez, New York: Columbia University Press, 1989.

Kristeva, Julia. *Desire in Language: A Semiotic Approach to Literature and Art*. Edited by Leon S. Roudiez, Translated by Thomas Gora et al., Oxford: Blackwell, 1993.

Kristeva, Julia. *Hatred and Forgiveness*. Translated by Jeanine Herman, New York: Columbia University Press, 2010.

Kristeva, Julia. *Powers of Horror: An Essay on Abjection*. Translated by Leon S. Roudiez, New York: Columbia University Press, 1982.

Lacan, Jacques. *Anxiety: The Seminar of Jacques Lacan: Book X*. Edited by Jacques-Alain Miller, Translated by Adrian Price, English edition, Cambridge: Polity, 2014.

Lacan, Jacques. *Ecrits*. Translated by Bruce Fink, 1st complete English edition, London: W.W. Norton and Co, 2002.

Lacan, Jacques. *The Psychoses: The Seminar of Jacques Lacan Book III 1955–1956*. Edited by Jacques-Alain Miller, Translated by Russell Grigg, Abingdon-on-Thames: Routledge, 1993.

LaCapra, Dominick. *Writing History, Writing Trauma*. Baltimore: The Johns Hopkins University Press, 2001.

Lackey, Douglas P. 'Reflections on Cavell's Ontology of Film.' *Journal of Aesthetics and Art Criticism*, vol. 32, no. 2, 1973, pp. 271–3, doi: 10.2307/429046.

Lafrance, Marc. 'From the Skin Ego to the Psychic Envelope: An Introduction to the Work of Didier Anzieu.' *Skin, Culture and Psychoanalysis*, edited by Sheila Cavanagh et al., London: Palgrave Macmillan, 2013, pp. 16–44.

Laine, Tarja. *Bodies in Pain: Emotion and the Cinema of Darren Aronofsky*. Oxford: Berghahn Books, 2015.

Laine, Tarja. *Feeling Cinema: Emotional Dynamics in Film Studies*. London: Continuum, 2011.

Landstrom, Catharina. 'Technosubjects on Film: Taking Feminist Technology Studies to the Movies.' *Kritikos: An International and Interdisciplinary Journal of Postmodern Cultural Sound, Text and Image*, vol. 1, November, 2004, https://intertheory.org/landstrom.htm.

Langkjær, Birger. 'Storytelling, Schemes, Realism, and Ambiguity: Susanne Bier's Danish Dramas.' *ReFocus: The Films of Susanne Bier*, edited by Missy Molloy et al., Edinburgh: Edinburgh University Press, 2018, pp. 19–35.

Laub, Dori. 'Truth and Testimony: The Process and the Struggle.' *Trauma: Explorations in Memory*, edited by Cathy Caruth, Baltimore: Johns Hopkins University Press, 1995, pp. 61–75.

Lechte, John. *Julia Kristeva*. Abingdon-on-Thames: Routledge, 1990.

Lechte, John, and Maria Margaroni. *Julia Kristeva: Live Theory*. London: Continuum, 2004.

Lerner, Richard M., et al. 'Toward a Science for and of the People: Promoting Civil Society through the Application of Developmental Science.' *Child Development*, vol. 71, no. 1, 2000, pp. 11–20, doi:10.1111/1467-8624.00113.

Lewis Herman, Judith. 'Complex PTSD: A Syndrome in Survivors of Prolonged and Repeated Trauma.' *Psychotraumatology: Key Papers and Core Concepts in Post-Traumatic Stress*, edited by George Everly Junior and Jeffrey Lating, New York: Plenum Press, 1995, pp. 87–100.

Marchant, Oliver. 'Acting and the Act: On Slavoj Žižek's Political Ontology.' *The Truth of Žižek*, edited by Paul Bowman and Richard Stamp, Continuum, 2007, pp. 99–116, http://public.eblib.com/choice/publicfullrecord.aspx?p=1983636.

Marinan, John. 'More Than Tattoos: Rhetorical Discourse and Autism in Girl with the Dragon Tattoo.' *PsyArt*, vol. 18, 2014, pp. 119–30.

Mark, Vernon, and Frank Ervin. *Violence and the Brain*. New York: Harper and Row, 1970.

Markert, John. *Post-9/11 Cinema: Through a Lens Darkly*. Lanham: Scarecrow Press, 2011.

Marston, Kendra. 'The Tragic Ballerina's Shadow Self: Troubling the Political Economy of Melancholy in Black Swan.' *Quarterly Review of Film and Video*, vol. 32, no. 8, 2015, pp. 695–711, doi: 10.1080/10509208.2015.1060825.

Massumi, Brian. 'The Future Birth of the Affective Fact: The Political Ontology of Threat.' *The Affect Theory Reader*, edited by Melissa Gregg and Gregory Seigworth, Durham: Duke University Press, 2010, pp. 52–70.

Masuda, Akihiko, and Robert D. Latzman. 'Examining Associations among Factor-Analytically Derived Components of Mental Health Stigma, Distress, and Psychological Flexibility.' *Personality and Individual Differences*, vol. 51, no. 4, 2011, pp. 435–8, doi:http://dx.doi.org/10.1016/j.paid.2011.04.008.

McGowan, Todd. *The Real Gaze: Film Theory after Lacan*. New York: State University of New York Press, 2007.

McSweeney, Terence. *The 'War on Terror' and American Film: 9/11 Frames Per Second*. Edinburgh: Edinburgh University Press, 2014.

Mercer, John. 'Two Basic Functions of Cinema.' *Journal of the University Film Producers Association*, vol. 5, no. 3, 1953, pp. 17–20. https://www-jstor-org.ezproxy.auckland.ac.nz/stable/20686324?seq=1#page_scan_tab_contents

Metz, Christian. *The Imaginary Signifier: Psychoanalysis and the Cinema*. Translated by Celia Britton et al., Bloomington: Indiana University Press, 1982.

Micale, Mark. *Hysterical Men: The Hidden History of Male Nervous Illness*. Cambridge, MA: Harvard University Press, 2008.

Midgley, Nick. 'Psychoanalysis and Qualitative Psychology: Complementary or Contradictory Paradigms?' *Qualitative Research in Psychology*, vol. 3, no. 3, 2006, pp. 213–31, doi:10.1191/1478088706qrp065oa.

Miller, Ronald B. 'Suffering in Psychology.' *Facing Human Suffering: Psychology and Psychotherapy as Moral Engagement*, Washington DC: American Psychological Association, 2004, pp. 39–69.

Miller, Toby. 'Introduction.' *A Companion to Film Theory*, edited by Toby Miller and Robert Stam, Oxford: Blackwell, 1999, pp. 1–8.

Molloy, Missy, et al. *ReFocus: The Films of Susanne Bier*. Edinburgh: Edinburgh University Press, 2018.

Molloy, Missy. 'Susanne Bier's Nomadic Perspective on Home.' *Journal of Scandinavian Cinema*, vol. 8, no. 3, 2018, pp. 193–208.

Mowitt, John. 'Trauma Envy.' *The Truth of Žižek*, edited by Paul Bowman and Richard Stamp, London: Continuum, 2007, pp. 117–43.

Mulvey, Laura. *Visual and Other Pleasures*. 2nd edition, London: Palgrave Macmillan, 2009.

Nasio, Juan-David. *Five Lessons on the Psychoanalytic Theory of Jacques Lacan*. Translated by David Pettigrew and Francois Raffoul, New York: State University of New York Press, 1998.

Nesselhauf, Jonas. 'The Story of My Body Is on My Body: Tattoos as Personalised Style in Late Modern Literature.' *Online Proceedings of the Annual Conference of the Poetics and Linguistics Association [PALA]*, PALA, 2014.

Ng, Andrew Hock Soon. 'Writing Skin: Esthetics and Transcendence in Junichiro Tanizaki's *The Tattooer*.' *Skin, Culture and Psychoanalysis*, edited by Sheila Cavanagh et al., London: Palgrave Macmillan, 2013, pp. 115–40.

Nielson, Mimi. 'Tracing Affect in Susanne Bier's Dramas.' *ReFocus: The Films of Susanne Bier*, edited by Missy Molloy et al., Edinburgh: Edinburgh University Press, 2018, pp. 155–72.

Nilges, Mathias. 'The Aesthetics of Destruction: Contemporary US Cinema and TV Culture.' *Reframing 9/11: Film, Popular Culture and the 'War on Terror,'* edited by Karen Randell et al., London: Continuum, 2010, pp. 23–33.

Noll Zimmerman, Jacqueline. *People Like Ourselves: Portrayals of Mental Illness in the Movies*. Lanham: Scarecrow Press, 2003.

Oliver, Kelly. *Reading Kristeva: Unraveling the Double-Bind*. Bloomington: Indiana University Press, 1993.

Oplev, Niels Arden. *Män som hatar kvinnor [The Girl with the Dragon Tattoo]*. Yellow Bird, 2009.

Ormel, Johan et al. 'Common Mental Disorders and Disability across Cultures: Results from the Who Collaborative Study on Psychological Problems in General Health Care.' *Journal of the American Medical Association*, vol. 272, no. 22, Dec. 1994, pp. 1741–8, doi:10.1001/jama.1994.03520220035028.

Ouweneel, Arij. *Freudian Fadeout: The Failings of Psychoanalysis in Film Criticism*. Jefferson: McFarland, 2012.

Packer, Sharon. *Movies and the Modern Psyche*. Westport: Praeger, 2007.

Paris, Joel. 'Preface.' *Making the DSM-5: Concepts and Controversies*, edited by Joel Paris and James Phillips, New York: Springer, 2013, pp. v–vi.

Pearson, Quinn M. 'Using the Film *The Hours* to Teach Diagnosis.' *The Journal of Humanistic Counseling, Education and Development*, vol. 45, no. 1, 2006, pp. 70–8, doi:10.1002/j.2161-1939.2006.tb00006.x.

Pheasant-Kelly, F. E. 'Institutions, Identity and Insanity: Abject Spaces in Shutter Island.' *New Review of Film and Television Studies*, vol. 10, no. 2, 2012, pp. 212–29. doi:10.10 80/17400309.2012.658677.

Pheasant-Kelly, Frances. *Abject Spaces in American Cinema: Institutional Settings, Identity and Psychoanalysis in Film*. London: I.B. Tauris, 2013.

Phelan, Jo C., et al. 'Public Conceptions of Mental Illness in 1950 and 1996: What Is Mental Illness and Is It to Be Feared?' *Journal of Health and Social Behavior*, vol. 41, no. 2, 2000, pp. 188–207, doi:10.2307/2676305.

Pile, Steve. *The Body and the City: Psychoanalysis, Space and Subjectivity*. Abingdon-on-Thames: Routledge, 1996.

Polack, Fiona. 'Taking the Waters: Abjection and Homecoming in *The Shipping News* and *Death of a River Guide*.' *The Journal of Commonwealth Literature*, vol. 41, no. 1, 2006, pp. 93–109.

Potter, Jonathan, and Jose Rey. '*The Machinist*: Two Perspectives.' *Mental Health Clinician*, vol. 1, no. 10, 2012, pp. 261–2.

Prince, Stephen. 'The Emergence of Filmic Artifacts: Cinema and Cinematography in the Digital Era.' *Film Quarterly*, vol. 57, no. 3, 2004, pp. 24–33.

Quinlivan, Davina. *Filming the Body in Crisis: Trauma, Healing and Hopefulness*. London: Palgrave Macmillan, 2015.

Ragland, Ellie. 'Lacan, the Death Drive, and the Dream of the Burning Child.' *Death and Representation*, edited by Elisabeth Bronfen and Sarah Webster Goodwin, Baltimore: Johns Hopkins University Press, 1993, pp. 80–102.

Ragland, Ellie. 'The Psychical Nature of Trauma: Freud's Dora, the Young Homosexual Woman, and the Fort! Da! Paradigm.' *Topologies of Trauma: Essays on the Limit of Knowedge and Memory*, edited by Linda Belau and Petar Ramadanovic, New York: Other Press, 2002, pp. 75–100.

Randell, Karen. '"It Was Like a Movie": The Impossibility of Representation in Oliver Stone's World Trade Centre.' *Reframing 9/11: Film, Popular Culture and the 'War on Terror,'* edited by Karen Randell et al., London: Continuum, 2010, pp. 141–52.

Rank, Otto. *The Double*. Translated by Harry Tucker Junior, 1st English edition, New York: Meridian, 1971.

Razinsky, Liran. *Freud, Psychoanalysis and Death*. Cambridge: Cambridge University Press, 2013.

Redmond, Sean. 'Introduction to Part Three.' *The War Body on Screen*, edited by Karen Randell and Sean Redmond, New York: Continuum, 2008, pp. 149–53.

Redmond, Sean. 'When Planes Fall out of the Sky: The War Body on Screen.' *The War Body on Screen*, edited by Karen Randell and Sean Redmond, New York: Continuum, 2008, pp. 22–49.

Reineke, Martha Jane. *Sacrificed Lives: Kristeva on Women and Violence*. Bloomington: Indiana University Press, 1997.

Reitz, Caroline. 'Nancy Drew, Dragon Tattoo: Female Detective Fiction and the Ethics of Care.' *Textus*, vol. 27, no. 2, 2014, pp. 19–46.

Requena-Pelegri, Teresa. 'Fathers Who Care: Alternative Father Figures in Annie E. Proulx's *The Shipping News* and Jonathan Franzen's *The Corrections*.' *Alternative Masculinities for a Changing World*, edited by Angels Carabi and Josep Armengol, London: Palgrave Macmillan, 2014, pp. 131–44, https://ebookcentral.proquest.com/lib/auckland/reader.action?docID=1839673.

Restuccia, Frances. 'Impossible Love in Breaking the Waves: Mystifying Hysteria.' *Lacan and Contemporary Film*, edited by Todd McGowan and Sheila Kunkle, New York: Other, 2004, pp. 187–208.

Robinson, David. 'Reel Psychiatry.' *International Review of Psychiatry*, vol. 21, no. 3, 2009, pp. 245–60.

Rose, Kate. 'Abuse or Be Abused: Traumatic Memory, Sex Inequality, and Millennium as a Socio-literary Device.' *Dignity: A Journal on Sexual Exploitation and Violence*, vol. 3, no. 3, 2018, p. Article 6.

Roth, Michael S. *Memory, Trauma, and History: Essays on Living with the Past*. New York: Columbia University Press, 2012.

Roth, Michael S. *The Ironist's Cage: Memory, Trauma, and the Construction of History.* New York: Columbia University Press, 1995.

Ruddell, Caroline. *The Besieged Ego: Doppelgangers and Split Identity Onscreen.* Edinburgh: Edinburgh University Press, 2013.

Rutherford, Anne. 'Film, Trauma, and the Enunciative Present.' *Traumatic Affect*, edited by Meera Atkinson and Michael Richardson, Newcastle upon Tyne: Cambridge Scholars Pub., 2013, pp. 80–102.

Sadler, John. 'Considering the Economy of DSM Alternatives.' *Making the DSM-5: Concepts and Controversies*, edited by Joel Paris and James Phillips, New York: Springer, 2013, pp. 21–38.

Sánchez-Escalonilla, Antonio. 'Hollywood and the Rhetoric of Panic: The Popular Genres of Action and Fantasy in the Wake of the 9/11 Attacks.' *Journal of Popular Film and Television*, vol. 38, no. 1, 2010, pp. 10–20, doi:10.1080/01956050903449640.

Sandino, Amanda. 'On Perfection: Pain and Arts-Making in Aronofsky's Black Swan.' *Journal of Visual Art Practice*, vol. 12, no. 3, 2013, pp. 305–17, doi: 10.1080/14702029.2013.10820084.

Sari, Efiyanti Puspita. *The Influence of Post Traumatic Experience on the Personality Development of Lisbeth Salander in Steig Larrson's* The Girl with the Dragon Tattoo *Novel (2008): A Psychoanalytic Criticism.* Surakarta: Muhammadiyah University of Surakarta, 2014.

Schneider, Steven Jay. 'Manifestations of the Literary Double in Modern Horror Cinema.' *Horror Film and Psychoanalysis: Freud's Worst Fear*, edited by Steven Jay Schneider, Cambridge: Cambridge University Press, 2004, pp. 106–21.

Schorn, Johanna. 'Empowerment through Violence: Feminism and the Rape-Revenge Narrative in *The Girl with the Dragon Tattoo*.' *Gender Forum: An Internet Journal for Gender Studies*, no. 41, 2013.

Sexeny, Julie. 'Identification and Mutual Recognition in Darren Aronotsky's *Black Swan*.' *Embodied Encounters: New Approaches to Psychoanalysis and Cinema*, edited by Agnieszka Piotrowska, Abingdon-on-Thames: Routledge, 2015, pp. 51–9.

Shaviro, Steven. 'Bodies of Fear: The Films of David Cronenberg.' *The Politics of Everyday Fear*, edited by Brian Massumi, Minneapolis: University of Minnesota Press, 1993, pp. 113–35.

Shepherdson, Charles. 'Foreword.' *Lacan's Seminar on 'Anxiety': An Introduction*, edited by Rico Franses, translated by Jane Lamb-Ruiz, New York: Other Press, 2001, pp. ix–lxii.

Shorter, Edward. 'The History of DSM.' *Making the DSM-5: Concepts and Controversies*, edited by Joel Paris and James Phillips, New York: Springer, 2013, pp. 3–19.

Shriver-Rice, Meryl. 'Adapting National Identity: Ethical Borders Made Suspect in the Hollywood Version of Susanne Bier's *Brothers*.' *Film International*, vol. 9, no. 2, 2011, pp. 8–19.

Shriver-Rice, Meryl. 'Danish Privilege and Responsibility in the Work of Susanne Bier.' *ReFocus: The Films of Susanne Bier*, edited by Missy Molloy et al., Edinburgh: Edinburgh University Press, 2018, pp. 243–60.

Simpson, Philip. 'Copycat, Serial Murder, and the (De)Terministic Screen Narrative.' *The Terministic Screen: Rhetorical Perspectives on Film*, edited by David Blakesley, Carbondale: Southern Illinois University Press, 2003, pp. 146–62.

Simpson, Philip. 'Introduction.' *Film Theory: Critical Concepts in Media and Cultural Studies*, edited by Philip Simpson et al., Abingdon-on-Thames: Routledge, 2003, pp. 1–22.

Singh, Shruti. 'Sweden: Tackling Mental Health Problems Is Critical to Boosting Job Prospects of Young Swedes.' *OECD – Better Policies for Better Lives*, 2013, http://www.oecd.org/sweden/swedentacklingmentalhealthproblemsiscriticaltoboostingjobprospectsofyoungswedes.htm. Accessed 7 November 2014.

Slethaug, Gordon. *The Play of the Double in Postmodern American Fiction*. Carbondale: Southern Illinois University Press, 1993.

Smaill, Belinda. 'The Male Sojourner, the Female Director, and the Popular European Cinema: The Worlds of Suzanne Bier.' *Camera Obscura: Feminism, Culture, and Media Studies*, vol. 29, no. 1, 2014, pp. 5–31.

Smith Jr, Claude J. 'Finding a Warm Place for Someone We Know: The Cultural Appeal of Recent Mental Patient and Asylum Films.' *Journal of Popular Film and Television*, vol. 27, no. 1, 1999, pp. 40–6, doi:10.1080/01956059909602796.

Smith, Vi D., et al. 'The Portrayal of Black Swan through a Multicontexual Framework.' *The Family Journal*, vol. 23, no. 1, 2015, pp. 97–101, doi:10.1177/1066480714555670.

Srinath, Shankarnarayan. 'Identificatory Processes in Trauma.' *Understanding Trauma: A Psychoanalytical Approach*, edited by Caroline Garland, Abingdon-on-Thames: Routledge, 1998, pp. 139–51.

Steward, Tom. 'Male Nutrition-Extreme Weight Loss, Socio-Cultural Transgression and the Male Body in Recent American Cinema.' *Transgression in Anglo-American Cinema – Gender, Sex and the Deviant Body*, edited by Joel Gwynne, New York: Wallflower Press, 2016, pp. 73–87.

Stutterheim, Kerstin. 'Traumatized Heroes: War and Distraction.' *The Horrors of Trauma in Cinema: Violence Void Visualization*, edited by Michael Elm et al., Newcastle-upon-Tyne: Cambridge Scholars, 2014, pp. 125–44.

Subramanian, Janani, and Jorie Lagerwey. 'Food, Sex, Love, and Bodies in *Eat Pray Love* and *Black Swan*.' *Studies in Popular Culture*, vol. 36, no. 1, 2013, pp. 1–20, ISSN: 0888-5753.

Sulaberidze, Salome. 'Aesthetics of Authentic Narrative in Scandinavian Films.' *Arthysteria: Film and Photographic Studies with Some Extras*, 6 February 2017, https://arthysteriablog.wordpress.com/2017/02/06/aesthetics-of-authentic-narrative-in-scandinavian-films/.

Summers-Bremner, Eluned. *Insomnia: A Cultural History*. London: Reaktion, 2010.

Szabados, Béla. 'Freud, Self-Knowledge and Psychoanalysis.' *Canadian Journal of Philosophy*, vol. 12, no. 4, 1982, pp. 691–707, doi: 10.1080/00455091.1982.10715811

Tambling, Jeremy. *Literature and Psychoanalysis*. Manchester: Manchester University Press, 2012.

Taubin, Amy. 'Sex, Politics, and Time Travel.' *Film Comment*, vol. 40, no. 2, 2004, pp. 54–6.

The Nordic Council Communications Department. 'Health in the Nordic Region.' *Norden.Org*, http://www.norden.org/en/about-nordic-co-operation/areas-of-co-operation/health/health-in-the-nordic-region. Accessed 10 April 2014.

Thomson, Shawn. 'Disrupting the Skin-Ego: See-Sickness and the Real in The Flagellation of a Virgin.' *Skin, Culture and Psychoanalysis*, edited by Sheila Cavanagh et al., London: Palgrave Macmillan, 2013, pp. 215–39.

Tietchen, Todd. 'Samplers and Copycats: The Cultural Implications of the Postmodern Slasher in Contemporary American Film.' *Journal of Popular Film and Television*, vol. 26, no. 3, 2010, pp. 98–107.

Turner, Graeme. 'Cultural Studies and Film.' *Film Studies: Critical Approaches*, edited by John Hill and Pamela Church Gibson, Oxford: Oxford University Press, 2000, pp. 193–9.

Tyrer, Ben. 'An Atheist's Guide to Feminine Jouissance: On *Black Swan* and the Other Satisfaction.' *Embodied Encounters: New Approaches to Psychoanalysis and Cinema*, edited by Agnieszka Piotrowska, Abingdon-on-Thames: Routledge, 2015, pp. 131–46.

United Nations [UN]. 'Convention against Torture and Other Cruel, Inhuman or Degrading Treatment or Punishment (Part 1, Article 1, Paragraph 1).' 1984, http://www.un.org/documents/ga/res/39/a39r046.htm. Accessed 7 March 2017.

Van Der Kolk, Bessel, and Onno Van Der Hart. 'The Intrusive Past: The Flexibility of Memory and the Engraving of Trauma.' *Trauma: Explorations in Memory*, edited by Cathy Caruth, Baltimore: Johns Hopkins University Press, 1995, pp. 158–82.

Vilhelmsson, Andreas. 'Depression and Antidepressants: A Nordic Perspective.' *Frontiers in Public Health*, vol. 1, no. 30, 2013, doi:10.3389/fpubh.2013.00030.

Voruz, Veronique. 'A Lacanian Reading of Dora.' *The Later Lacan: An Introduction*, edited by Veronique Voruz and Bogdan Wolf, New York: State University of New York Press, 2007, pp. 158–79.

Wagner, Matthew. 'A King(Dom) for a Stage The War Body in and as Performance.' *The War Body on Screen*, edited by Karen Randell and Sean Redmond, London: Continuum, 2008, pp. 50–63.

Walton, Priscilla. *Detective Agency: Women Rewriting the Hardboiled Tradition*. Oakland: University of California Press, 1999.

Wang, Yixuan. 'Memory, Space and Self Identification: Reading the "Knot" Image in Annie Proulx's Novel *The Shipping News*.' *Journal of Henan Institute of Education (Philosophy and Social Sciences)*, vol. 2, 2012, p. 26.

Weber, Samuel. 'Vertigo: The Question of Anxiety in Freud.' *Lacan in the German-Speaking World*, edited by Elizabeth Stewart et al., translated by Elizabeth Stewart, New York: State University of New York Press, 2004, pp. 203–20.

Wedding, Danny, and Christina McCrae. '*The Machinist*: Taking Insomnia to Its Extreme.' *Psyccritiques*, vol. 50, no. 26, 2005.

Weiss, Joseph. 'The Nature of the Patient's Problems and How in Psychoanalysis the Individual Works to Solve Them.' *Psychoanalytic Psychology Winter 1990*, vol. 7, no. 1, 1990, pp. 105–13, doi:10.1037/h0079148.

Westerink, Herman. *A Dark Trace: Sigmund Freud on the Sense of Guilt*. Translated by Language Centre, University of Groningen, Leuven: Leuven University Press, 2009.

Westerståhl Stenport, Anna. 'Nordic Remakes in Hollywood: Reconfiguring Originals and Copies.' *A Companion to Nordic Cinema*, edited by Mette Hjort and Ursula Lindqvist, Hoboken: Wiley & Sons, 2016, pp. 436–55.

Westwell, Guy. *War Cinema: Hollywood on the Front Line*. New York: Wallflower Press, 2006.

Whitaker, Robert. *Anatomy of an Epidemic: Magic Bullets, Psychiatric Drugs, and the Astonishing Rise of Mental Illness in America*. 1st edition, New York: Broadway Books, 2011.

White-Stabley, Debra. 'I Don't Know How She Lives with This Kitchen the Way It Is: Military Heroism, Gender, and Race in *Brothers* (2004 and 2009).' *Heroism and Gender in War Films*, edited by Karen Ritzenhoff and Jakub Kazecki, London: Palgrave Macmillan, 2014, pp. 133–51.

Williams, Simon J. *Sleep and Society: Sociological Ventures into the (Un)Known*. Abingdon-on-Thames: Routledge, 2005.

Wolf-Meyer, Matthew. 'Fantasies of Extremes: Sports, War and the Science of Sleep.' *BioSocieties*, vol. 4, no. 2–3, 2009, pp. 257–71.

World Health Organization [WHO]. *World Health Organization*, 2020, http://www.who.int/. Accessed 20 January 2018.

Wright, Elizabeth. *Lacan and Postfeminism*. London: Icon, 2000.

Žižek, Slavoj. *Enjoy Your Symptom: Jacques Lacan in Hollywood and Out*. 2nd edition, Abingdon-on-Thames: Routledge, 2008.

Žižek, Slavoj. *Event: A Philosophical Journey through a Concept*. New York: Melville House, 2014.

Index

abject, the 9, 12–16, 20, 88, 92–8, 143, 147–8, 185, 194
   cadaver 56, 92
   corpse 52, 74, 90, 92, 123–4, 185
   decay 56–8, 92
   expel 20, 93–4, 101, 194
absent-event 117–18, 195, 198
adaptation 77, 106, 162–3
   Hollywood 8, 15, 17, 20–1, 77, 106, 108
adjustment disorder 16–18, 21, 103–4, 110, 113, 120, 123–4, 126, 131, 195, 198
aesthetic profession 26, 28, 45, 47, 197
   ballet 26, 36, 45, 192, 197
agency 31, 47, 77, 90–1, 99, 101–2, 119, 129, 133, 143, 156, 160, 177, 196
analysand 7
anger 86–7, 93, 95, 103–4, 113, 125–7, 129, 170, 183, 194, 197
annihilation 63, 116–18
anxiety 9, 14–16, 19, 22, 26, 29, 32–3, 49, 78, 107, 109, 124, 135–7, 140–2, 144, 149–54, 158–9, 166, 196–8
   fear 5, 22, 29–30, 32, 36, 41, 48, 51, 63–5, 70–1, 80, 86, 90, 94, 97, 116, 120, 124, 133, 135–6, 139, 142–7, 149, 152–4, 157–9, 167, 185–6, 188, 193, 196–8
   panic 14–15, 18, 22, 59, 80, 133, 135–6, 140–6, 148–50, 153–4, 156, 159, 185, 196–8
   threat 12–13, 37–8, 51, 64–5, 81, 90, 92, 112, 135–7, 142, 147, 149–54, 159, 183, 186
assault 21, 75–7, 81, 83, 84–5, 90, 94, 97–8, 100–1, 134, 136, 139, 142, 148, 154, 157–9, 194, 196, 198
   abuse 75, 85–7, 90, 94, 98, 162–4, 170–1, 174–5, 186
   attack 76–7, 79, 84–5, 87, 96–8, 100–1, 121, 128, 133–57, 159, 196
   physical assault 21, 76, 83, 98, 154, 157–9, 196
   rape 75–7, 79–87, 90–4, 96, 98–101, 116, 136, 194, 196
   sexual assault 75–7, 81, 98, 101, 194
   violation 78, 93, 102
asymbolia 162, 166, 171–3, 180–4, 187–8, 197
avoidance behaviours 18, 22, 78, 135–6, 145, 149, 196

body 11, 19, 20, 22, 27–34, 38–45, 50, 54, 58–9, 67–8, 73, 80, 83, 92–6, 98–100, 103, 107–8, 112, 123, 137, 139–40, 144, 146, 149–50, 152, 156, 166, 176–7, 192–4, 197–8
   corporeal reality 19, 29–30, 36, 39–41, 45–7, 50, 53, 58–60, 80–1, 93–4, 96, 99–100, 102–3, 105, 110, 133, 140–2, 144, 156, 158, 160, 165, 171, 182, 185, 197–8
   corporeal space 30, 80–1
   emaciation and wasting 50–2, 58–61, 74, 193, 198
   embodiment 38, 43, 48, 66, 70, 74, 102, 105–6, 131, 165, 194, 199
   hyperventilation 22, 135, 141–4, 146, 150, 153
   malformation 42
   malfunction 13, 29
   muscle memory 80
   physicality 19–21, 23, 51, 59, 67, 74, 78, 80, 92, 94, 100, 141, 156, 187, 198
   physical manifestation 21, 32, 64, 142, 198
   vertigo 22, 135, 141, 143–4, 148, 153
   visceral 13, 60, 93, 182
boundaries 20–1, 30, 33, 39, 41, 45, 76, 92–9, 103, 105, 109, 111–13, 115, 122, 124, 129–30, 134, 144, 146–8, 154, 158–9, 185, 194–7

ethical 94, 96–7, 111–12, 115, 120, 130, 194
legal 20, 54, 94, 96–7, 111–12
moral 20, 54, 94, 97–8, 103, 111–12, 116, 130
physical 34, 44, 46, 83, 93–4, 98–9, 128, 147, 159, 194, 196–7
spatial 69, 95, 134, 147, 196
temporal 20, 95, 129

Caruth, Cathy 20, 78, 80, 82, 95, 109, 136
clinical psychology 1–5, 9, 18, 25, 76, 135, 159, 161, 187, 190–1, 199
    Diagnostic and Statistical Manual (DSM) 2–4, 10, 14–15, 18–19, 23, 49, 54, 73, 75, 79, 84, 103, 113, 159, 161–2, 164–5, 187, 190–2

death drive, the 23, 45, 120
depression 14–16, 18, 22, 125, 135, 161–2, 164–5, 173–4, 180, 187, 197–8
    lack 8, 12, 23, 140, 142, 148, 152, 155, 159–60, 169–74, 181, 197
    melancholia 9, 13–14, 22, 161–2, 164–88, 197–8
desire 7, 10–11, 13, 19, 23, 31–7, 45, 47–8, 50–1, 61, 63–6, 111–12, 119–20, 132, 145
development stage 1, 22, 29, 38, 154
    infancy 31, 33, 47, 89, 137, 196
    psychosexual development 31–2
diegesis 6, 20, 50, 52, 56–7, 62, 74, 167
    diegetic 20, 47, 50, 68, 74, 114, 192
disability 15, 22, 96–7
disavowal 27
doppelganger 44, 51, 55, 64–7, 70–2, 74
    double 30, 51, 55, 67–72
    replica 43, 159, 178, 196
drowning 167, 172, 174, 186

ego ideal 74, 112, 117, 122, 125, 132
Eros 181, 188
event, the 9, 12, 17, 113–18, 121, 126, 130–1, 198

fantasy 7, 19, 67, 69
foreclosure 27, 34–9, 42

gender 13, 17, 19, 31, 51, 59, 63, 77–8, 94, 99–102, 192
    feminine 13, 38
    feminization 38
    masculine 13, 63
    pousse à la femme 38
genre 7, 13, 15–17, 51–2, 54, 56, 67, 70, 106–9, 151, 154, 159, 195
    Nordic-noir 16, 106
guilt 8, 12, 20–1, 50–74, 105, 111–12, 119–26, 130–1, 193, 195, 197–9
    displacement 123–4
    guilt-residue 123–4
    projection 63, 65, 69, 71, 74, 124–6, 193–4

human condition 5–7, 23, 44

identification 9, 11, 89, 90–1, 93–4, 97, 101
    fragmentation 29–30, 32, 39, 41–6, 70, 89, 139–41, 155–6, 159, 176
    perpetrator identification 90
    projective identification 90–2
    self-actualization 23, 193
    self-hood 193
    subjective destitution 41–2
    unified self 27–8, 192
insomnia 15–16, 18, 20, 49–59, 61–2, 65–6, 73–4, 193, 198
intimacy 33, 36–8, 180

jouissance 21, 33, 44–6, 111–12, 114, 116, 119, 122–8, 130–1

Lacanian registers 10–11, 29–30, 37–8
    Imaginary, the 10–14, 22, 29–30, 35, 38, 42, 76, 92–3, 113, 139–43, 145, 169, 175, 180, 193
    Real, the 10, 12, 20–1, 29–30, 34–6, 38–40, 42–3, 45, 62, 73, 76, 83–4, 93–4, 100–2, 111, 113, 116, 118–19, 142, 148, 153, 193–4, 196
    Symbolic, the 4, 10–14, 22–3, 29, 33–40, 44, 48, 62, 88–93, 95, 113–14, 117–19, 129–30, 133–4, 137–43, 145–48, 151, 153–62, 164–9, 172–5, 178, 180–8, 192–3, 195–8

libido 31
  libidinal relations 31–3, 37–8, 43, 45–6
liminal 51, 58, 61, 96, 178–9
lived experience 1–3, 5–7, 15, 17, 84, 96, 110, 113, 164–5, 170, 187, 189–92, 195, 197–9
living death, a 13, 22, 56–7, 164, 185
  already dead 56
  living corpse 74, 124

madness 7, 25, 47, 63, 166
marginalization 96–7
memory 12, 49, 51, 58, 61–3, 70–1, 73, 75, 79–83, 87–9, 95, 116–17, 123–4, 128, 132, 148, 151, 159, 167, 182, 186, 193, 195
Metz, Christian 8, 10
mirror stage/phase 4, 9, 13, 22, 27–32, 43, 46–7, 60, 89, 137–40, 147–8, 154–5, 159–60, 192–3, 196
  imago 19, 30–2, 40–8, 140, 156, 192
  misrecognition 11, 19, 54
  reflection 9, 11, 27–30, 41–8, 60, 72, 89, 155–6, 192
  reflective surfaces 19, 25, 27–8, 30, 41, 60, 67–8, 72, 89, 193, 196
  reverse mirror stage 137–40, 148, 159–60, 196
mourning 13, 23, 161–2, 168–9, 179–81, 184, 186, 187–8, 197

narcissism 11, 175–7, 188
narrativize 1, 5, 18, 23, 57, 133
negation (language) 70, 171–2, 174, 176, 187–8, 197

Oedipus 31–3, 35, 37, 41, 192
  Oedipal trajectory 31, 35–6, 38
  Oedipus complex 11, 32–3, 35, 37, 41, 192
  pre-Oedipal dyad 4, 8, 13, 34, 37, 120, 140, 192
Other, the 50, 57, 86, 89, 107–9, 114, 139, 143, 145–8, 152–5, 158–9, 170, 174, 176–7, 180, 195–6, 199
  big Other 9, 57, 111, 115

m(other) 23, 113–14, 137, 139–40, 143, 168–9, 178, 183–4, 186–8, 199
Otherness/Othering/Othered 17, 47, 77, 90, 163
West/Other dichotomy 107–8

paradox 1, 16, 57, 60, 91, 111–12, 122, 141, 143–6, 148, 159, 171
passivity 77, 90–1, 162, 165, 167, 170, 174, 184, 186, 197
perfectionism/ist 45, 47–8, 105–6, 112, 120, 193
phallus 13, 32–3, 36, 38, 101
  Master signifier 13, 36
  Name-of-the-Father/paternal metaphor 4, 32–3, 34–7, 39, 43, 45, 64–5, 192–3
  phallic 31–2, 36, 102
  primordial signifier 35–7, 39
phenomena/phenomenon 6, 25, 38, 40, 42, 54, 69, 79, 111, 117, 192
phobia 140, 144, 152–3, 158
  agoraphobia 15–16, 18, 22, 135–53, 156–60, 196–8
  safe zone 22, 133, 137, 139–49, 151, 153–4, 159, 196
primal wounding 178, 188
psychical splitting 60, 82–3, 136
  dissociation 117, 127–8, 136, 198–99
  dissociative splitting 82–3
psychological disorder 1–10, 14–23, 47–51, 53, 56–7, 73–5, 78–80, 94–5, 104, 112, 114, 119–20, 127–8, 137–40, 143–4, 156, 158, 165–6, 189–99
  categorization 1, 3–4, 14, 49, 69, 75, 78–9, 100, 103, 135, 159, 191
  co-morbid 16, 162
  disturbance 5, 10, 19–21, 49, 66, 103, 111, 128, 178
  manifestation 5, 20–3, 27, 29, 31–6, 39–40, 42, 53, 75, 81, 103–4, 110, 121, 123–5, 130, 135–6, 140, 142–3, 145, 153, 159, 161, 164–5, 169, 189–94, 197–8
  mechanism 1, 3, 5, 7, 9, 19, 23, 25, 27, 33–5, 40, 51, 63, 73, 88, 90, 111, 119, 121–3, 136, 170–3, 180, 183, 187, 191–2, 198–9

origin 1, 5, 19, 52, 73, 119, 151, 168, 187, 189–92, 199
pro-dromal 16, 49
recovery 5, 19, 88, 104, 118, 120, 123, 125, 132, 156, 158, 170, 192, 195
symptomatology 4, 9, 18, 187, 190–1
treatment 2–4, 14, 18, 53, 85, 187, 189–90
psychological suffering 1–8, 15–20, 22–3, 25, 45, 49–50, 52, 57–8, 69, 73–5, 80, 96, 101–2, 106, 110–12, 114, 118, 127, 133, 141, 143, 156, 159, 166, 174, 182, 187, 189–199
distress 1, 5, 21, 47, 113, 130, 133, 135, 146, 161, 166, 182
stress 19, 26, 29, 36, 47, 49, 74
psychosis 19, 25–7, 29–47, 80, 192–3, 197–8
delusions 15, 18, 25–6, 40, 48, 56, 63, 68, 193
hallucinations 12, 15, 18, 25–6, 29–30, 34–6, 42, 50–2, 55, 63–4, 65–8, 71–4, 92, 192–3, 198
paranoia 15, 18, 25–6, 36, 39–40, 43, 50, 52, 55–6, 59, 61–7, 69, 71, 73, 193, 198
psychotic episode 18, 26, 37–8, 43, 192

reframing 110, 195
regression 22, 141, 147–8, 198
repetition symptoms 78–9, 82–4, 95, 194
flashbacks 12, 20, 71, 77–9, 83, 95, 101, 103, 109, 136, 182, 185, 194
nightmares 12, 20, 51, 78–80, 83, 95, 101, 194
re-experiencing 18, 20, 78–81, 84–5, 91, 95, 101, 136, 167, 182, 194, 198
repression 10, 12, 27, 30, 34–5, 37, 39, 51, 63, 70, 135, 192

sadness 5, 13, 162, 164–6, 169–71, 174, 183, 187, 197
self-harm 85, 100
tattoos 94, 99–102
silence 89, 93, 101, 116–19, 129, 132, 166, 187
skin ego 99
sociocultural context 108

cultural climate 6, 9
international context 17
modern culture 7, 107
reflexivity 5–7, 23, 191–2
social climate 9
socio-political climate 17, 107, 110
spectre 32, 42, 57
spectral 20, 56, 185, 198
speech (language) 14, 26, 45, 56, 118–19, 127, 129, 130, 164, 166, 172, 181, 187
suicide 23, 71, 125, 130–1, 165–6, 170, 172–5, 186
super ego/conscience 4, 11, 21, 52–3, 64–74, 68, 105–6, 112–13, 119–24, 130–2, 193, 196
survival 21, 56, 70, 76, 83, 86–93, 96, 99–102, 112, 115–17, 125, 127, 134, 142, 158, 160, 184, 186, 194, 198

temporality/temporal reality 6, 12, 20, 80, 96, 102, 127, 133, 151, 158, 160, 165–6, 168, 185, 187, 197–8
atemporal 30, 34, 39, 41, 56–7, 114, 118, 138–9, 141, 143, 147, 152, 158, 169, 175, 198
textual analysis 6–7, 23
Thing, the (das Ding) 161, 169, 171–3, 180–1, 197
transcendence 80, 82, 95, 127, 131, 166–7, 169, 182, 199
trauma 10, 12, 14, 16–9, 20–2, 43, 51–2, 60–2, 69–73, 75–104, 107, 109–11, 113–21, 123, 127–31, 136–8, 141–2, 147–54, 158–9, 167, 182, 186, 193
belatedness 79, 81–3, 109, 136, 188, 194, 198
complex-post-traumatic stress disorder (C-PTSD) 85–7, 91
hypervigilance 78, 101, 194
latency 81–3
post-traumatic stress disorder (PTSD) 16–18, 20, 75–87, 91, 93–6, 103, 109–10, 135–6, 194, 198

uncanny, the 69–70
'unknown knowns' 51–2, 74, 193
unrepresentable, the 10, 12, 34, 62, 73, 94, 101, 118, 153, 194

'beyond words' 82, 119
    unspeakable 34–5, 89, 94, 115, 118, 153, 182
    uterine 139–41, 143, 145, 147–8, 157–8, 196
    womb 139, 141, 143, 148, 198

violence 13, 71, 75, 84, 90, 104, 109–10, 112, 114, 121, 170–1
Void, the 165, 168, 174, 178–81, 186–8
vulnerability 85–6, 96–7, 135, 144, 164

war 17, 107–10, 114–15, 195
    captivity 21, 86, 104, 116, 125–8, 195, 198
    combat 17, 106–8, 115
    post-9/11 17, 21, 107–10, 114–15, 195
    torture 55–6, 77, 90, 104, 115, 126, 128
    war zones 17, 75, 115
witnessing 85–7, 102, 116–19, 139
World Health Organization (WHO) 2, 14–15

www.ingramcontent.com/pod-product-compliance
Lightning Source LLC
Chambersburg PA
CBHW052039300426
44117CB00012B/1885